LEADERSHIP DEVELOPMENT

LEADERSHIP DEVELOPMENT

Change from the inside out

Torin M. Finser, PhD

SteinerBooks | 2016

STEINERBOOKS

An imprint of Anthroposophic Press, Inc.

610 Main Street, Great Barrington, MA 01230

www.steinerbooks.org

Note: Some quoted translations have been revised.

Design: William Jens Jensen
Cover image: Spiral staircase at
the Goetheanum, Dornach, Switzerland
Cover photo © by Diccon Bewes (www.dicconbewes.com)

LIBRARY OF CONGRESS CONTROL NUMBER: 2016900302

ISBN: 978-1-62148-148-5 (paperback)
ISBN: 978-1-62148-149-2 (eBook)

Printed in the United States of America

TABLE OF CONTENTS

PART TWO: VOICES FROM THE FIELD

This book is dedicated to my father,

Siegfried E. Finser,

who more than any other person in my life

has exemplified servant leadership.

Modest, creative, clear-thinking and a visionary,

he is dedicated to bringing ideals into practice

and teaches those around him through example.

Acknowledgements

I am deeply grateful to my students in the Administration Program at Antioch University New England and leaders in the field who have brought my attention to both the need to practice leadership development and for their many helpful suggestions. I want to thank my colleague Laura Thomas, Director of Antioch's Center for School Renewal, for her co-facilitation of our Administration Program and Sarah Wilson, Education Department Administrator, for her constant support for all we do as a department.

I am grateful for many years of collaboration with Leonore Russell and Barbara Richardson, who brought eurythmy in the workplace and wisdom to many of our training sessions over the past two decades. I thank Craig Giddens for looking over the chapter on speech and making many helpful suggestions and edits. This volume includes a section, "Voices from the Field," featuring individuals who have agreed to include their articles or selections to enhance the breadth and scope of the book. In many cases, I found a segment and said to myself, "This person has done a better job than I could have on this subject; let's see if we can include it." I thank Holly Koteen-Soule, Claire Stanley, Milan Daler, Rea Gill, John Cunningham, Barbara Richardson, Lynn Jericho, Reg Down, Angeles Ariene, Christof Wiechert and Siegfried Finser.

Once again, I have been fortunate to have the editorial help of Jens Jensen and the wonderful team at SteinerBooks. All of us are also grateful to our donors and sponsors for their enthusiastic support for this project.

Finally, everything I do is possible only because of the wonderful family that surrounds my professional work: my dear wife Karine Munk Finser and our six children, Thomas, Nikolai, Kira, Ewen, Louisa and Ionas. They help me practice work–life balance!

PART ONE

HOW TO BECOME THE LEADER
YOUR ORGANIZATION NEEDS

"I want to demonstrate to the world the architecture of a new and beautiful social commonwealth. The secret of my harmony? I alone know it. Each instrument in counterpoint, and as many contrapuntal parts as there are instruments. It is the enlightened self-discipline of the various parts, each voluntarily imposing on itself the limits of its individual freedom for the wellbeing of the community.

"That is my message. Not the autocracy of a single stubborn melody on the one hand, nor the anarchy of the unchecked noise of the other. No, a delicate balance between the two; an enlightened freedom. The science of my art. The harmony of the stars in the heavens, the yearning for brotherhood in the human heart.

"This is the secret of my music."

—Johann Sebastian Bach

1

INTRODUCTION

Waldorf schools are very fortunate to have a highly developed curriculum based on an articulate description of child development given by Rudolf Steiner at the start of the last century. Although not prescriptive, it is detailed and expansive. Since the first one was founded in Stuttgart in 1919, Waldorf schools have grown all over the world and now number more than one thousand one hundred today. In my visits to some of these schools on all the continents where they exist, I have found marvelous instances of adaptation to local cultures and geography. Yet one has only to walk into a Waldorf school to recognize it as such, and much of that quality has to do with the archetypes that stand behind the teaching and the essential view of the human being. Rather than looking to "learning outcomes" and testing, Waldorf teachers strive to understand the unfolding capacities of each child as a creative process with tremendous implications for the future of humanity.

In many countries professional organizations have arisen with the aim, at least in part, to further enhance the development of Waldorf schools. In the United States we have an Association of Waldorf Schools that supports teacher education, professional development and school accreditation as a continuing effort to ensure the highest possible standards while respecting the basic freedom of each school. The self-administration and policy development in most schools is based on the real needs of the students in their care. These professional organizations have supported mentorship and pedagogical conferences, as well as various research projects. The result is that at least in my lifetime, I have seen considerable progress regarding faculty development and collaborative projects regarding the curriculum and teacher mentoring.

This story of success has not been replicated to the same extent in the areas of school governance and administration. Although our schools continue to attract talented professionals to serve in administrative roles, they often face considerable challenges:

1. Pedagogical leaders selected by the faculty often have the goodwill of their colleagues but not the necessary skill sets to the do the job.
2. Waldorf teacher education programs give little time and attention to issues of leadership development and administration.
3. Yet often within months, teachers are asked to participate in meetings that include personnel and HR matters in which they have little experience.
4. Decision-making is often more a matter of rendering an opinion than doing a thorough analysis of the options and the available data.
5. Administrators often have the skill sets needed in their area of specialization (finance, development, admissions etc.) but sometimes lack a thorough understanding of the school's philosophy or culture.
6. As a result of some of the above, there is often a disconnection between those in administrative roles and the teaching faculty.
7. These differences can play out in way that there are different expectations arising from the trustees vs. the faculty. Parents are sometimes caught in the middle.
8. Much work is accomplished through dedication and long hour of work, but much human capital and energy are expended. Burnout is sometimes a result among parent volunteers, administrators and teachers.
9. Even when systems are in place and good policies have been developed, communication can at times be erratic and support for the schools suffers.
10. Many of the above factors have an effect on institution development and fund-raising, which in turn can result in tuition dependence and an endless cycle of budget discussions.
11. Whereas schools seem to strongly support mentorship for teachers, there is much less evidence of any real investment in leadership development or professional development for administrators. In some cases, there is evidence of negative attitudes, though often not verbalized, to anyone who tries to exercise real leadership.
12. Lack of professionalism in governance matters affects morale and can cause a preoccupation with internal matters at the expense of community outreach and development.

Many of these issues (of which the above is but a sample) can create a negative feedback loop. For instance, poor decision-making can result in a bad hiring decision, which can lead to endless internal discussion and neglect of other needs. Parents can become frustrated and some may depart, which in turn affects the budget and results in more cuts. The cuts lead to a diminished program that is less attractive to new families. Especially since the great recession in 2008, many independent schools have been in retrenchment mode. At best, flat (enrollment/finances) is often now called "the new normal."

The good news is that one can also create a positive feedback loop in which strong governance attracts the best teachers, new families enroll, additional funds are available for new programs, the school's reputation grows and the community notices the good work.

Yet far less attention and far fewer resources have been devoted to school governance than to other legitimate needs. We need to change that dynamic. Dedication and good teaching can hold a school together in the face of many challenges, but poor governance and leadership can destroy all the good work in a matter of weeks. We need to expand our strategic planning and yearly goal setting to include serious investment in leadership if Waldorf education is to take its rightful place in the forefront of educational renewal. We need good teachers and administrators, *and* we need healthy governance.

In the 1990s a few of us at Antioch offered collaborative leadership institutes across the country. These were three-to-four-day intensives in which parents, trustees, administrators and teachers participated in day-long trainings. We used a movement training called eurythmy in the workplace (see chapter on that subject), conventional training in subjects such as communication, leadership, conflict etc. as well as interactive role-plays and in-depth discussion of Anthroposophy as a basis for understanding Waldorf pedagogy. These institutes were well received but cumbersome to deliver: we insisted on at least two instructors which increased the costs, and we always demanded participation by all the major groups in the schools: administrators, teachers, trustees etc. After a few years we realized that not all schools could organize these institutes, and many could not afford them. So the effort was suspended.

In the meantime others tried a variety of training modules, most of which also had a limited shelf life. In 2014, the volume of emails increased around the needs of the schools in regard to governance. New administrators were being hired with little background in Waldorf education, an older generation of teacher–leaders was about to retire, charter schools were expanding with a host of new needs, and trustees were becoming inpatient with the lack of professionalism at their schools.

So we went back to the drawing boards and began to design a new training initiative. In consultation with our faculty, experts in the field, leaders at AWSNA and DANA (a development and administrators' network) we took up the question of forming a program that would be practical, anthroposophic and affordable. We (Antioch) then sent out an announcement and within weeks we had a group ready and eager to begin. We entered our first cohort group in April 2015 with a five-day retreat in Keene, New Hampshire, and continued with online and mentoring work throughout the next year with a second face-to-face retreat in April 2016. Many others have signed up for future cohort groups.

The program balances group work with independent readings and mentorship. Although a multi-year program would do a more thorough job, we set our sights on thirteen months and practicality: the five day retreat in Keene in April, a Renewal course or alternative offering elsewhere in the country in the following summer, independent readings from an assigned list of anthroposophic and mainstream sources in the fall, mentorship online and by phone in the winter and a final face-to-face session in Keene the following April. Participants in the program thus far have included administrators from charter and independent schools, faculty leaders, board members and those preparing for a change in jobs. We hope we can offer support as well as insight to those most involved in school governance.

As part of the preparation for working with these school leaders, I intensified my research in content areas I knew were essential for their work. Some of the subjects had been a focus of my consultations and action research for many years, whereas others were recent inspirations arising out of my inner work with Anthroposophy. I also reached out to several thought leaders in the movement for guest presentations in the program and articles. In several cases I found an article or chapter that did such a good job on a theme that I felt: If someone else says it better than I can, let's use it! Thus I am very grateful to these colleagues, their collaboration and permission to use their material. I am ever so happy to offer this new book on Leadership Development.

This book is for leaders and administrators in Waldorf schools, Camphill communities, farms, clinics and other not-for-profit initiatives. It could be used for personal study or in a team or board meeting. The themes are a sampling of issues that may be helpful, but are by no means an exhaustive coverage of governance. The hope is to stimulate discussion and awareness of these topics in a way that promotes self-reflection as well as personal and professional growth. Even if one is not in a formal leadership role at the present time, consideration of some of these topics can help us become better participants and followers.

In the end, we are servant leaders, doing what needs to be done for the sake of real human beings in our care. Our children believe in us. This devotion gives us the strength and courage to continue. We need the tools and insight to serve the high ideals we espouse. This leadership effort is not just about "a job"; it is a calling. Let us work together to respond!

2

BREATHING

"Music is a moral law. It gives soul to the universe, wings to the mind, flight to the imagination and charm and gaiety to life and to everything." —PLATO

For all of us fortunate to be alive on the Earth at this time, breathing is a routine bodily function. We breathe more rapidly when doing exercise, and more gently when asleep. Unless there is a problem in the respiratory system, such as bronchitis, few give breathing much attention (unless one meditates, but more on that later).

Those of us who have learned to observe group dynamics have observed that there is a breathing process in how people meet each other in conversation. There is an in-breath when one listens to and absorbs new information, and then an out-breath as one lets it go again or shares something in return. If people in a group have to take in too much information without an out-breath it can produce discomfort, even headaches. If there is too much outflow it can result in chaos and a feeling of exhaustion. Healthy meetings, as with human beings, need a balance of the in flow and outflow. A crucial function of the facilitator is to attend to this balance, calibrating the presentations with adequate time for questions and discussion. Groups need to breathe.

But let us go deeper. What is actually happening when one breathes? Of course we take in oxygen and expels CO_2. But that is only the most fundamental level. We are taking in air from the world around us, using it, and then letting it go again. How we do this says a lot about who we are as human beings. Those who are fearful, for example, might breathe in air in short gulps and then have trouble letting it go again. Someone in anger may expel too much air and even get dizzy afterward. So we see right away that breathing is connected to our feelings, our state of soul.

At the very beginning of his lectures for the teachers of the first Waldorf school given just before it opened in September 1919, Rudolf Steiner said that one of the essential tasks of the teacher was to help children learn to breathe rightly (Steiner, *Foundations of Human Experience,* pp. 38ff). When one first reads this comment it can come across as odd, even tangential to the obvious tasks of learning to read, write and compute numbers. Yet the more I have worked with this notion the more I have learned to respect what it stands for in terms of healthy development. For breathing has a great deal to do with a child's circulatory system, metabolic system and nervous system. Breathing is the mediator between these internal systems and the outer world surrounding the child. For instance, the young child "has not yet learned to breathe in such as way that breathing maintains the nerve–sense process rightly" (ibid., p. 40). Put another way, by harmonizing breathing with the nerve–sense process we draw the soul–spirit aspect of the child into the right relationship to the particular physical body the child has found in this current life. In other words, we are seeking to help the "genius" of children to find their home in the physical body inherited from their parents. To the extent that children find good teachers who see beyond the materialism of test scores and can lift their gaze to the actual living being of the children before of them, we can expect healthy human development. Waldorf schools are dedicated to human and social health as a fundamental basis of pedagogy.

Now how does all this relate to administration and leadership? First of all, we have not all had the benefit of a Waldorf education, and even those who have still have issues to resolve and inner work to do. But in the case of most people who are hired for administrative tasks in our schools, there is serious unfinished work to do particularly in the realm of breathing and inner harmony. Some have developed more in the realm of nerve senses, with the result that they are quick to perceive and name what is wrong, but have less skill in doing anything about it. Others have great strength of will and commitment to do good, but have not developed a clear understanding of how to apply their energy. There are many other examples one could give of people who come to the party with all sorts of costumes, and the organization is expected to assimilate and work with what is given.

To use a sports analogy, it is as if some come to the game with a basketball, others with bats and mitts, and others with golf balls. They all run out onto the field and expect to "play ball." And we see what happens!

On the other hand, anyone who has had the pleasure of watching a really good basketball game, for instance, will notice the clarity of roles and harmonious working of the team. Even a "star player" cannot score without a team. The passing of the ball and the collaboration of the players is a very visible form of breathing. The ball itself actually moves in patterns of receiving and throwing, in and out breath. How did they get to that place? Lots of practice... (breathing).

We all need to work on our breathing. There is something about my iPhone that has changed my breathing, at least it is easy to say it is the iPhone. I get pinged when emails come in, I receive interesting text messages, and when the phone rings I never know if is important or not until I answer it. (I find it very hard to disregard a ring or ping if I am nearby.) Turning the whole thing off or onto vibrate is like turning off life support; I find it very hard to do. *It*, the iPhone, has become my breathing with the world.

Yet of course, I know I am in charge of my iPhone, MacBook Pro, iPad and all the other things I have acquired in recent years. Yet it is curious that I have given them so much control of my life. My breathing, feeling good or frustrated at any point in the day, is highly dependent on the latest email or text message I have received. Even a person with spirit striving and meditative practice needs to summon extra resolve to overcome the allure of these external devices.

So, just as we have made great strides in technology (and I am grateful for the tools I have that allow me to type and process these thoughts), we need to take equally great strides in our inner development and the sharpening of our moral compass. This is essential if we are to retain our freedom to act as self-directed human beings.

Where do we begin? I suggest that one point of entry is the same as the one Steiner used in preparing teachers: in breathing. The notion is not new; ancient practices such as yoga focus on right breathing. There are many exercises given in a variety of spiritual practices than can assist in the development of healthy breathing. There are many places and opportunities to look these up and take up the practices best suited for ones own needs. (See, for instance, my book *Finding Your Self*, which focuses on meditative practices for teachers.)

Here is one more perspective that demonstrates the importance of breathing: Now we focus on breathing very much from the pulse-beat perspective, the "counting" and quantifying of heart and lung functioning. This is real time and very much focused on the here and now. Yet as told by Rudolf Steiner, in ancient times people had a longer view, a slow breathing approach that was very different. It consisted of this:

> At the beginning of earthly life, human beings become capable of receiving the thoughts. Just as we hold the breath within us for a certain time—between breathing in and breathing out—likewise those people conceived a certain fact, as follows: They imagined that they held the thoughts within themselves, yet only in the sense in which we hold the oxygen that belongs to the outer air. They imagined that they held the thoughts during the time of their earthly life and breathed them out again—out into the cosmic spaces—when they passed through the gate of death. Thus it was a question of breathing in (the beginning of life), holding the breath (the duration of earthly life), breathing out (sending forth the thoughts into the universe). (Steiner, *Karmic Relationships,* vol. 3, p. 16)

This is a remarkable picture, connecting breathing with thinking. As an author, I have long learned to value the importance living with thoughts, breathing with them day in and out before writing. The old Platonic law is that what is outer must become inner. So when vacationing in Bornholm in 2013 I visiting an old Medieval castle, and that outer perceptive experience transformed itself in my overnight sleeping into a chapter on Hammerhus and the insiders and outsiders of Waldorf schools (see my book, *A Second Classroom*). Again and again in life, what is perceived outwardly can become the stimulus for an idea. Perceptions give birth to concepts as described in Steiner's *Intuitive Thinking as a Spiritual Path*. In our soul life, we continuously process outer experiences and transform them into feelings and thoughts.

However, when we go a step further and do not just process things but also exercise some inner effort, it is possible, at least once in a while, to connect a newfound idea with an archetype, or what speaks to a larger truth. When this happens, it is a moment of great joy and recognition. From the welter of many ideas and thoughts, every once in a while something rises to the surface that speaks to a larger reality, something that has value beyond my little self and my daily struggle to get through life. When these connections are made from the idea of archetype, suddenly the day becomes radiant; meaning arises from the morass of information-overload, and I can hold on to something that becomes inner nourishment. This in turn gives me the strength to go on.

So to recap, perception can become concept; concepts can mature into ideas; over time, ideas can lead us to connect with a larger truth or archetype. That in turn gives us direction and meaning in life, and we can reenter the fray with renewed courage and inspiration. Then an author has something from which to write, the musician can compose rather than just play, and the painter is inspired anew. Creativity is at the heart of all original work, and the source of creativity is the human encounter with the archetype. Our breathing the thoughts in and out is a kind of intuitive bridge between our ordinary selves and the greater truths that are available, waiting to awaken in human consciousness.

Leaders and administrators need to find this fertile ground of inspiration. It cannot be programmed or organized; it can only be cultivated. I would like to suggest that attending to healthy breathing is a way to prepare the soil of the soul for the important work that stands before us.

3

MANAGEMENT AND LEADERSHIP

"Leaders must encourage their organizations to dance to forms of music yet to be heard." —WARREN G. BENNIS

The world today is filled with managers, while true leadership is hard to find. In part, this is due to the sheer press of work to do, the multitasking, the nature of the workplace today and societal expectations of performance. When good leaders are given too much to do, they can easily become managers. We are faced with a social phenomena of "get results today," solve problems in the moment, deliver profits each quarter, and this tends to place a higher premium on management skills. In contrast, leaders think strategically, look to the future and are often willing to endure short-term hardship if there is reasonable hope that decisions will bear fruit later on. Leaders tend to take an investment approach to resource allocation and decision-making; they see the horizon and emerging trends.

In his book *Leading Change,* John Kotter (Harvard Business Review Books, 2012) has a nice chart that clearly differentiates between management and leadership (see following page). He further points out that today's emphasis on management has been institutionalized in corporate cultures in a way that discourages employees from learning how to lead. Even success can lead to greater emphasis on management, as once one has achieved a certain level of performance the natural tendency is to try to maintain one's position. Sheer size can also hinder leadership, just as huge investment funds tend to be less nimble and "winners" are often buried in the averages of other investments. Some of the most

MANAGEMENT VERSUS LEADERSHIP

Management	Leadership
• Planning and budgeting: establishing detailed steps and timetables for achieving needed results, and then allocating the resources needed to make it happen	• Establishing Direction: developing a vision of the future—often the distant future—and strategies for producing the changes needed to achieve that vision
• Organizing and staffing: Establishing some structure for accomplishing plan requirements, staffing that structure with individuals, delegating responsibility and authority for carrying out the plan, providing policies and procedures to help guide people and procedures to help guide people and creating methods or systems to monitor implementation	• Aligning people: communicating direction in words and deeds to all those whose cooperation may be needed to influence the creation of teams and coalitions that understand the vision and strategies, and that accept their validity
• Controlling and problem solving: monitoring results, identifying deviations from plan and then planning and organizing to solve these problems	• Motivating and inspiring: energizing people to overcome major political, bureaucratic and resource barriers, to change by satisfying basic, but often unfulfilled, human needs

Produces a degree of predictability and order, and has the potential to consistently produce the short-term results expected by various stakeholders (e.g., for customers, always being on time; for stockholders, being on budget)	Produces change, often to a dramatic degree, and has the potential to produce extremely useful change (e.g., new products that customers want, new approaches to labor relations that help make a firm more competitive)

Adapted with permission from John P. Kotter, *A Force for Change: How Leadership Differs from Management* (Simon and Schuster, 1990).

serious turnaround challenges involve large entities such as McDonald's, Sears or Microsoft in the corporate world, or state universities in higher education. A tanker is harder to turn than a tugboat.

Yet change is not an option; it is a necessity. An organization is either leading change efforts or at least participating in new trends, or it is left in the wake of others. When Steve Jobs passed away, there were legitimate questions as to the future of Apple. Much to the relief of many, it appears thus far that Tim Cooke has continued to innovate and introduce new and improved products (although I do not have an Apple Watch). If one does not do this, to stay with the corporate model, the massive presence of an ITT or Xerox of the 1970s can become the mini-entity of today. If change is not forthcoming as a part of a growth strategy, change will be thrust upon one as part of downsizing if not outright closure.

For years higher education seemed to view itself as immune to change. Long traditions, tenure, ivy-covered brick buildings and so on seemed to defy the notion of change. Yet endowments can only shield an institution for a certain amount of time. In the end, one cannot survive without students. In my view, only those colleges and universities that innovate are sustainable. And technology is only one tool in what needs to be both content and delivery innovation. Technology is necessary for today's innovation in higher education, but not sufficient. (Someday I will write a piece just on higher education.)

Returning to the theme of change and leadership, I would like to once again cite John Kotter, this time in regard to his eight-stage process of creating major change:

1. ESTABLISHING A SENSE OF URGENCY
   · Examining the market and competitive realities
   · Identifying and discussing crises, or major opportunities
2. CREATING THE GUIDING COALITION
   · Putting together a group with enough power to lead the change
   · Getting the group to work together like a team.
3. DEVELOPING A VISION AND STRATEGY
   · Creating a vision to help direct the change effort
   · Developing strategies for achieving that vision

4. COMMUNICATING THE CHANGE VISION
   · Using every vehicle possible to constantly communicate the new vision and strategies
   · Having the guiding coalition role model the behavior expected of employees

5. EMPOWERING BROAD-BASED ACTION
   · Getting rid of obstacles
   · Changing systems or structures that undermine the change vision
   · Encouraging risk taking and nontraditional ideas, activities and actions

6. GENERATING SHORT-TERM WINS
   · Planning for visible improvements in performance, or "wins"
   · Creating those wins
   · Visibly recognizing and rewarding people who made the wins possible

7. CONSOLIDATING GAINS AND PRODUCING MORE CHANGE
   · Using increased credibility to change all systems, structures, and policies that don't fit together and don't fit the transformation vision
   · Hiring, promoting and developing people who can implement the change vision
   Reinvigorating the process with new projects, themes and change agents

8. ANCHORING NEW APPROACHES IN THE CULTURE
   · Creating better performance through customer-and productivity-oriented behavior, more and better leadership, and more effective management
   · Articulating the connections between new behaviors and organizational success
   · Developing means to ensure leadership development and succession[*]

Kotter shows, in many different ways, how skipping a step or moving too quickly through them can hinder lasting progress. Many leaders think that a few key decisions, such as reorganization, making an acquisition or laying some people off will be enough, and because short-term results often improve, the urgency for change can diminish after a few initial steps. Often leaders jump right to steps 5, 6 and 7, hoping that everything else will take care of itself. Kotter is adamant that the eight steps are necessary and must be carried out with a high level of intentionality.

---

[*] Adapted from John P. Kotter, "Why Transformation Efforts Fail," *Harvard Business Review* (Mar./Apr. 1995), p. 23.

A CEO or university president needs to be an active leader of the change effort, but there are many ways to lead. The traditional format is for the formal leader to organize some strategy sessions, develop a plan, announce it and then become its champion. All too often (in my view), the change effort becomes too closely identified with the specific leader. This can build in the possibility for change mortality when that specific leader moves on, or it can become too personalized. A collaborative leadership structure is less vulnerable to these tendencies, and the more the change effort is perceived as a whole-systems endeavor the better it will be implemented and sustained.

During the passing of Nelson Mandela some time ago, I went back to the book, *Mandela's Way: Lessons on Life, Love, and Courage* by Richard Stengel, in which Mandela's remarkable leadership is described from a variety of perspectives. Perhaps no other leader of his era had such a great challenge as that faced by him with apartheid. Talk about change efforts! Mandela had an entire nation and years of hurt and violence to contend with. Yet he took on a leadership role as the first president of a united country with remarkable modesty and charm. One of the characteristics of his unusual style was what he called "leading from behind," told in this memorable story:

> He turned to me and said, "You have never herded cattle, have you, Richard?" I said I had not. He nodded. As a young boy—as early as eight or nine years old—Mandela had spent long afternoons herding cattle. His mother owned some cattle of her own, but there was a collective herd belonging to the village that he and other boys would look after. He then explained to me the rudiments of herding cattle.
>
> "You know, when you want to get the cattle to move in a certain direction, you stand at the back with a stick, and then you get a few of the cleverer cattle to go to the front and move in the direction that you want them to go. The rest of the cattle follow the few more-energetic cattle in the front, but you are really guiding them from the back."
>
> He paused. "That is how a leader should do his work."
>
> This story is a parable, but the idea is that leadership at its most fundamental is about moving people in a certain direction—usually through changing the direction that is not necessarily by charging out

front and saying, "Follow me," but by empowering or pushing others to move forward ahead of you. (Stengel, pp. 76–77)

The author goes on to say:

That is what Mandela means by leading from behind. A good chief does not grandly state his opinion and command others to follow him. He listens, he summarizes, and then he seeks to mold opinion and steer people toward an action, not unlike the young boy herding cattle from the back. Mandela regards this as the best of African tradition of leadership. He sees the West as the bastion of personal ambition, where people fight to get ahead and leave others behind. The Renaissance idea of individualism never penetrated Africa like it did Europe and America. The African model of leadership is better expressed as ubuntu, the idea that people are empowered by other people, that we become our best selves through unselfish interaction with others.

I remember arriving one weekend morning at Mandela's house in Houghton. In the driveway, beyond the front gate, Mandela and a group of his advisers sat in discussion. I pulled up a chair just outside the circle. What struck me most forcefully was that these men were talking animatedly, some of them criticizing Mandela and telling him very directly that he was wrong about certain positions. All the men were respectful (a few just barely), and were quite fiery and outspoken. Mandela sat straight, almost unmoving, listening intently with a neutral expression. He would make an excellent poker player. Only at the end of the meeting, as the fellows were getting ready to go, did Mandela speak, and he summarized their views without saying exactly where he stood. I noticed that the men seemed more jovial once they had gotten their opinions off their chest, regardless of whether or not they had persuaded Mandela. Mandela knew that the surest way to defuse an argument is to listen patiently to the opposing point of view. (ibid. p. 81)

And these qualities are related to basic assumptions about other human beings:

Some call it a blind spot, others naiveté, but Mandela sees almost everyone as virtuous until proven otherwise. He starts with an assumption that you are dealing with him in good faith. He believes that, just as pretending to be brave can lead to acts of real bravery, seeing good in other people improves the chances that they will reveal their better selves.

It is extraordinary that a man who was ill treated for most of his life can see so much good in others. In fact, it was something frustrating to talk with him because he almost never had a bad word to say about anyone. He would not even say a disapproving word about the man who tried to have him hanged. I once asked him about John Vorster, the Nazi-sympathizing president of South Africa who tightened apartheid and rued the fact that Mandela and his comrades had not been executed.

"He was a very decent chap," Mandela said with complete sincerity. "In the first place, he was very polite. In referring to us, he used courteous terminology."

One of the leadership characteristics I most admired in Mandela was his ability to turn negative experiences into something positive, to see the best in every human being. Here is a further example:

We were talking one day about a prisoner who had been rival of Mandela's on Robin Island and who had actually put together a list of grievances about Mandela. When I asked him about the fellow, Mandela did not address the man's hostility but said, "What I took from him was his ability to work hard." . . .

What I took from him. Mandela seeks out the positive, the constructive. He chooses to look past the negative. He does this for two reasons: because he instinctively sees the good in people and because he intellectually believes that seeing good in others might actually make them better. If you expect more of people, whether they are coworkers or family members, they often contribute more. Or at least feel guilty if they do not. (ibid., pp. 117–118)

Another key quality of a true leader is the ability to take a few personal steps for each outer one (i.e., to demand change of oneself). In some of our classes at Antioch we challenge our students to learn something new, a skill or hobby. They are asked to observe themselves in the learning process. It is remarkable how changing just one thing can have repercussions for many other areas of life. Change is a kind of yeast; it affects the whole.

In the case of Mandela, one change was learning Afrikaans:

He also began studying manuals of a different kind: handbooks of Afrikaans grammar.

His comrades could understand his studying *The Art of War,* but not the art of Afrikaans poetry. They used to tease him about learning the language of the oppressor. But Mandela knew he could not defeat his enemy if he did not understand him, and that he could not understand him if he did not speak his language. Literally. And he was thinking even further ahead: There could be no dispensation in South Africa, no peaceful resolution of the conflict that did not somehow include the Afrikaner. Even as head of MK,* he did not envision driving Afrikaners into the sea; there would eventually need to be accommodation and negoiation.

When I asked him why he had started studying Afrikaans, he gave a very forthright answer, "Well, it's obvious because as a public figure, you do want to know the two main languages of the country, and Afrikaans is an important language spoken by the majority of the white population in the country and by the majority of the Colored people, and it's a disadvantage not to know it." He paused, then added: "When you speak Afrikaans, you know, you go straight to their hearts."

You go straight to their hearts. It was an echo of something else he had famously said about the art of persuasion: "Don't address their brains. Address their hearts." This is true in many arenas of our lives—whether we are trying to persuade a colleague to see our point of view, win someone's vote, or attract new customers. If you want to make the sale, address the heart. Mandela did this with his own supporters as well as the Afrikaner. But in the case of the Afrikaner, he had much more to overcome. Mandela knew that prejudice was not rational and that he could not address it only in a rational way. He needed whites to accept democracy and the idea of a diverse nation not only intellectually but also emotionally. Only then would he achieve the accommodation he truly sought. He had appealed to people's minds, but he knew that his unlimited victory would only come when he won over their hearts. (ibid., p. 134)

It is hard to find a book on leadership without frequent references to vision, long term planning or strategic thinking. As said earlier, managers deal mostly with the present, whereas leaders help people move forward into the future. Once again, Mandela gives us a good example in what he calls the "long game":

---

* MK (*Umkhonto we Sizwe*) was the armed wing of the African National Congress (ANC) party in South Africa.

Twenty-seven years in prison teaches you many things, but one of them is to play a long game. As a young man, Mandela was impatient: He wanted change yesterday. Prison taught him to slow down, and it reinforced his sense that haste often leads to error and misjudgment. Above all, he learned how to postpone gratification—his whole life embodies that." (ibid., p. 174)

"In the long run"—it is a phrase he uses often. That is the way he thinks, the distance at which his mind works best. He is not quick or facile; he likes to marinate in ideas. If everyone has a natural distance— sprinting, middle-distance, long-distance—Mandela is a long-distance runner, a long-distance *thinker*. And prison was a marathon. When we were talking about an issue or a problem, he would sometimes say, "It will be better in the long run" (ibid., p. 174).

So here we have the key ingredients of leadership: the long game, vision, going straight to the heart of the matter, self-development, positivity, leading from behind, recognizing others. All this can then become a powerful impulse for change.

4

FACILITATION

"A jazz musician is a juggler who uses harmonies instead of oranges."
—BENNY GREEN

In my book *Organizational Integrity,* I refer to facilitation as a heart function in an organization. Like the heart, it is absolutely vital to the health of the entire organism. When facilitation is done skillfully it can take a challenging situation and turn it into an opportunity. But when facilitation is inept, even gifted people can run amok. In fact, the role of facilitator is so crucial that I wish to devote several pages to the basic "nuts and bolts" of the craft, as represented in the pages below that come from a text I found very helpful: *Effective Meeting Planning and Facilitating* by Robert DeGroot (2012).

> For many organizations, meetings are a way of life. Clearly, making these meetings as productive as possible goes a long way toward increasing organizational productivity.... Many types of meetings can benefit from having a facilitator present. Some of the more common include strategic planning or visioning, brainstorming, stakeholder input, project evaluation, staff retreats, policy development or review, project design, and prioritization of goals and actions.
>
> A common misconception is that good results will occur simply by getting all the experts together in the same room. Getting the right people together is certainly important, but that's just a first step. A facilitator supports the meeting process by keeping the group on track to produce the desired objectives.

THE ROLE OF A FACILITATOR

A facilitator is someone who uses knowledge of group processes to design and deliver the structure needed for effective meetings. Facilitators can be individuals from outside the group or organization, or an internal team member or meeting leader. Helping plan the agenda is a key function of this role. Facilitators help the group members decide where they want to go, but the group itself deliberates and makes the final decisions.

At the meeting, a facilitator acts as a "content-neutral" person who leads the group through the agenda—but does not contribute to the substance of the discussion and has no decision-making authority.

Facilitator functions:

- Helps group define its meeting purpose and desired objectives for a meeting
- Designs processes for the group to meet its goals, create products or make decisions
- Guides group discussions to keep meeting participants on track by asking key questions and reminding groups of their stated goals
- Ensures that group assumptions are stated and tested, and that all participants' voices are heard
- Acts as a "neutral party" that has no stake in the outcome of a meeting
- Takes notes to record key points of conversation and group decisions
- Helps group plan to carry out decisions made at a meeting

Facilitator beliefs:

- A group of informed individuals, working together, can accomplish more than one person working alone
- Everyone's opinion is of equal value, regardless of rank or position
- People are more committed to ideas and plans that they have helped to create
- Participants will act responsibly in assuming accountability for their decisions
- The process—if designed well and sincerely applied—can be trusted to achieve results

Key facilitator characteristics:

- Neutrality on the issue being discussed or decided upon
- No decision-making authority
- Acceptable to all members of the group
- Some knowledge of the issues being discussed so facilitator can follow the conversation and keep it on track
- Trust in the group to make the right decisions for itself
- Ability to synthesize and organize ideas quickly

A few comments on the preceding: I have found that one of the greatest challenges for effective facilitation is working to break old meeting habits. People bring a variety of experiences from other meetings in other organizations, and sometimes unconsciously play them out in the present situation. Thus one might have shades of corporate meetings, some with habits from other nonprofits, some from educational settings...all these collective experiences play into the present. In addition, participants in your organization have sometimes been together for years, and habits have developed. Although experience is often a good thing, when meeting habits surreptitiously creep in, one can have a United Nations type situation, and the facilitator ends up being a translator as well as process coach. Some behaviors can be outright dysfunctional.

One way to deal with old habits is to take the time to discuss the new protocols in depth, practice them and then reflect on progress. This has the effect of making behaviors more conscious, which in turn tends to at least sideline old habits while new skills are learned.

PLANNING A PRODUCTIVE MEETING OR WORKSHOP

The following steps for planning a productive meeting do not necessarily have to be done in the order listed. In fact, facilitators often work through a few steps simultaneously, with one exception: defining the meeting purpose and desired objectives always come first.

1. Define the meeting purpose and objectives
2. Create the participant list
3. Establish roles
4. Develop the agenda
5. Identify background materials
6. Plan the meeting space

1. Define the Meeting Purpose and Objectives

The first step should always be to ask, "Why are we having this meeting?" Typical reasons include planning or visioning, decision-making, team building, problem solving, evaluating or tracking a program or process and information sharing.

Objectives are the expected, concrete outputs of a meeting. Objectives should be specific and measurable, such as a tangible product or a potentially measurable increase in knowledge or understanding on a specific subject. A tangible product might be a strategic plan or a funding priority list.

If the desired objective is an increase in knowledge or understanding, it is important for the desired objective to shed light on why this is needed. The desired objective should therefore include a "so that" statement. For example, "Increased understanding of customer needs is necessary so that new decision-support tools can be developed to address the impacts of climate change."

2. Create the Participant List

For a meeting to be truly successful, the right people need to participate. During the planning phase, organizers should think about the people needed to finalize decisions and commitments.

If the meeting requires that a decision be made, then the decision makers should be present. Meeting size is also important, since more than twenty participants can be difficult to manage if consensus is needed. If some people in the room are attending to observe, not participate, then their roles should be made clear to everyone before the meeting begins.

3. Establish Roles

It is important to determine the roles people will play at the meeting. Roles can shift during a meeting, but assigning roles in advance will lead to a more organized and productive experience for all. The following are common roles for a typical facilitated meeting:

Facilitator: The facilitator is the one who contributes structure and process to interactions so groups are able to function effectively. The facilitator moves the meeting along and keeps it focused. Ideally, a facilitator is neutral toward the outcome of the meeting. When complete neutrality is needed, or when dealing with contentious issues, the group will benefit by using a facilitator from outside the office or organization. Using a professional facilitator is strongly encouraged when the meeting will have forty or more participants.

Breakout Group Facilitator: Breakout group facilitators guide the small discussion groups within a meeting. For the people acting in this role, having some facilitation training or experience is helpful.

Meeting Leader: This is typically the person who convenes the meeting and serves as the "team captain," providing direction on the purpose and desired objectives of the meeting. Meeting leaders are often content experts for the issues being discussed.

Facilitative Leaders: Whereas the use of a facilitator from outside the group is ideal for many situations, groups do not always have the resources to hire one. In these instances, a group member or the meeting leader will serve as a facilitative leader. When serving in this dual role, the facilitative leader may or may not be neutral on the issue at hand, but can still provide the effective facilitation practices needed.

Meeting Planner: A meeting planner organizes the logistics of the meeting, which involves contracting with the meeting location, arranging for catering, purchasing supplies, and so forth. Although there is often overlap between this role and that of the meeting leader or facilitator, it can be extremely helpful, especially for larger meetings of fifty or more people, to designate a meeting planner.

Recorder: The recorder documents the process, deliberations, decisions, actions taken (or to be taken), and outcomes of a meeting, with varying degrees of detail as needed. The facilitator can also act as the recorder by writing main points of the discussion on a flip chart. For taking more detailed notes, however, it is necessary to have a separate person in the recorder role. A multi-day meeting or a meeting involving breakout groups can use many recorders.

A few additional words on minute-taking; I find it important to reflect accurately the collective memory of decisions and even some discussions, otherwise individual participants will write their own history of what happened, and those individual versions then live on into future meetings. Thus one can imagine three parts to minute taking:

1. The actual minutes of decisions made. These need to be stated as clearly as possible, need to be read back to the group at the end of the meeting and ideally approved while everyone is still present.

2. A summary of some of the main points from the discussions. When dealing with a nonprofit, the minutes of decisions are usually available to all interested parties, but the summary of discussion points can be an internal document to facilitate the formulation of future agendas and for future reference. It is good to try to listen for the threads that connect topics and that can lead to progress on any issue. This then makes possible one last aspect....

3. In reviewing the decisions and the discussion summary, it is possible for the facilitator to look for the intent of the group and guide future meetings accordingly. Sometimes a group is really saying something collectively that is not really reflected in any decision or any one statement. This awareness of the collective intent and direction is like knowing whether one is playing Bach or Scott Joplin; it makes a difference. In this third stage one is looking at the entire "score" not the individual notes.

Participants: The participants provide input, discussion and feedback on the topics provided on the agenda. Participants can also provide feedback on the meeting design after the meeting has concluded.

4. Develop the Agenda

The agenda provides the focusing framework for the meeting, puts tasks in a logical order and time frame, and offers an outline for writing the summary report at the meeting's conclusion.

In the hands of a skilled facilitator, an agenda should be considered a guideline, not a law. Flexibility is essential to ensure that topics are resolved or tasks accomplished in the best manner possible. Facilitators should anticipate which items could be postponed and be prepared to table them until a more appropriate time.

There are typically two versions of an agenda. The participant agenda is the concise version participants receive before a meeting. At a minimum, the participant agenda includes the meeting title, location, start and end times, objectives, discussion topics, and information about how and when attendees will participate. The participant agenda is a clear and streamlined version of the detailed process agenda.

The process agenda has the additional information the facilitator and meeting leaders need to ensure that the meeting runs smoothly. Putting together the detailed process agenda helps the meeting leaders think through the details of the entire session.

The letters "OPQRST" provide an easy way to remember the six components of a process agenda:

- **Order** of the facilitation processes (the agenda) and specific objective for each **Process,** techniques used to gather information throughout each process (e.g., listing, brainstorming, grouping, prioritizing, sticky-dot voting, etc.).
- **Question** (starting question) and the explanation given to initiate each facilitated process
- **Recording** method used to document the information as it is received during each process (e.g., three-column matrix)
- **Supplies** needed to perform each process (Post-it notes, for example)
- **Timing** and estimated duration for each process

5. Identify Background Materials

Background materials should provide participants with the information needed to meaningfully participate in the meeting. Ideally, participants should receive this information at least one week in advance. Materials to include in a meeting background package:

- The participant agenda
- List of participants
- Any relevant information participants should read before the meeting—including topical information on issues that will be discussed; it is also a good practice to let participants know if materials will be available at the meeting or if they should bring their own copies of the digital materials that were provided before the meeting

6. Plan the Meeting Space

An important part of meeting dynamics is the meeting environment. A convenient location for all participants is a plus. A neutral location should be considered for contentious discussions. If participants are traveling, send hotel information well in advance so everyone can stay in the same place.

How the room is set up should depend on how the content will be delivered and what type of interaction is expected between participants.

QUESTIONS TO CONSIDER WHEN DESIGNING AN AGENDA

Purpose and desired objectives
- What is the primary purpose of this meeting? Can the meeting purpose be posed as a single phrase or sentence that will guide meeting planning?
- What are the desired objectives? What will the participants walk out of this meeting with (products or knowledge)?
- What decisions, if any, will be made at this meeting?
- How much can the group realistically expect to accomplish in the time allotted?

Participants and roles
- Who are the group members (both the individuals and the organizations they represent)?
- What are the backgrounds of the individuals and organizations? What are the interpersonal dynamics? Do they know each other well?
- Who will serve as the meeting leader?
- Is the facilitator neutral and perceived as such? How important is neutrality?
- Are there any objectives or motivations that need to be addressed up front?
- Will there be other people helping (other leaders, facilitators, recorders etc.)?
- Will the appropriate people be present to finalize decisions or ensure that commitments can be made and the decisions carried out?

Logistics
- Where will the meeting be held?
- Who is the contact person for facility and logistical arrangements?
- Is this the most appropriate location? (Consider "territory" issues, convenience, comfort, accessibility.)
- What kind of space, furniture, wall space (if needed for posters or flip-chart notes), lighting and audiovisual equipment does the site have?
- What are the starting and ending times? Are there adequate breaks in the agenda?
- Have arrangements been made for food and beverages?
- Is any additional equipment needed (audiovisual, displays, computers etc.)?

(DeGroot 2012, p. 7.)

Different setups will allow for different types of learning and participation. Common room setup options include the following.

Conference Style: Participants are seated on four sides of a table. This style is often used for small committee meetings or similar meetings of this type, where interaction between participants is anticipated and expected.

Hollow Square: Tables are arranged in a square in which the center is open. Chairs are placed around the perimeter of the square. This setup is used for larger committee-type meetings where interaction among participants is important.

U-shape: Rectangular tables are positioned to form a "U," with chairs placed around the outside. This setup is used for committee meetings as well, but is particularly helpful when using audiovisual equipment so that all participants can see a presentation when a screen is placed at the open part of the U.

Theater Style: Rows of chairs are placed next to each other facing the front of the room. A speaker or presenter is at the front of the room. This style maximizes the available seating and works well when the audience needs to take minimal notes and when participant interaction will be minimal.

Classroom Style? Rows of tables face the front of the room with two to four chairs at each. This setup is appropriate when there is a presentation at the front of the room and participants are expected to take notes. There usually will be some dialogue between the presenter and the audience. Participation between audience members will be limited.

Roundtables: Eight to ten chairs are arranged around small, round tables. This style can be used for small breakout groups. Participants can easily converse with one another.

Executing a Productive Meeting

Setting Expectations: Setting realistic expectations of what will be achieved is an important part of meeting planning and facilitation. If the agenda is overly ambitious, participants may feel let down if all the objectives are not met, even when substantial progress has been made. Conversely, participants may be caught off guard if more input is needed from them than originally anticipated. Articulating meeting expectations and participant roles is important both before and during the meeting.

The meeting leader or facilitator also should explain how the input gathered at the meeting will be used and what the next steps in the process will be (e.g., a draft report will go out for review, actions identified at the meeting will be completed and so on). Participants should know if the decisions they reach will be final or if their input will be viewed as a recommendation for someone else to use.

Meeting leaders should give participants clear expectations about what is being covered at the meeting. There may be topics that participants would like to discuss that are not appropriate for the meeting or that will be discussed at a future meeting. The facilitator and meeting leader should make this clear before the meeting and reiterate the point, when appropriate, by reviewing the meeting agenda and objectives.

Managing Time: Limiting time is an essential part of well-run meetings. Although time limits can create anxiety, most participants will appreciate starting and ending on time more than they will resent the pressure of time limits. The first step is to map out time limitations for each activity on the agenda. Make sure each activity is given a specific amount of time that is adequate to address the issue. Practice activities before the meeting to test the time assumptions, and, using this information, establish time limits for speakers, discussion and less-structured activities. Consider appointing a timekeeper and giving that person authority to stop people, with ample warning (e.g., a "two-minute sign" or other signal), when their time is up. Having a visible clock in the room is also helpful.

Here again, the need to be flexible is paramount. The facilitator or meeting leader must know what agenda items can be put off to another meeting, decided quickly or delegated to a participant or subcommittee to decide. Facilitators must be ready to tweak the agenda during the meeting, as needed, with the ultimate goal of accomplishing meeting objectives while letting everyone leave on time.

Establishing Ground Rules: Setting ground rules is important. While most ground rules reiterate common sense, it is still beneficial to draw attention to them at the beginning of a meeting. After presenting the ground rules, the facilitator may ask, "Does anyone disagree with sticking to these ground rules during our meeting?" If no one has any objections, the ground rules can be referred to if there are problematic interactions during the workshop, such as people interrupting each other or not coming back from breaks on time. Some of the more common ground rules are:

- Don't make or receive phone calls or use any personal electronics during the meeting; set phones to silent or vibrate.
- Start and end sessions on time.
- Commit to being back from breaks on time.
- Everyone participates.
- All participants are considered equal.
- Only one person talks at a time—don't interrupt.
- Raise your hand to speak (if the group has more than six participants).
- Listen to ideas without judging.
- Clean up after yourself.
- Groups can decide on their own ground rules at the beginning of a meeting if needed." (DeGroot, pp. 9–10)

The next section deals with decision-making, which is also covered in a separate chapter in this book.

PROCESS TOOLS FOR MAKING DECISIONS

Professional facilitators draw from a library of tools to aid groups in making decisions collaboratively. The following are a few of the most commonly used and easiest to implement.

Consensus Decision-making: The stated objective of many meetings is to reach consensus, but participants need to know the degree of consensus needed. In a perfect world, all group members would leave the meeting with a high degree of satisfaction with the decisions made at the meeting, a perfect consensus. While this is sometimes possible, resource and time constraints and strong opinions make perfect consensus difficult to achieve. It is important to think strategically about the degree of consensus needed.

In many instances a "comfortable consensus" is enough. This term refers to final agreements that all participants can at least live with and group members will not try to actively derail. On the other hand, issues that affect group members personally, or that group members have passionate feelings about, may need a high degree of consensus to get everyone on board with the group decision.

Facilitators have to be flexible with the level of consensus that is possible. When no degree of consensus is forthcoming at a time when a decision has to be made, the facilitator can default to majority voting. The easiest way to do this is by a simple show of hands.

By the way, to change a consensus decision one needs consensus, which is not so easy to achieve!

Consultation: When holding a public meeting or dealing with diverse groups of stakeholders or parties that have already agreed to disagree on some issues, the meeting objective might be to come up with a list of suggested recommendations. Facilitating a conversation between such groups can help them better understand each other's viewpoints and interests and may open up the possibility of consensus-based decision-making in the future.

Prioritization: Sometimes the desired objective of a meeting is to assign a priority level to a list of needs, options or solutions for the decision makers. An excellent technique for determining which of the components are most important to a group is "sticky-dot voting" (in which) a list of items is provided. Participants are given a number of small dots with an adhesive backing and told to place the dots next to the ideas they like the best. Specific selection criteria can be used to guide this exercise. Participants can be given the option of placing all their dots next to one item, or they may be directed to distribute them among the items. The facilitator tallies up the number of dots next to each item to determine the overall priorities of the group.

THEORIES OF GROUP INTERACTION

The following concepts are helpful models for facilitators and meeting leaders. The models enhance insight into group interactions and will help to design the agenda and facilitate discussion.

Stages of a Discussion: Meetings can be viewed as a series of discussions with three phases.

- Opening—multiple ideas are generated and clarified, or information is gathered. This phase includes brainstorming, general discussion, and question and answer sessions.
- Narrowing—the information gathered is organized by eliminating duplicate ideas, combining similar ideas or evaluating options.
- Closing—decisions are made, priorities are set.

Viewing discussions in this way helps facilitators keep the group focused on specific tasks. For example, during the opening phase of a discussion, a facilitator will encourage participants not to evaluate any ideas but just to generate as many ideas as possible.

During the closing phase of a discussion, it can be useful for the group to use specific criteria for deciding on a preferred solution or prioritizing options. For example, if the organization is trying to decide on the best projects to take on over the next year, the criteria for prioritizing may be that the project (a) be feasible given current resources and (b) advance the mission of the organization.

Positions versus Interests: Facilitators need to be adept at knowing the difference between positions and interests. When a group is having trouble agreeing on a solution to a problem, it is often because participants are focused on their positions instead of their interests or values.

A "position" is an opinion about how a problem should be solved or how a group should go about accomplishing an objective. An "interest" is an underlying value or area of importance for an individual or group. Focusing on interests instead of positions increases the chance of forming consensus within a group. An example of a position might be that "the development should be allowed." The underlying interest, however, is concern about jobs, tax revenue and community quality of life.

When a group comes to an impasse, a facilitator can attempt to guide the discussion down to the level of underlying interests and values by asking probing questions such as "Why do you think this is the best solution?" and "What makes you feel so strongly about this issue?" Focusing on interests instead of positions can be useful when working with groups with a high degree of conflict.

FACILITATION TECHNIQUES

The following techniques are used by facilitators during meetings to assist groups in accomplishing their objectives.

Breakout Groups: Some groups can be too large to enable in-depth discussion. For example, in a one-hour discussion session involving 100 people, many participants would not be able to share their thoughts. Depending on the nature of the issue, the facilitator may decide to break a large group into smaller groups of five to twenty participants. These groups usually "report" back to the larger group to share the results of their discussion or any decisions made.

Active Listening: The facilitator should look people in the eye, use attentive body language, and make participants understand that they are being heard. Body language should neither show support for or disapproval of any suggestions, comments or ideas, since this can discourage open communication. The facilitator should face and take a step toward the person who is speaking to show interest.

Asking Questions: Question test assumptions, invite participation, gather information and probe for hidden points. The facilitator can ask open-ended questions to encourage thorough discussion of all ideas presented.

Paraphrasing: This involves repeating what has been said to let participants know they are being heard, to let others hear the point a second time and to clarify key ideas. This also provides an opportunity to ascertain if the facilitator has correctly "heard" or interpreted what was said.

Summarizing: After listening attentively to all that has been said, a facilitator should offer a concise and timely summary. Summarizing is a good way to revive a discussion, or to end one when things seem to be wrapping up.

Synthesizing: Although it may be appropriate sometimes to record individual ideas of each participant, in other situations the facilitator may encourage attendees to comment on and build on each other's ideas and then record the "collective idea" on a flip chart. This builds consensus and commitment.

Negative Polling: It is sometimes easier to reveal disagreement within a group than to confirm agreement. Often used during the "closing" part of a discussion, the negative poll is a way to find out if the group is ready to confirm a decision and move on to the next task. When using this tool, the facilitator can ask the group if anyone disagrees with what has been suggested or put forth by participants. If no one speaks up, it is usually safe to move on. If any individual has hesitation, he or she will usually speak up in a negative poll.

Boomeranging: Participants will often look to the facilitator to answer questions about content or suggest solutions. However, the facilitator is the process expert, not the content expert, and must resist the temptation to solve content problems for the group. Instead, the facilitator can "boomerang" the question back to the group by asking the following questions: What do *you* think the groups should do? What does the *group* feel is the best choice? How would *you* suggest solving this problem?

Restating the Purpose: When a discussion gets off track and participants are talking about issues that are not on the agenda, the facilitator can ask the group to pause and reconsider the meeting purpose or desired objectives. The facilitator may say, "I sense this issue is important to the group, but the purpose of our meeting today is _____, so would it be okay to table this discussion until a later time?"

Three-step Intervention to Deal with Disruptive Behaviors: The facilitator can use this intervention when a person's behavior is disruptive to the meeting. Step 1—Describe problematic behaviors. For example, "Allen and Sue, both of you have left and returned three times during the meeting." Step 2—Make an impact statement to tell group members how their actions are affecting the facilitator, the process or other people. For example, "We had to stop our discussion and start over on three occasions because of this." Step 3—Redirect the person's behavior. This can be done by asking members for their suggestions about what to do. For example, "What can we do to make sure this doesn't happen again?" or "Would everyone like a short break so that when we return everyone will be able to participate fully?"

Labeling Sidetracks: The facilitator should let the group know when it gets off track. The group can decide if it wants to pursue the sidetrack or get back to the agenda.

Parking Lot: The facilitator can use a flip-chart page or ask the recorder to keep a sheet labeled "Parking Lot." Sidetrack items are placed in the parking lot and reviewed later to determine if any should be included in a future agenda. Questions and concerns recorded in the parking lot need to be followed up—either by the facilitator or (more often) by the meeting leader.

Mirroring: The facilitator can periodically tell group members how they appear so they can interpret their actions and make corrections. This is particularly effective for drawing the entire group's attention back to the tasks at hand or dealing with disruptive behaviors. This is also a good way to see if the pace is too slow, too fast, or if the group needs a break. "I see some confused faces out there. Do we need to clarify the process? Or perhaps take a break?"

Remaining Neutral: The facilitator must focus on the "process" role and avoid the temptation to offer an opinion on the topic under discussion. A facilitator who becomes involved in the content discussion must let the group know that he or she is stepping out of the facilitator role.

FACILITATING TELECONFERENCES, VIDEO CONFERENCES, AND WEBINARS

There are special considerations for facilitating meetings where one or all group members are participating via phone, video or the Web. Below are some of the techniques used for virtual meetings.

Before the meeting:

- Make any special arrangements for the delivery of background information and all meeting materials.
- Make sure that all participants have directions for how to gain access to the meeting, including conference-call code, directions for joining the webinar and so on.

During the meeting:

- Conduct a roll call to establish that people are engaged and ready to proceed, and to let everyone know who is participating.
- Keep a list of participant names in front of the facilitator. As the meeting progresses, the facilitator should make a check mark beside people's names every time they speak to keep track of who is on the line and help identify the people who need to be brought into the conversation.
- Ask participants to identify themselves before they speak.
- Ask participants to mute their phones when they are not speaking to minimize interference on the line.
- Periodically check in with participants who are not physically in the room, because in-room participants may not be able to pick up on important nonverbal cues.

Meeting Evaluation: Collecting information from meeting participants on how well they thought the meeting went can be used to make future meetings more productive. An evaluation form is a common way to get this feedback.

Another tactic is to spend a few minutes at the end of the meeting asking participants what went well and what could be changed or improved. The facilitator then records the responses on two different sheets of flip-chart paper or on one sheet with two columns for the aforementioned questions. Some facilitators call this a "Plus/Delta Exercise." Asking the group to answer these questions in a round-robin format is also a productive approach.

Meeting Follow-up: Meeting follow-up starts before the meeting begins. During the planning stage, the meeting leader, facilitator, and planning team should discuss what type of meeting follow-up will be done and who is responsible. This will help guide the recorders at the meeting in knowing what information should be captured, to what level of detail, and in what format.

A short meeting summary document should be drafted within two weeks of the meeting, if possible. The summary should contain, at a minimum, the action items and next steps, including due dates and responsible parties. More formal summary reports can include background information, main points of discussion and answers to questions asked by participants. Participants should know what type of meeting summary will be compiled and if they will be asked to review such a document before it is final.

CONCLUSION

Knowing how to plan and facilitate an effective meeting is a highly valuable skill. There is a growing need for increased facilitation skills as decision processes become more collaborative and input is needed from many perspectives.

Whereas written materials cannot replace formal facilitation training, this primer provides the basic concepts and techniques. Using the material put forth in this publication will help people new to this process design and conduct effective meetings and group interactions" (DeGroot, pp. 15–18).

↓

There is an old Quaker saying that goes something like this: "There is that of God in every person." My read of this wonderful expression is that a facilitator always needs to remember the spirit in each human being in the room. Old behaviors and habits start to fade away when a facilitator works with the spirit in each person, the higher Self that is in a process of becoming. A facilitator always needs to see the best in each person and believe in positive outcomes. To this end, the person in the role of facilitator needs to do everything possible to model what is expected of others.

To facilitate means to "make easy," to help the group do what it could not do alone. One is a servant to the group, always working to make everyone feel a sense of ownership and participation in the results.

This also involves the inner work of the facilitator. One has to enter a meeting centered, focused, and well prepared. If the "center" in one-self is strong one will not be bothered by some of the inevitable challenges to group work and they will not linger afterward. It is easier to release things if one is inwardly strong. It can help to think of oneself as a clear stream: the logs and stones will come along, but they can be guided to the shore a put at rest if one works with the current and flow of the meeting. One needs to be fully present for everyone, silent as to personal feelings to the extent possible so that one can "attend" fully to what is happening. One has to walk a fine line between being a "friend" but not a counselor, accessible but not partial to any one sub group or special interest. In short, facilitation is an art every bit as refined as playing the *Goldberg Variations* on a piano…a crucial building block of all social architecture.

Decision-making:
A Litmus Test for Leaders

"Jazz will endure just as long people hear it through their feet instead of their brains." — John Philip Sousa

Just as a musical score is for an orchestra or numbers are for an accountant, decisions are the foundation of leadership. Although one can discuss leadership styles and a variety of other attributes, in the end a leader has to be able to make decisions if she or he is to have the confidence of others. One can procrastinate for a while, delegate and defer to others, but in the end no other aspect goes as close to the core of leadership than does decision-making. Others, especially those outside the organization may not know all that transpires within, but a decision is a clear statement of action that reflects a leader's philosophical orientation, ability to work with others and sense of priorities. Collectively, the decisions emanating from an organization are a crucial "tell" of what is happening within. You may not know the details, but a good decision inspires confidence, a poor decision often does not pass the "smell test" of even the most peripheral players. Decision-making goes to the "heart" of an organization.

Yet relatively little has been researched or written about the anatomy of decision-making. What is a decision anyway? Are there stages in making good decisions? How can we prepare ourselves and our leaders to make good decisions?

What is a decision? Although it might later appear in an email or hard copy letter, these artifacts are the *results* of decisions, they appear *after* a decision is made. In fact, even as the words are spoken in a meeting or a conversation, they are already referring to a past event. A decision happens in a split second, and we know it mostly because it has already happened.

I like to compare awareness of a decision to taking a photograph, or catching an autumn leaf floating down in the breeze. It is there for a flash, and then it is gone. We often even miss opportunities for making a decision, and then the circumstances have changed and we need to move on.... First, it is important to appreciate that a decision is an ephemeral phenomena. It has almost no substance on the physical plane; in fact, one could say a decision is a spiritual event in the consciousness of an individual.

Now just as nutrition is essential for physical health, there are certain conditions and processes that can promote healthy decision-making. One of the most important aspects is to attend to process:

What are the stages of decision-making? In the March 2014 edition of *Anthroposophy Worldwide*, Paul Mackay describes Heinz Zimmermann's approach to meetings. They worked together on the Executive Council of the Anthroposophical Society and came to understand three stages:

1. Intention. This has the character of exploring a certain direction, looking at a goal that meets a perceived need, an idea that is worthy of further work.
2. Discussion. This stage has a quality of drafting, of sketching the options, looking at the objective situation at hand and the broader social context. Different perspectives are shared and that can result in modification to the originally stated intention.
3. Decision. This takes the project or plan into the realm of reality, it sets in motion an action, or at least a series of steps, that has the possibility of changing the environment.

There are other ways to describe these stages. I have learned to appreciate the first stage as a time of assimilation in which those who will be involved in a later decision need to immerse themselves in data and information that cluster around the stated intention. It is helpful to ask: Are we looking at the right data or just at what the "system" produced?

Is the data accurate? Has it been "tested" or at least questioned? The second stage, or discussion, has the quality of sifting and digesting. What does all this mean? Are there patterns, trends? A good discussion goes beyond synthesis to some analysis. Are there different scenarios that can be imagined? How will the different possible solutions affect the people concerned? What about our image and reputation? Then the third phase can be seen as bringing the original intention into a "form" that can be sent out into the world. That is why in many meetings participants will turn to the scribe at this stage and ask: What are we really saying with this decision? The wording and boundaries have to be clear. If not, groups tend to revisit the same decisions again and again.

This is not a fixed method, but I urge groups and leaders to attend to process, or at least to have a process and honor it. Even if the act of making a decision remains a mystery, the process should not be...the process needs to be transparent to all those within and even those outside the decisive group. It is great when a leader can say: We are taking up this topic so that...[intention] and we will hold open a period for discussion that will involve the following groups and people...and we (the executive team or some other) will make the final decision at such and such a date. This is an exercise in transparency, even if the content of the decision does not allow for full participation.

In all of this, time management is an issue. Process is often understood to be a kind of license to take as long as it takes, but there are positives and negatives associated with too much or too little time for a decision-making process. In a hierarchical, rigid organization the tendency is to take too little time for process and simply "announce" decisions. There are good reasons to have this structure, such as when the firemen/women arrive on the scene of a blaze. There are many cases in which all one wants is swift, effective decision-making from the top down. The more urgent the need the greater the case may be for top-down management. Yet there are other situations in which it is best to give things some time, to let a process unfold gradually so time can "inform" the participants. Learning to know the land before planting, practicing child observation before changing lesson plans, reviewing the accounts before budgeting are just three examples of using time as a friend. Generally, the more one is dealing with developmental growth the more we want to err on the side of healthy process, and the more one has specific outcomes in mind (a factory) the more one wants to speed things up. An essential leadership function is to learn to discern the time needed or available in a given situation and set a course accordingly. A leader is like the conductor of an orchestra, setting the tempo but knowing that real music will only arise when everyone is playing their individual instruments. (Playing from the same score is also crucial, but that is a topic unto itself.)

Another factor is the relative complexity of a decision. If there are multiple parties involved, or stages of implementation, or the chess pieces are in constant motion, one has to do things differently from when one is making a simple or routine decision (putting out a fire). The danger occurs when complex situations are handled in a routine way, or when simple issues are made complex because participants are using the occasion to surface pet projects. I have seen a discussion about setting up a room for an assembly or meeting become a surrogate for power and control issues in a group. It is not about the chairs, an observer might say, but the folks in this room certainly seem excited about things.... Why? Especially in resource scarce nonprofits, often the simplest issues become complex decisions because everyone wants to have an oar in the pond.

Now let's look at the different types of decisions that can be made. Groups do not make decisions, individuals do. Yet for the sake of time, one needs to have a variety of methods to quickly "collect" the sum of individual decisions so one can understand the will of the group. Most often what happens is someone makes a declarative statement that summarizes the sense of the meeting, and then the facilitator asks if that meets with general approval. At times there are still some reservations, and when they can be incorporated into the final statement that is great. Other times they can simply be noted in the minutes. A group tends to coalesce around a common understanding, especially since there is a growing desire to "get on with it" and move to the next topic. If one waits too long and accommodates the particular nuances of individuals too much, people start repeating themselves and time is wasted. If decisions are made too quickly and differences are not heard, they usually do not hang together very long and need to be revisited. So the facilitator needs to hold a delicate balance between efficiency and inclusion.

This balancing act is served when some distinction is made according to the type of decision at hand:

1. For procedural matters, such as lengthening the meeting, adding agenda items, calling a break etc., I find a show of hands or majority vote works well. It is better to see where the group stands on a ten-minute break rather than take ten minutes discussing whether to have one!

2. For major decisions that affect the core values and mission of the organization, the launching of new programs, moving or restructuring, it is good to try for consensus. In *School Renewal* (p. 147) I cite a wonderful passage from M. Scott Peck that deserves repeating here:

> Consensus is a group decision (which some members may not feel is the best decision, but which they can all live with, support, and commit themselves not to undermine), arrived at without voting, through a process whereby the issues are fully aired, all members feel they have been adequately heard, in which everyone has equal power and responsibility, and different degrees of influence by virtue of individual stubbornness or charisma are avoided so that all are satisfied with the process. The process requires the members to be emotionally present and engaged; frank in a loving, mutually respectful manner; sensitive to each other; to be selfless, dispassionate, and capable of emptying themselves, and possessing a paradoxical awareness of the preciousness of both people and time (including knowing when the solution is satisfactory; and that it is time to stop and not reopen the discussion until such time as the group determines a need for revision).

When used well, consensus can pull a group together and be a solid foundation for implementation.

1. Then there are times when one needs to take an informal "temperature of the group" to see how to allocate time and energy. In this case the facilitator might list several options and give each person

three "votes" to be cast by making marks on a whiteboard or flip chart. This way, in a matter of minutes, one can see where people stand and make a course correction if needed.

2. Finally, I am a great believer in unilateral decision-making. These are decisions made by individuals or small groups that have been mandated to take action by the sponsoring group (board, college, faculty etc.) If the mandate is clear and reporting has been regular, an individual or group can exercise considerable latitude in doing the needed research, consulting with others and then making a decision that is mindful of the purposes and mission of the whole. I find that when there is a lot of unilateral decision-making in a school it is often a sign of trust and healthy group dynamics. When everyone wants to be in on everything it is either due to lack of attention to organizational needs or lack of trust. Indeed, trust is the "glue" that holds an organization together.

In the end, we each need to take responsibility for the decisions that fall within our purview. If we each take care of our own sphere it helps others do their work. I have found this vividly illustrated in exercises done through eurythmy in the workplace (see separate chapter). When passing copper balls for instance, all we can do is fix what happens to the left and right of us. Stressing about the problem across the circle does no good at all, except perhaps as an observation or a "learning" to reflect upon after the exercise is over. We each need to take care in our personal and professional decision-making, for they become the building blocks for the whole.

And this involves working with the utmost integrity, as Rudolf Steiner states in chapter 6 of *How to Know Higher Worlds:*

> Any decision, even the most trivial, should be made only after thorough, well-reasoned deliberation. We should remove all thoughtless activity and meaningless action from our souls. We must have well-thought-out reasons for all we do. Anything we cannot find a reason for, we must refrain from doing. (pp. 112–113)

6

AGREEMENTS

"To achieve great things two things are needed; a plan and not quite enough time." —LEONARD BERNSTEIN

What do you think of first when you hear the word "agreements"? Some might think of legal contracts, appointments or decisions reached in meetings. It is an area of social life that is often relegated to such ordinary contractual functions, but my experience has shown that agreements are the fabric that holds an organizational garment together. When they are clear, honored by all concerned and reviewed periodically, people are "freed" to work with initiative and confidence. When they are murky, undefined and continuously undermined, then an organization becomes threadbare, good people leave, and those that remain are either transients or just serving time until retirement. So I have come to the opinion that agreements are a barometer of organizational health.

Having said this, it is not easy to really understand the DNA of an agreement. What are the essential elements, and how does one achieve agreement in an organizational setting? To get at the heart of this issue, one has to look more deeply at human nature and the creative tensions that flow into social interactions.

1. The individual and the group. As individuals we want to act out of freedom, take initiative, and get things done. This is a unique characteristic of the age in which we live, referred to by Rudolf Steiner as the time of the "consciousness soul." Rather than just acting out of duty or loyalty, we want to know the reasons behind policies and job requirements.

We seek to understand, and we want to be seen as who we are—as individuals with a unique biography that very much includes a particular set of childhood circumstances, a given gender (even the freedom to change it), but also a shared cultural, racial or religious heritage. We want to be seen as who we are, and we do not want to be bound blindly by the dictates of others.

At the same time we spend most of our lives in groups, both in the workplace and in a family/friends context. People need each other, and our mutual needs bring us into groups and a wide range of social contexts. We also need groups and teams to get things done, whether as a member of a sports team, a committee or musical band. As a member of a group we work out of a sense of the "collective" needs of others or of the organization. Sometimes we do things out of duty and a sense of responsibility for "the whole," even if it may cause personal stress or interpersonal friction. In groups we often have to give up some of our personal freedom in order to serve broader goals. Yet, when the peer pressure becomes too great or the politics too extreme, something in us rebels. Often we are not aware until afterward when a line has been crossed, and we have to reassert our individuality. For some, a crude remark might be ignored, but when witness to workplace harassment one feels compelled to speak up. For each of us, that "line" may be slightly different, but we know when the social norm has gone too far and we need to step away. We can say: "enough is enough; I will not let this stand." Individuality asserts itself in opposition to the group. If too many object, the group may shrink or even disband. So we are faced with an existential question: How is it possible for humans to live together socially if everyone is striving merely to express his or her own individuality?

To explore this theme further, we can also experience freedom that has gone too far, that has become license to do as one wants, regardless of others. Many people are attracted to Waldorf schools in particular because of a climate of freedom, and that is a huge benefit when it comes to teaching. But sometimes the freedom afforded adults in a community leads to a few who push their way upon others, who use freedom to exploit circumstances in their own favor. Then freedom can become the self-will of the individual.

The creative tension between individuality and group can be bridged through consciously reached agreements. This happens when each person, as an individual, makes a personal decision to commit to the agreement, and the group as a collective agrees to protect the rights and privileges of each person living within that agreement. The group becomes the guarantor of the individual and the individual commits to the group agreement. The two forces become interlocked in a mutually supportive system. The individual retrains freedom by freely agreeing, and the group can function collectively by respecting the needs of the individuals within it. An ethical individual is someone who holds equal commitment to freedom of action and consciously chosen agreements.

From Rudolf Steiner's *Intuitive Thinking as a Spiritual Path:* "To live in love of action, and to let live in understanding of the other's will, is the fundamental maxim of *free human beings*" (ibid., p. 155). Only because individuals are of one spirit can they live out their lives side by side. A free person lives in trust that the other free person belongs to the same spiritual world and that they will concur with each other in their intentions. Those who are free demand no agreement from their fellows, but they expect it, because it is inherent in human nature. This is not meant to indicate the necessity of this or that outer arrangement. Rather, it is meant to indicate the attitude, the state of the soul, with which a human being, experiencing himself or herself amid esteemed fellow human beings, can best do justice to human dignity" (ibid., p. 183). To summarize, we cannot demand agreement, but we need to expect it in order to have a functioning organization.

2. The needs of Self and the wish to serve others: Most of those drawn to administration, teaching, nursing, environmental preservation and so on have a strong desire to serve the greater good, to help others, to make the world a better place. This idealism brings many to work in not-for-profit organizations and/or give time and energy as volunteers. Our communities would not be the same without the food pantry, the local library, after-school sports or the theater company. Many people simply want to help others, especially those less fortunate.

On the other hand, we live at a time of rampant egoism. It seems many people think a lot about themselves, their money, career and social standing. Some are willing to step on others to advance their goals or those of loved ones (many an otherwise normal parent can become obnoxious when incited by a Little League game). Some will do almost anything to advance the interests of their children in particular over the interests of others.

How can we negoiate our way through this quagmire of idealism vs. egoism? The place where the two can meet is on the playing field of agreements. An agreement can reflect most of the ideals held by individuals or special group, while still serving the practical purposes and needs to get things done. An agreement is a marriage of the stars and the minerals, the highest striving of humans and the realities of earthly laws. Despite it's flaws, the U.S. Constitution is a good example. The high language was met with the reality of need to compromise. Without an agreement such as the Declaration or the Constitution it is doubtful the thirteen colonies could have stayed together. Our founding fathers recognized the delicate balance between the "pursuit of happiness" and the moral imperative of the greater good. And they knew that for democracy to work each citizen would have to take responsibility for his or her free speech and actions:

> The principle of producing through one's actions the greatest amount of pleasure for oneself—that is, of attaining individual happiness— is called egoism. This individual happiness is sought either through thinking ruthlessly only of one's own welfare and striving for it even at the expense of the happiness of other individuals (pure egoism), or through promoting the good of others because one hopes for indirect advantages from their happiness, or through fear of endangering one's own interests by harming others (morality of prudence)....
>
> A special kind of moral principle is involved when the commandment does not announce itself to us through outer authority, but from within ourselves. We may call this moral autonomy. We then hear within ourselves the voice to which we must submit. The expression of this voice is *conscience*. (Steiner, *Intuitive Thinking as a Spiritual Path*, pp. 145–146)

3. Freedom and accountability: When I visit Waldorf schools, I often hear from teachers how much they appreciate the freedom to teach based upon the perceived needs of the children. Although we have a given curriculum founded on a highly articulated view of child development, much in the selection of content on a day-to-day basis rests with the conscience and intuition of the teacher. At the same time I often hear from board members who ask about accountability. How do we hold each other accountable to agree upon goals? Who holds the teachers accountable? What if something goes astray, who has the authority to step in?

Thus freedom and accountability are another one of the creative tensions that can live in schools and community organizations (and is played out in spades in public debate today around common core and standards!) Again, I would like to postulate that rather than political legislation at the state or federal level, mutual agreements within a school or association is a preferred way to handle the tension between freedom and accountability. For a good agreement, say around curriculum goals, needs to respect the insight freely arrived at by those trained in the profession (teachers) and at the same time hold everyone accountable for what they have agreed to. One cannot just spend the whole year teaching ancient India, as happened in one school. There is a "collective expectation" that a certain curriculum will be covered in fifth grade.

Given these creative tensions living in many of our schools, how can we begin to arrive at agreements that serve the core principles of Waldorf education and the needs of a particular community? This is where our discussions can really get interesting, and rather than share a lengthy discourse on the subject I would like to point to some signposts that can help us navigate our way to healthy agreements:

1. Rather than always focusing on content, look to process early on. How do we intend to address this issue, who needs to be involved, how much time is needed, how do we want to communicate with others along the way, and at what date do we want to conclude our process and realize an agreement? All too often I find groups stumble into a process and self-correct only after mistakes, often around the omission of key stakeholders, and then steps need to be retraced.

2. HR (human resource management) is often a litmus test for some of the most crucial agreements. Because of our ideals and views of spiritually striving human beings, those working in Waldorf

schools tend to have high expectations for interpersonal relations. When we fall short in how we treat each other it can be devastating to morale and the social fabric of the school. So many key issues come into focus in the area of HR. For instance: how do we conduct a search, who do we include in the interviews, do we have policies around recusal for conflict of interest, and who gets to make the hiring decision? Another whole area involves evaluation of faculty and staff: do we have clear guidelines that are transparent and applied to all or do we do too many informal, mini-evaluations in our hallways? Finally, how do we handle compensation and categories of employment? Are policies established to protect the interests of those in leadership roles or to safeguard the interests of parents and the children we all serve? HR is a huge field that needs much more conscious attention in our schools.

3. An agreement is a photo of a moment in time. It is a statement of where the school stands regarding a particular issue or subject and is meant to serve the needs of the present. Yet as time goes by, these agreements need to be reviewed and updated. We also need to be mindful of new employees who may not have been part of the original discussions and need to be brought onboard. I suggest yearly retreats to review key agreements among other tasks.

4. In addition to school-wide agreements (we could call them policies) there are also many little agreements made on a daily basis, such as making an appointment to meet at such and such a time. Honoring these smaller agreements can help build a culture of trust and confidence in a school, and it is important that these appointments are kept.

5. In agreements, we are dealing with what Rudolf Steiner called the "rights life," that area in which people relate to each other as equals. If I agree to meet with a student in my office at Antioch, we are each equally responsible to show up, and I cannot plead status as professor in breaking the appointment (notice of inability to meet is more than a common courtesy). Whether rich or poor, wise or ignorant, as human beings we stand as equals in the rights life, and each person needs to be respected. When smaller agreements are honored, it is easier for an organization to build and maintain a culture of trust.

6. Having mentioned five areas to look at for the sake of achieving healthy agreements, can you name a few out of your experience? Are there areas in the life of your school that need greater consciousness around forming and holding to

agreements? Please share them with your colleagues, and let us learn from one another!

Finally, I would like to end with something that is much harder to describe: the role of intuition in forming agreements. We have all experienced something we can call intuition, but can we learn to trust it?

> People vary in their capacity for intuition. For one person, ideas just bubble up, while another achieves them by much labor. The situations in which people live, and which serve as the scene of their activity, are no less varied. How I act will therefore depend on how my capacity for intuition works in relation to a particular situation. The sum of ideas active within us, the real content of our intuitions, constitutes what is individual in each of us, notwithstanding the universality of the world of ideas. To the extent that the intuitive content turns into action, it is the ethical content of the individual. Allowing this intuitive content to live itself out fully is the highest driving force of morality. At the same time, it is the highest motive of those who realize that, in the end, all other moral principles unite within it. We can call this standpoint ethical individualism. (Steiner 1995, pp. 149–150)

Thus we can say that agreements are the products of ethical individualism, they are social contracts arrived at through the utmost freedom and with the greatest possible consciousness. Groups exist in part to help us be accountable to each other and ourselves. This is then a virtuous cycle: individuals are able to act out of free initiative because members of the group have extended confidence, and by holding one another to agreements, trust "warms" the group and allows for more latitude and the exercise of initiative arising out of insight and intuition. As individuals become more and more successful, the group can step back and attend to strategic direction and periodic review. An organization can then become a living organism, one that inhales and exhales with life-supporting rhythm. Human beings can feel recognized and supported, and thus want to do more for the "whole." In the end, the process leads to the creation of spiritual capital, an unseen but palpable substance that serves as a living resource for years to come.

7

ROLE CLARITY

"I am hitting my head against the walls, but the walls are giving way."
—GUSTAV MAHLER

In my experience as a teacher, parent, board member and consultant, the issue of role clarity has often taken center stage. Especially in a self-administered Waldorf school, it seems that we attract highly committed, dedicated people who are not always sure as to how they are supposed to interact. Here are a few of the confusions:

1. For the teacher, especially the new ones, it can be overwhelming at first to find out that in addition to teaching a curriculum and working with children all day, they are expected to serve on committees, engage in a variety of faculty activities, help recruit new students, engage in conflict resolution when needed and at times deal with school finances. They may sincerely ask: Which hat am I wearing and when?

2. For the parent, engagement in a Waldorf school is far more than dropping the kids off at the curb or attending an occasional parent meeting. Instead, they are expected to raise funds, help beautify the school, join a committee or even the board. So the parent may also ask: Which hat am I wearing and when?

3. For the administrator, rather than just working with a straightforward job description as defined in many other schools, we have a peculiar way of mixing and matching, such as: admissions and outreach with a few little extras thrown in such as the annual appeal. Or the finance manager may suddenly also be put

in charge of the physical plant and grounds maintenance, organizing the after-school bus schedules or working summers on deferred maintenance. The list can go on, but again, the administrative person might ask: Which hat am I wearing and when?

Some might say that this is all part of a pioneering venture (and it is amazing how many schools remain in the pioneering stage for years!), but there is a serious downside to fractured roles and lack of clarity: too many chefs in the kitchen can lead to frayed nerves at best, or serious conflict in the worst-case situations. Here are a few symptoms:

1. A super-dedicated teacher who ends up on virtually every committee and guides the discussions in the faculty and board meetings can eventually become a lightning rod for any issue and eventually she/he burns out.

2. A super-dedicated board president notices that the school is understaffed and that the administration is not functioning well, so he or she starts coming in each morning to "help out." Eventually one has become a quasi-administrator and starts making decisions. Soon the faculty members feel they are working for a "boss" and start to distance themselves.

3. A parent with many professional skills notices that teachers are not being evaluated and she designs an evaluation process and brings it to the board for approval. They are more than happy to see a solution to a long-perceived problem, and approve the procedure. You can imagine how the faculty will respond.

When I get a phone call the first words often involve "communication issues," "struggles between the board and faculty" or "personnel matters," but after a bit of investigation one often finds that role clarity is the underlying issue.

So how can one achieve role clarity in a Waldorf school? Although most schools have a description of the role of the board, PTO and faculty leadership (such as the College of Teachers), there is a need to do more. Here are a few things to consider:

1. At an annual retreat, share the job descriptions of the board, PTO, College, Administrative Committee or any other leadership group. Ask for questions of clarification.

2. Then, at the same retreat, it is helpful to ask for examples in which things played out as intended, and instances in the last year in which there was some role confusion. Simply name them, as that will aid in the further suggested steps.

3. Look at areas of differentiation and integration. There is a reason why the faculty meets on Thursdays just as faculty/staff: they need to apply their pedagogical insight to the needs of the students, deepen their understanding of the curriculum and Anthroposophy and share classroom issues. Likewise, there is a reason the board meets as a board etc. These meetings are a result of differentiation. But each group has a natural overlap with the others (i.e., a few faculty members may serve on the board). Are we clear about the purpose and role of these integrative functions? For instance, even though the faculty meets only with teachers and staff, who is in charge of communicating with the PTO and the board and vice versa? How often will there be all-school retreats? These aspects are integrative functions, and by looking at them formally there is less chance things will morph informally with the result of role confusions.

4. Ask parents who have been at the school for some years as well as a few who have just joined how they perceive their roles. Their perceptions are valid.

5. Listen to those in administrative roles, for they often have their "ears on the ground" and can identify issues quickly. And please do not shoot the messenger(s).

6. In faculty, board and PTO meetings have the courage to ask: Are the roles and responsibilities in our leadership structure working? What can we improve? The more our schools become learning organizations (and not just regarding our children) the better off we will be, for learning organizations are more adept at self-correcting

and evolving over time. Sclerotic organizations need revolutions to change; living systems evolve.

7. From time to time ask an external consultant or experienced person from another school to do an assessment of roles and responsibilities. Their findings may stimulate positive changes or confirm good practices. A small note: some schools do what is called an "administrative audit" from time to time. These can be helpful, but I urge schools to define "administration" as all those who ad-minister to the needs of others within the school. Thus one should not, restrict the review to just those with offices and desktop computers. It is essential to get an accurate picture of all who carry responsibility for tasks and how they work together. The flow patterns and interpersonal dynamics then become very interesting.

8. Every one to three years each person in a leadership role should be evaluated, and that often begins with a hard look at job descriptions and discussions about who is doing what.

A Waldorf school is much like a visiting troupe of characters, minstrels of sorts. Some have considerable expertise and others are learning on the job. That is not such a bad thing, as it can keep things dynamic (in contrast to fostering a staid bureaucracy). But a lively troupe of players needs to sing (or speak) from the same score (long-range plan, mission statement, yearly goals) and they need to know who is playing which part. There are many, many ways to do things successfully, and in the end, if it works there must be something to it. But I urge all concerned to pay more attention to roles and responsibilities; know what you are asking of your leaders and then give them all the support you can!

8

Strategic vs. Tactical Leadership

"A real leader faces the music, even when he doesn't like the tune."
—ANONYMOUS

Here is a classic case study: The Waldorf School of the Shining River has a deficit. It is not so large as to threaten the closure of the school, but large enough to render small cuts and deferments useless. It is serious. So how will your school leaders respond?

Possible solutions from tactical leaders:

"We will do across-the-board ten-percent cuts in salaries."
"The board wants us to fund development at current levels, so we will cut elsewhere in administration, say the receptionist at the front desk."
"Teachers did not use all their professional development funds last year, so let's cut that line item in half."
"We can wait another year to replace the roof."

And so on. The picture is clear: tactical leaders look to piecemeal solutions that follow the paths of least resistance. No one will be happy with the cuts, but since every aspect of the school suffers somewhat, there is no major outcry. In fact, I have known nonprofits that do round after round of these kinds of cuts over years. In one case the school cut themselves out of existence, but it was a gradual process and most were asleep to what was really going on. It was a colossal failure of leadership.

Now let's look at some alternative that might come from strategic leaders:

"This deficit is an opportunity to finally establish our donor circle and create an additional source of financial and human support surrounding our school."

"Let's hold an all-school retreat and discuss our vision for our
    programs, why we do them and the level of support needed.
    Perhaps ideas will surface that can help, and some teachers and
    parents may be willing to make voluntary sacrifices to help a
    program continue or even expand. Perhaps this is even the time
    to start a new program in response to a perceived need."

"Where do we want to be in three to five years? Let's build that pic-
    ture and then work backward to the present situation."

"Are there strategic partners in our community who could work
    with us to realize our long-range plan (i.e., a local music school
    or summer music festival that may want to collaborate with our
    strings offerings)?"

A strategic leader looks to the horizon and does not try to solve current issues just with bean counting. Although we need accurate records
of all we do, yearly audits (or at least financial reviews depending on
the size of the organization and state laws), in the end the numbers
tell the story of the present. We need to have good reporting so we
know on a monthly basis where we stand. But an organism is either
growing or dying, and simply reporting does not change the story line.
Leaders are needed to articulate a vision and help an organization gal-
vanize the resources to create a preferred future, one that both inspires
and motivates. Leaders bring the right people together to generate new
resources, human and financial. New opportunities can then open up,
and effective leaders must know how to seize the moment!

To summarize: tactical moves are often needed on a short-term basis,
but they usually fail to change the essential dynamic. Strategic moves
open up new possibilities and allow the future to work in on the present.

Waldorf teachers are perhaps uniquely suited to develop strategic
capabilities for their schools, in that they work on a daily basis with the
development of capacities in their students. They are by nature future
oriented, and know the importance of imagination and the flow of time.
The danger is that they may overlook the basics of "minding the store"
and attending to daily administrative chores (even things like returning
phone calls and writing reports). Those who work full time in administrative jobs are often extremely adept at managing the daily flow of
tasks, often multitasking to serve the many diverse needs that come at

them from a variety of directions. The danger here is that management trumps leadership.

So we need to take care of each other. Administrators need to draw faculty into meaningful planning meetings so the school can access their commitment to the pedagogy and their fertile imaginations. And teachers need to respect the vital role of administration in keeping the Waldorf ship afloat through adherence to best practices such as consistent policies and agreements. We need each other.

Finally, in setting the stage for more conversation on collaborative leadership later on, I would like to share a personal observation. Although a balance in terms of tactical and strategic leadership is desirable, I have found that most organizations tend to tilt in one direction more than the other. There are schools that administratively run like a Swiss watch...you don't need a calendar because on such and such a date financial aid forms are mailed to parents etc. These schools run efficiently, and there is much to be said for that! But sometimes one can sense a "coldness" creeping in, like Carl Sandburg's fog that creeps in "on little cat feet." It happens gradually until one day people realize they are part of a corporate entity, and the school spirit has departed.

The other extreme is that no one seems to be "minding the store," the teachers want to be in control of everything and they refuse to empower administrative personnel with anything more than routine duties. Here there may be a lot of creative energy including even some extravagant community events, but sooner or later someone finds out that no one has conducted a fire alarm in years, or the furnace breaks down due to lack of servicing. Then parents step in to take the reins from those "incompetent" teachers (who may quite naturally have been spending most of their time in the classroom). My point in drawing out these extremes is that schools can tip at least slightly more one way or the other: administrative efficiency or creative chaos. The founding years tend to favor more of the latter, and subsequent years the former, with an occasional crisis thrown in to rebalance things.

The essential point is that we can in fact be both tactical and strategic, cultivating both efficient administration and creative visioning. (And we need to avoid stereotypes, as I have often experienced an administrator who suggests the most creative solution to an issue, or a teacher who takes hold of a process and brings forth greater clarity and efficiency) We can sail this vessel called Governance together, especially if we are self-aware and learn to observe what is going on around us.

> A vision without a task is but a dream.
> A task without a vision is but drudgery.
> A vision with a task is the hope of the world.

9

TAKING A BREAK

HOW TO GET WORKPLACE ISSUES OUT OF YOUR MIND:
A BIOGRAPHY OF THOMAS EDISON

"There was no one near to confuse me, so I was forced to become original." —JOSEPH HEYDEN

Leaders and administrators tend to work long hours. Even when at home or on vacation, it is easy to let school and workplace issues churn around in our thoughts and feelings. It can be really hard to let go.

Doing nothing, trying to "veg out" does not work. As soon as one sits down on a lawn chair, the thoughts, feelings, and "to do" items creep into one's consciousness. Watching a movie or TV can perhaps give temporary relief, but often one feels more tired and pressured afterward, with tinges of guilt that so much time was wasted. So I have found that when I want to let go, the best thing is to put something else in the place of work: a long walk in nature, social time with friends, a good book, gardening, playing the cello. There is something about an *alternative activity* that does wonders. If one is having a good conversation with friends at a restaurant it is hard to go back to work issues...something else is now occupying one's inner life. Other people come into focus, preferably folks who are not connected to work, and their interests, issues and stories occupy our consciousness. So many people seem to defer social time with friends with the comment "when we retire," only to waste valuable years in-between. We all need to do the things that bring us joy and relaxation now, rather than just defer to the future. One of my recently retired colleagues said just that: he wishes he had cultivated more hobbies and friendships while he was younger. Retirement can otherwise come as a shock.

For me, writing is a creative outlet, my hobby. I do not depend on it for a living, and although it is nice when people purchase my books or express appreciation for something they have read, I did not start out with these goals in mind. I do it because it makes me feel whole and it gives me a sense of purpose. When a question or issue finds me, I enjoy following it through all sorts of highways and byways. It becomes a traveling companion and everything I see or read seems to miraculously connect to the question I am pursuing! My overall wish is to lift everyday issues into a wider perspective that comes through spiritual practice, in my case Anthroposophy. I like to build bridges between the Earth and the wisdom-filled starry heavens. And I try to do it in a way that leaves people free to cross those bridges when and if they want to...thus most of what I write is invitation. Rather than "prove" a point, I try to describe things enough so pathways open up.

Of course I, too, have struggled with balancing work and personal life, especially since most of my life I have had more than one job. The long hours are one thing, but the carrying in full consciousness the affairs of others is at times a burden. If one is doing meaningful work, it does not stop when one leaves the office or school. We carry it around with us.

So one tool that I have found very helpful is the study of biography. There are many reasons to learn to know one's own, but for the purposes of this chapter I would like to concentrate on learning to know the biography of others: people we meet and historical figures we can read about, both those who are well known and some who are not. One of my favorite historical novelists, Barbara Tuchman, once wrote that biography is the prism of history. Her books are a testament to that. One can read about Vinegar Joe Stillwell in China or the Black Plague in the Middle Ages, and suddenly one is right there. Space and time are suspended. If I read a good biography, my inner world changes. I am suddenly thinking new thoughts, making discoveries that want to be shared with friends and family. And the issues of the everyday workplace fade into the background.

Why is that? I suspect it has a lot to do with attention and consciousness. What we choose to attend to becomes foremost in our consciousness. A biography is like looking at a stunning painting; it works in on the senses; it affects our feelings it stirs us in places we did not know. The soul is a vast territory, and a good biography can help us explore new landscapes. A biography gives us food for thought, and helps us integrate another person into our own striving, hopes and dreams. Just as we are changed by meeting new people in everyday life, likewise the meeting of someone in a biography from way back in history can change our inner lives.

Of course, one can read biography just for the entertainment value. There is nothing wrong with that. But if one takes this practice up over many years, one can begin to develop a method called self-education. Each person may have their own way, but after a while one starts to compare and contrast, as questions as to why and how, and then the tapestry of life becomes even more interesting. Recently I did this with the life of Thomas Edison, which I include here not just as an example, but also as a representative biography for the American spirit. Since most of my readers work in North America, it might be of service to spend some time looking at essential characteristics such as innovation, individuality and the human will. These qualities are found abundantly in the people we work with... and they lead to serious questions regarding the nature of collaboration.

My methodology is taken from Rudolf Steiner, the foremost esotericist of the last century. The following paragraphs take up the theme of individualism, first from the perspective of fact, then feeling, and then essence. Rather than writing just in the abstract, I have chosen to bring forward one historical personality from U.S. history, and will first describe his life from the factual point of view, then my feeling relationship to him and finally, with the help of Anthroposophy, seek for the essence of his life in relation to the mission of America. As an example of a "representative" biography, I chose Thomas Edison, the famous inventor of the phonograph, the light bulb, movies and much more.

- Thomas Alva Edison was born on February 11, 1847, in Milan, Ohio, located in the central part of the U.S.

- As a baby he was single minded: he would fix his attention on some object and then try and try again until he could get hold of it. Once he learned to walk he went everywhere.

- He often got himself into trouble: he fell into a pile of wheat chaff in a grain elevator and had to be hauled out by his legs, he fell into a canal and, at age six, he set his father's barn on fire, for which he was whipped publicly in the town square.

- At the age of eleven, he used picture-framing wire to build his first telegraph.

- At twelve, he became a "candy butcher" on the local train, selling fruit and snacks to the passengers. He soon figured out that he could hire a helper to do the selling so he was free to set up a lab in the baggage car. Soon he was also selling newspapers at each train stop.

- In a teenage episode of publishing a newspaper aboard a train, we see his particular ability as an entrepreneur (Baldwin 1995, pp. 30–32).

- Battle of Shiloh, telegraphed news ahead of train, bought 1,000 copies of newspaper, sold them to large crowds, upping the price in the end from five cents to a dollar.

- Once when he was late boarding, a conductor grabbed him by the ears and lifted him aboard. Something snapped in his ears and from then on he had difficulty hearing. It made him even shier, as he could not hear casual conversation well. Combined with his looks: rough clothes, uncombed hair, crooked hat...he was not comfortable in large groups. Instead, when he had a four-hour wait for the return train in Detroit he would go to the library and read one book after another.

- At age fifteen he rescued a small child playing on the tracks. The baby's father gave him training and then a job as a telegraph operator. He quickly learned to send the fastest telegraphs and held one job after another all over the region. He worked at night and invented devices on the side, including a vote-recording machine and a stock ticker.

- One could say he invented the word *workaholic;* he stayed in the lab long hours, totally absorbed in an invention. Once when he was somewhat older and had a crew working for him he had a problem with a machine. Edison locked the doors and told everyone they could not go home until the problem was solved. Wives and family members pleaded at the door, entreating to be allowed to give their husbands food, but Edison refused to open the doors. They worked for sixty hours until it was fixed.

- Despite his unkempt appearance and lifestyle, Edison met a beautiful girl whom he courted in his own way, visiting her parent's house and sitting in the parlor communicating by Morse code so they could talk confidentially. In fact, when he proposed, he tapped Morse code on her knee, to which she responded in the affirmative. Yet, on their wedding day, when they got arrived at their new apartment, Edison said he had to check on something in the lab. Many hours later, a friend found him there at midnight and dragged him home to a very distraught wife, who had waited twelve hours.

- Edison now had a series of successes, including perfecting the telephone and inventing the phonograph (record player), but it was the invention of the light bulb that brought him his greatest fame.

- Edison also invented the first moving pictures. At the opening performance, the lights dimmed but there seemed to be a problem. He ran down to the basement and fiddled with the equipment until it was fixed and then resumed his place in the audience—a classic example of his "can-do" approach.

- Tragedy also entered his life: his first wife died young, and his uninsured lab burned to the ground. Nonetheless, he became famous and was even invited to the White House, went on tours and became friends with Henry Ford and other well-known Americans. But, as applied to himself, he never agreed to the term *genius*. He said, "There is no such thing as genius. What people choose to call genius is simply hard work—one percent inspiration and ninety nine percent perspiration." What is work? "Bringing the secrets out of nature and applying them to the happiness of man." Even in regard to his hearing problems, which grew worse as he aged, he said, "Think of all the nonsense I haven't had to listen to."

- Thomas Edison worked right up until the end of his life and passed away on October 21, 1931. President Hover suggested that the entire nation turn off all electricity for one minute as a tribute to Edison, but everyone quickly realized that chaos would ensue. Edison's contribution was so great that even one minute without electricity would now be considered extremely dangerous.

The preceding are *facts* from the life of Thomas Edison. Now for the next level—establishing a *feeling* connection to what arises from the facts, for which we can turn to a key symptom. Imagine Edison's studio in Florida: a long table, a stuffed owl on the wall, many books piled all around and a large chair on sat. Edison frequently placed a heavy book on his lap, read for a while and meditated. Often he would fall asleep, the book would drop to the floor and he would wake up with a new inspiration.

This key characteristic tells us something special. Edison could find his new insights when he entered his etheric body consciously. We know that we can find true living thinking in the etheric, the life body. When talking about life between death and a new birth Steiner once said, "During this entire time, human beings absorb the will, and now, coming again into physical existence, we see how what works in from the cosmos, what they absorbed from the previous incarnation, is as in a picture, and the will is still within that picture. Thus, here we have will-saturated Imagination" (Steiner, *Therapeutic Insights: Earthly and Cosmic Laws,* p. 78). This is Thomas Edison in his full being—will-saturated imagination.

We know that in our will, our metabolism, we sleep during the day, and only gradually awaken in regard to head-human, our conceptual life. Again, we have a perfect example from Edison, who once said he had done more than 200 experiments (will exercises, so to speak) and learned 199 ways *not* to do it. He was grateful for the lessons of 199 failed experiments. Here we have will forces and the pure practical application of knowledge, an essential characteristic of the American folk soul.

Edison worked out of very strong sympathy, a great love of the task. Through great effort and persistence he raised the will impulses up into the conscious sphere of thought life. He united cosmic will with cosmic thought. This enlivens thinking but keeps it grounded. Otherwise...human beings would increasingly become subject to compulsive thoughts.

As many readers will know, Rudolf Steiner seldom referred to Americans, and when he did, he could be quite critical, as he was of Woodrow Wilson. Thus, you can imagine how delighted I was to find the following reference to Edison:

> I was overjoyed recently when I read that there are still people who, going beyond the ordinary routine of life, have already perceived the practical life as something important. Recently, a news item spread through the world describing how Edison tested the people he wished to prepare for some sort of practical work. It did not interest him at all if a merchant was able to keep books. That, he said, can be learned in three weeks if one is a reasonable, intelligent person. None of these specialties interested him at all; one can

learn them. When Edison wished to know if people could be of any use in practical life, however, he tested them by asking questions such as "How large is Siberia?" ... or "If a room is five meters long, three meters wide, and four meters high, how many cubic meters of air are contained in this room?" and similar questions.... He knew that if people could answer such a general question it proved that their schooling had not been in vain, that as children they had developed mobile thoughts, and this is what Edison demanded.... When you look at life, there are few "Edisons" who have such practical principles. It is necessary to work toward a pictorial quality of concepts. (Steiner 1984, p. 89)

It was toward the end of my research process when I came across a reference to a connection between Edison and Madam Blavatsky. In 1873, she responded to a spiritual "call" to move to the U.S., where she founded the Theosophical Society two years later. She was captivated by the invention of the phonograph and sent Edison a letter, a copy of her book *Isis Unveiled* and forms for joining the Theosophical Society. Edison signed the papers and sent a thank-you note saying, "I shall read between the lines" (Baldwin, p. 93). Sometime later, her colleague Henry Steel Olcott traveled to Menlo Park, New Jersey, to visit Edison. They talked about "occult forces," and Olcott asked Edison about the sources of his creativity and innovation. Edison replied that often he would be out walking with a friend on the busy streets of New York, and amid the din and roar a thought would flash into his mind, whereupon he would rush home and set to work on the idea "and not give it up until he had either succeeded or found the thing impracticable" (ibid., p. 94).

The connections continued for some time, with Blavatsky even referring to "brother Edison" in her publications. Some years later, when there was an uproar in the UK over the theosophists, Edison denied any connection, but when he died, among his books were those of Blavatsky and a copy of Swedenborg's *Heaven and Hell*.

In its essence, the biography of Thomas Edison illustrates a particular way of meeting the world: we learn by doing. Even today America, North and South, is the land of doing, experimenting, inventing, forging ahead, lately particularly in technology. It is not an accident that

Apple Computer, Oracle, Intel and Microsoft come from American, not European soil. Technology is intellect put into the immediate service of the will. In America ideas seek direct application, often known now as "apps." (It is interesting that, parallel to my study of Edison, I happened to read the biography of Steve Jobs just after his passing. It was amazing to compare and contrast the two figures, two giants in the history of innovation and American ingenuity.)

With a particular intensity of intellect and an extraordinary will (as represented by Thomas Edison), we are left with an American challenge: Can we develop the middle sphere, the lung–heart realm, the soul forces that balance intellect and will? Thus we encounter some of the major social challenges that have characterized the social landscape of the brief history of the United States (though we can find them also in Canada and Central and South America). Here we have the troubled history of relations with the native peoples on these continents. We have the huge social issue of slaves, which the founding fathers could not resolve, leading to the costly Civil War a century later, as well as the lingering effects of racism. We have seen the social challenges presented by mixed attitudes toward immigration and the great "melting pot," as it has been called, the challenges of class and economic strata, whereby the rich get richer and the poor get poorer. We could go on, but it is remarkable that almost all the major challenges in the Americas reside in the social sphere, the middle realm between intellect and will.

So the study of this representative biography of Edison points to the social challenge that is still with us today: How can we work together? We have to look at the social architecture needed to take this great experiment we call the Americas into the next millennium.

Administrators and leaders are, whether they know it or not, modern social architects. They are a microcosm within the social macrocosm. Their actions, often even the smallest decisions make in the course of a school day, contribute to the larger scaffolding we call an organization. We may think globally, but in the end we all need to act locally.

10

AUTHORITY, INFLUENCE AND POWER DYNAMICS IN WALDORF SCHOOLS

"Works of art make rules; rules do not make works of art."
—CLAUDE DEBUSSY

In 1994, when doing a survey of teachers at an AWSNA conference, I was pulled aside by an "elder" and told that surveys (especially one having to do with stress) are not "the way we do things." I was speechless in the moment, and after some consideration, went ahead and did the survey anyway. It proved very helpful in gathering material for my second book, *School Renewal,* which many schools have since used as a study text to discuss some of the common issues they face regarding personal and organizational renewal. But looking back on that AWSNA encounter, I now realize that "stress" was a taboo subject. The focus of this chapter is yet another example.

It's not that authority is a bad word in Waldorf circles; in fact, teachers rely a good deal on authority to educate, first through imitation in the younger years, and then the authority that comes through knowing a subject well in the high-school years. Many who work in our schools have also come to appreciate the authority of wise mentors, not to mention Rudolf Steiner. There is indeed nothing wrong with authority, and few would take a discussion on the subject as misplaced. The discomfort, I feel, comes when addressing issues of power and influence. Why?

These terms are most often associated with traditional examples of authority, such as military generals, political leaders, corporate executives and some of the one percent, who are very wealthy. History is full of examples of the abuse of power, and many who are drawn to Waldorf education and nonprofit work have rejected certain lifestyles in favor of others. In my experience working with many schools, I have found that a majority of parents and teachers have a more-than-healthy skepticism of anyone in a position of authority. So even when a school is fortunate to have a skilled board president or faculty chair, there are many who keep a close eye on things to be sure he/she does not become too influential. We all know the saying: "power corrupts."

All this is fine, but there are some untended consequences of this aversion to authority. One of them is that it tends to promote management over leadership (see chapter 3). It also supports short-term service, with the result that schools and other nonprofits are often in continuous transition between leaders. Even a term of three years is short, as it takes about a year to learn a job and another to perform, followed by a period of transitioning out during the third year. This is one reason I prefer that some of the leadership positions become professional appointments, with at-will service and regular performance reviews. If things are working well, why not enjoy successful leadership for six or nine years?

Ironically, the troubles around leadership authority happen less with formal leaders (faculty chairs, board presidents and such) than with informal leaders. Here is where one often finds unusual pockets of influence and, yes, power. To examine this further, one has to understand first of all where power comes from:

1. formal authority
2. expertise
3. control of information
4. control of rewards
5. coercive power
6. personal influence
7. demographic or social influence
8. control of resources
9. control of access—who gets to see whom

Any of these items themselves (except coercive power) can be okay and even helpful in certain situations. For example, who has not benefited from expertise when timely and helpful? Teachers control the rewards in every classroom, so it is not surprising that some might be recognized or rewarded more than others in the adult realm. And of course, some people have extensive personal influence, sometimes just through years of experience. So these factors are not in themselves totally inappropriate.

However, it is the exercise of these attributes, especially when more than one is brought to bear, that the situation becomes problematic. For example, a former mentor who also has personal influence in the school and has a role in distributing professional development funds can become a seat of undue influence. Even an office assistant who learns the ropes and starts to exert personal influence on the control of access (who gets to see the business manager) can become a problem. And when one has a team of husband/wife or two partners who jointly exercise power, serious issues can develop. It is far better to give someone formal authority, a title and job description, than to have weak formal leaders with many power centers exercising influence behind the scenes. And to err on the side of repetition, it is not the notion of authority in itself that is wrong, but the misuse or manipulation of influence when it occurs for personal gain or to further one's own agenda.

When one senses something is amiss, it is like the smell test. Your nose may communicate to you before your thoughts catch up. But if one is part of an organization and one senses that something is out of balance regarding power and influence, there are a few common-sense strategies that can help:

1. Share your observation with a colleague or friend and ask if that person sees things in a similar light. Sometimes I have been dead wrong, and it is good to let go early on before making a fuss.
2. Ask a question that prompts others to reflect, such as, "How did you experience that moment in the meeting when...?"
3. Observe and question yourself over several days. It could be you are only seeing part of the story.
4. Try having a conversation with the person at the center of the concern.
5. Ask for a discussion on the theme of mandates and authority, to see if there are related issues living in the group.
6. Establish good policy around issues such as nepotism, conflict of interest etc.
7. If all else fails, and especially if one has tried less-intrusive avenues, come right out and say, "I have observed that every time we discuss

the budget, no matter how many points of view there seem to be in the room, when J speaks it is as if the decision has been made. Do others experience this?"

The wonderful thing about whole-systems work (see *Organizational Integrity,* chap. 18) is that even a small intervention—asking a simple question, for example—can have positive ripple-effects throughout the system. The group soon becomes aware that there are a few of us who notice, who "see through" what is happening, and it acts as a kind of antidote against further abuse. This is connected on a deeper level with the working of human conscience. Even when just one person acts out of higher ideals it serves as a stimulus to awaken the conscience of others (see reference to ethical individualism in the chapter on decision-making). Some of the most remarkable things in human history have happened because one person exercised the voice of conscience and it sparked a ripple effect through thousands of followers (Martin Luther King, Jr., in regard to racism; Jane Addams and pacifism during World War I; Rachel Carson and the environment). Fortunately for us, the list of such individuals is extensive.

We need to develop a positive relationship to authority. Within the word itself, one has "authorship," which implies a relationship to the material that is intimate and substantial. When one speaks out of this direct experience of the material, as Rudolf Steiner did with his research, then it draws an audience. Most of us can remember a teacher, say a high school chemistry whiz, who year after year astounds students with amazing experiments and stimulating class debates, bringing the subject to life. Likewise, many of us remember a certain violinist or jazz player we heard at a particular concert. We need people on this Earth who engage in first-hand experience, wrestling with their material, transforming it to a special level of excellence and offering it to humanity.

When my mother was diagnosed with cancer of the esophagus our family went through all sorts of emotional reactions. For a while we were flailing around for something to hang onto, some form of certainty, a way forward. Then my parents found a doctor at Massachusetts General Hospital who was at the top of his field. His credentials in regard to surgery and this type of cancer were stellar. But that was all on paper until we met him. Our pre-op conversations were among the most memorable of my life. It wasn't just that he knew the esophagus so well, it was *how he engaged us in conversation, how he answered our questions and the confidence and natural authority he exuded from his entire being.* He was able to see through our fears, meet us as ever-so-frail human beings and give us hope. I left those meetings a different person. He was an authority in the very best sense of the word.

And a footnote: His wonderful expertise resulted in a successful operation, removing the esophagus, and my mother was blessed with more than ten more years, until she passed over recently at the age of eighty-seven.

Finally, some food for further thought:

- What is the ultimate authority in my life?
- Who has served as an authority figure in my childhood?
- How do the spiritual worlds exercise authority?
- Why do I respect some in authority and not others?
- In which instances have I experienced myself as an authority?

11

PETER DRUCKER

"It is not hard to compose, but what is fabulously hard is to leave the superfluous notes under the table." — JOHANNES BRAHMS

This short chapter features three thought-provoking concepts from the collected works of Peter Drucker who pioneered the discipline of professional management in the 1940s. Prior to his passing in 2005, he consulted with executives for many Fortune 500 companies while teaching, lecturing and writing. Although his books have been on the market for many decades, the essential ideas remain underexplored by most. Unlike the endless parade of management consulting books published each year, this timeless wisdom will never go out of style. Those of us in the Waldorf world need to access the best thinking on management and leadership and not turn aside due to language issues and what might at first appear as "pure business" thinking. Schools need to operate effectively, and although they are not strictly a business, they need to employ best practices in human resource management, innovation and budgeting.

Several essential ideas from Drucker include, but are certainly not limited to the following: Employees are assets rather than costs. In a knowledge-based economy, work will be defined by results rather than quantity or cost of labor. Employees must be redefined as partners who are invited to participate in a venture (rather than cogs from a nineteenth-century industrial machine). Knowledge workers need a deeper level of engagement that goes beyond the old carrot of more money. Shared values may be of equal or greater importance than financial compensation.

My comments on these thoughts: Certainly most teachers sign on based upon values and ideals more than they do for reasons of compensation.

But sometimes in administration and in board deliberations we can slip into the notion that they "cost us" so and so much per year. I really like the idea of seeing all human beings involved in a school as assets, not costs. Parents, grandparents, board members and others are indeed partners, and when treated in that way we can achieve much more. We need to become ever more explicit about our shared values, and be sure to work hard on developing strategic goals together.

The concept of organized abandonment: Those who cannot abandon yesterday are doomed to irrelevance. Sometimes we must shrink to grow—cull the herd of milk cows to reinvest elsewhere. What you choose to abandon, whether it be an investment, research project or a business, defines who you are and, in many cases, determines your ultimate success.

MY COMMENTS

1. In one of his books on innovation Drucker actually says that one should look at each program and division every three years and ask the question: Would we start this activity today if we did not already have it? If the answer is No, then we need to be prepared to abandon it. Why? I see two reasons:

First, it involves a kind of fresh thinking that continuously forces us to realign our practices with our mission. Are we doing what we said we would do? Are we succeeding?

Second, by abandoning or "pruning" some activities, we make room for new growth. Too often we add and add only to run ever harder (like a hamster in a cage) just to keep up with present demands. To innovate, we need to cut back from time to time. This frees human and financial resources to try new things. This applies to the school calendar, after-school programs, festivals, fund-raising events and so on. Just because we have had a spring auction for several years does not mean we have to continue doing so, especially if the key carriers have moved on and the impulse has faded. It is better to make room for the new rather than dragging on with the old beyond its usefulness.

Future success in business will be less about controlling costs and more about the creation of value and wealth. Cost is merely one input. Most information systems in use today are stuck in the past, focused on preserving brick and mortar assets and controlling costs. One can see this with the GAAP (Generally Accepted Accounting Principles) system, in which the measurement of historic costs often takes precedence over the accumulation of intangible assets (patents, contractual relationships and market position to name but a few). Our information systems are increasingly out of touch with the forces of modern wealth creation.

One can determine the quality of management by the priorities it sets. This requires deep understanding of what an organization really is and what it should be. Consider the Steinway piano company in the early twentieth century. The Steinway people thought they were in the piano-manufacturing business. While this may have been true in the late nineteenth century, they were competing against Henry Ford for middle-class appliances by 1910. Cars had more utility and status than did pianos for the parlor. The piano business suffered devastating losses and was nearly lost until Steinway pivoted to a new niche.

When an independent Waldorf school has a financial shortfall, the most frequent response is to cut expenses. That is a natural reaction, and in many cases it is a necessary step. Yet Drucker helps us remember that the real reason parents sacrifice so much to send their children to an independent school is that they perceive value. The education has worth. So if a school has needs, it is a good idea to look to highlight the value, even increasing the value of the offerings rather than simply cutting back. I know some schools after 2008 cut back so much they practically eliminated all their "special" programs such as foreign languages, sports and music. After a while, a parent could ask: Why send my child if now the program closely resembles a good public school? We need to distinguish ourselves not only through the breadth of our programs but also through the depth of our work, commitment to the children and the ability to see them as they can become, as light-filled beings. We teach to the potential in each child; we see more in them than the rest of the world might see. And thanks to Anthroposophy, we are able to give them a curriculum that meets their developmental needs and inspires them to learn and grow. We need to articulate the worth and value of each subject and program so our work is visible to parents and the wider community. If that is possible, we will not have to spend as much time cutting costs.

A development effort at a school is mostly about making the values and worth of the enterprise visible, celebrating success and connecting people with similar values to the mission of the school. If we do this well, we expand the financial base of the school and make the education more accessible to children of many different backgrounds. Development work is not an "add on," but rather an integral part of everything we do.

12

The Double: The Shadow Side of Groups

"If you can walk, you can dance. If you can talk, you can sing."
—ZIMBABWE PROVERB

For a long time, I have wondered whether groups have a double or shadow that can be recognized and, if so, whether we can do anything about it. We know from Jung (see *School Renewal*) that individuals have a shadow side, and Rudolf Steiner speaks in several places about the human double. Freud describes the id, the home of desires and lower passions. These all hold certain common characteristics: that which has not been fully penetrated by consciousness and consequently shows itself in unplanned and unpredictable ways. It could be seen as negative attributes that have not been engaged and worked upon, or old habits and patterns of behavior.

Groups are of course a collection of individuals, so naturally they bring all the various dimensions of their personality to any meeting or event. But when a specific group of individuals, such as a working group, spend long amounts of time together, is there the possibility that a kind of "group double" can come into existence? So with this question foremost in mind, I went back to a lecture Dr. Philip Incao gave some years ago, in which he focused on the medical aspects of the double. Yet as I suspected, his imaginative treatment of the subject provides a foundation for my further exploration of groups.

Excerpts from "Illness and the Double: The Scales of the Dragon," by Philip Incao, MD:

Rudolf Steiner tells us that with the eating of the apple, the serpent himself entered right into the human constitution, deeply and catastrophically into the human physiology, to remain to this day. As a consequence of this indwelling of the Serpent, or Dragon, or the Double in us, many of our bodily functions, from thinking and perceiving to digesting, procreating, and even sweating, are very different from what they would have been had Adam and Eve not eaten of the apple.

And God said to Adam: "In the seat of your face you shall eat bread, and you shall eat the plants of the field." Why? Rudolf Steiner says that before Adam's fall, human beings did not need to eat and digest coarse material foodstuffs in order to nourish themselves, this only became necessary as a consequence of the Serpent taking up residence in the human body. God therefore said, "you shall eat the plants of the field, and in the sweat of your face you shall eat bread."

Rudolf Steiner says yes, at a definite time, a short time before birth, we are permeated by an Ahrimanic being who comes to be within us in the same way that our own soul is within us: That is the Double!

The Double remains within us for our entire life, below the threshold of our consciousness, but it always leaves us a short time, a matter of hours or perhaps days, before we die. The Double cannot tolerate death, it cannot bear to be with a human being who is passing though death, so it always leaves us beforehand. This gives the loved ones of the one who has died the opportunity to see his or her beauty that can only be achieved when the Double is no longer influencing the human countenance.

Rudolf Steiner tells us that, as a consequence of the great shift, the great displacement in the members of our being that occurred when Adam and Eve ate the apple, in all the descendants of Adam, the individual human soul simply cannot fully penetrate the body, cannot fill up the human body. Thus there is always a part of us, which remains more or less un-ensouled and unpenetrated by the human spirit. And it is this un-ensouled, unconscious part of the human body, which becomes the home of the Double.

This unconscious unpenetrated part of ourselves indwelt by the Double is what Freud called the "Id," the source of all human desires, instincts and passions, and the source of fear—the strongest of all passions.

In another context, Rudolf Steiner called this unconscious, un-ensouled, unpenetrated part of the human being the realm of subnature within us. Where and when we are conscious, we are living in nature; to be living at the level of nature is to live in the realm where Christ is active. As Rudolf Steiner said in the Pastoral Medical course,

Christ is the spiritual life in nature. Nature is permeated by Christ. We live in nature and have the possibility to live in Christ, when we are awake and where we are awake in our body and soul.

But when we are asleep, it is different. In sleep, our spirit and soul could leave our body and go into the spiritual world, where they have the possibility to meet spiritual beings, to meet human souls who have died and even the possibility to meet Christ. But also, in sleep, the part of us that's left lying on the bed, without the benefit of a conscious spirit and soul, this physical and etheric body goes in the opposite direction from the soul and spirit and descends into a realm that Rudolf Steiner calls subnature.

Thus, when we are asleep, or when our thinking, feeling, and willing are derived from the un-ensouled part of ourselves, then we are living in subnature—and subnature is the realm where, not Christ, but the Double, or the Dragon, or Ahriman is active—but it is also the realm of the Father of God or Creator God. Subnature belongs to the Father God, but it is a realm, which, since Adam's sin, has become infected—infected with our ahrimanic Double, with the Dragon....

Now we have the picture of Ahriman living in the subnature below the Earth, in Hell, in Hades, and we have the Dragon or the Double, the servant of Ahriman, living in the un-ensouled, unconscious sleeping realm of subnature within us.

If we do not take care to balance our sleeping and waking time, we can become ill. This happens not only for the obvious reasons of sleep deprivation, but also, as in the state of disequilibrium, it is possible for the double (as Steiner calls it) or the shadow (in Jungian terms) to enter our essential being.

Looking at what Dr. Incao has said in these passages, we can see that the work of the double is quite a natural phenomenon of human existence today. Just as we all sleep, and we all have times when we walk around in a state of semiconsciousness, so also we continuously open the door for the double to enter our subnature. Especially in those acts that are un-ensouled, we give space to the double. What is an un-ensouled situation? This occurs far more frequently than we may want to imagine. Simply going through the check-out line, packing things in grocery bags with our thoughts elsewhere. That can be an instance of un-ensouled actions. Deeds that are divorced from feeling, or thoughts that live in total abstraction can be opportunities for the double.

When we get together in groups, it is possible to open with a community activity, a verse, song or ritual that serves to "warm the space" and connect people. Or, one might do things in a rote way, rattle through the agenda, follow the same empty protocols, and those meetings could serve as invitations for the double. What makes things really interesting is when several people come to the meeting in a state of tiredness or stress, and if their consciousness is not strong enough to counteract those conditions, one can start to see a kind of dance of the doubles; the double in one person entices the double in someone else to step out onto the dance floor so to speak. One then has an unreal situation, in which people are speaking and interacting out of a sub-natural world, a place of semiconscious, reactive behaviors. Sometimes this goes on for a while and then another person will jolt things into greater consciousness (even a comment such as "what is going on here?") and the dance will end.

Fear is food for the double. Dr. Incao provides a medical example of this phenomenon:

> People today are haunted by a fear we can compare with the medieval fear of ghosts. It is fear of germs. Objectively, both states of fear are the same. Both fit their respective age: People of the Middle Ages held a certain belief in the spiritual world; therefore, quite naturally they had a fear of spiritual beings. The modern age has lost this belief in the spiritual world; it believes in material things. It therefore has a fear of material beings, be they ever so small. Objectively speaking, the greatest difference we might find between the two periods is that ghosts are at any rate sizable and respectable. The tiny germs, on the other hand, are nothing much to speak of as far as frightening people is concerned. I do not mean to imply by this that we should encourage germs, and that it is good to have as many as possible.
>
> However, the important point is that germs can be dangerous only if they are allowed to flourish.... Germs flourish most intensively when we take nothing but materialistic thoughts into sleep with us. There is no better way to encourage them to flourish than to enter sleep with only materialistic ideas (Steiner).
>
> When Hippocrates, the ancient Greek physician who is considered to be the father of Western medicine, said that inflammation is the fire that cleanses the body, the concealed wisdom of that statement is that really the only unclean thing in us, that which defiles us and puts us in need of cleansing is nothing more or less than our

Double, our Dragon. And every inflammatory, so-called infectious disease is not caused by germs, but in reality is caused by the immune system, which serves like Michael's fiery sword, and creates a fire in us, a fever, an inflammation in order to burn up a bit of our Dragon and to discharge his ashes out of our body.

Contagion is a spiritual phenomenon, not a material phenomenon. Contagion is a vibrating of one's own soul, one's own astral body, in resonance with the disturbed or diseased or merely passionate astral body of another person.

The original Latin and Greek meaning of *passion* was suffering. Could it be that passion is actually a kind of suffering? The original Latin meaning of *suffer* meant "to bear up," more specifically, "to carry up from under."

Now let's return to group dynamics. One of the chief characteristics, known to all who have spent significant time in meetings, is that in groups we have to "suffer" each other. This can take many forms: listening to someone who goes on and on, or hearing the same information repeated at each meeting or simply knowing how someone will respond in a typical fashion to what has just been said by someone else. Meeting can try our patience and test our goodwill. Many people emerge from meetings exhausted, having had to "bear up" while sitting uncomfortably for so long. Yet many organizations respond to any challenge or problem with the refrain, "Let's call a meeting."

Now back to Dr. Incao:

The ancient root of the word *passion* has two original meanings: to suffer and to harm. It is like one tree that gives rise to two branches— the branch with the meaning "suffering" and the branch with the meaning "harming." And both branches arise from the same Indo-European root. The words *harming* and *suffering* have a common origin. Along the branch of *suffering*, the modern words *patient, passive, compassion* and *passion* have been derived. And along the branch of harming, the modern word *fiend* has been derived, and the related meanings given on this branch are hating, hostile, enemy, and devil. So the word *passion* and the word *fiend* are like brothers; they come from a common origin, the same parent!

Every illness is a kind of passion, and every passion is a kind of illness. Both of them are a suffering, a carrying up and a bearing up that has the possibility of becoming an offering up for redemption and healing, of that which comes from our own personal Dragon, from our Double, from the Fiend in us.

Now I would like to go back to the words with which I began: "The strongest passion is fear." Fear is the inseparable companion of materialistic thinking, and both of them exist in us only by virtue of the Double. Without the Double, there would be no materialistic knowledge and understanding; the more we are able to know and understand our Double and how he works in us in practical details, the less we will fear him or fear germs or fear Lyme disease or AIDS or anything else.

The Double is like a house guest who may have been unwelcome at first, but by now we need him. We have adapted and accommodated our whole being to his presence, and we literally could not function in our physical body, on Earth without him.

Rather it is a matter of knowing, understanding and taming our Double, of letting him work for us, rather than our working for him. It is a matter of becoming the master of our Double, rather than being his servant.... When we realize, as Christ says in the Gospel of St. Matthew, "It is not what goes into the mouth that defiles a man, it's what comes out of the mouth that defiles a man."

With these reflections to work with, one can come to some new understanding of group work:

- Groups may not begin with a "double" but through the repetition of certain predictable interactions between individuals, they can sometimes take on the appearance of a "dance of the double."
- Fear is a root cause of some of the shadow or double behaviors. When individuals bring fear to a group or meeting, it can serve as an invitation for the appearance of shadows. For instance, if a nonprofit is under budgetary constraints and some are fearful they may loose their jobs, that undertone will pervade meetings and could influence interpersonal interactions.
- Look to dialogue as a litmus test of the presence or absence of the double. How do people speak with each other? Is there intentionality and consciousness in the language used, or is the speaking reactive? The later tends to be more accommodative of the double.
- Like attracts like—i.e., if one person is working out of the double it tends to attract others, thus the appearance eventually of what can look like group double. By the same token, all it takes is for one person to step into the strong light of heightened consciousness for others to see the benefit and join in. This often happens in groups when one person comes back to an ideal, asks a stimulating question or makes an

affirmative statement about the mission of the organization, and suddenly everyone starts to pull themselves back into greater consciousness. Light can dispel shadow.

In a lecture on reincarnation and karma Rudolf Steiner gave on January 23, 1912, he describes a human counterpart. In order to paint a picture in the mind's eye of such a counterpart, he asks that we begin by taking inventory of the things in our life that have pleased us least of all. When I do this with a class I ask each individual to make a list of human traits that they find repugnant. For one person it might be someone who is slovenly, lazy or rude. Other members of the class will list different characteristics. The point is to come up with things that really repel us, not just in a mild sort of way, but in a visceral, gut-wrenching manner.

Then I ask that they write a paragraph describing a person who embodies many of the characteristics just listed. They even give the despicable person a name! For the fun of it, we always ask for volunteers to read a few aloud. The descriptions are often so vivid and startling that they are sometimes humorous. The point is that these "counterparts" stand in vividly before our imagination.

Then we turn back to the lecture mentioned previously and hear this remarkable challenge: "We must desire and will everything that we have not desired or willed...for in the picture we have thus been able to make of our own personality there will arise something that we have not been in this present incarnation but that we have introduced into it. Our deeper being will emerge from the picture built up in this way" (Steiner 1992, p. 16).

This is a very complicated thing to grasp. The counterpart, that often grotesque image that has been described through the exercise, is not us now, yet it is somehow related to us. No one in the exercise was forced to write down certain characteristics...people created their own counterpart. Steiner says "you cannot disown it. Once it appears, it will follow you, hover before your soul and crystallize in such a way that you will realize it has something to do with you, but certainly not with your present life. And then the perception develops that this picture is derived from an earlier life" (ibid., p. 17).

So we have come to a point in which the influence of the counterpart, which I feel is related to the double, comes from life before birth. The double or shadow is very much a phenomena of this life, but the counterpart is something we brought with us from a longer journey. It may be related to people we have known, to family dynamics or especially poignant encounters in a last life. But we have brought a counterpart with us as a kind of uninvited companion.

How does this influence group work? Well, let us image you are sitting in a meeting and a new person enters the room. He or she says a few things, perhaps has certain gestures or mannerisms, and you find yourself recoiling. It is as if a few simple behaviors trigger something in you. It becomes a challenge to welcome that new person in the whole-hearted way you do with others. Why? It could be, if one goes back to the inventory of characteristics made in the above exercise, that the person across from you in the room exhibits a few of them. It may be nothing significant, and one might soon find out that one is overreacting, but in some cases we will find ourselves confronted by people for whom we feel a natural antipathy.

There are of course a myriad of reasons for this, including things such as gender issues, cultural factors or language, but for the purposes of this chapter, I would like to suggest that it is helpful to once in a while return to the previously mentioned inventory and see if there are any connections. For if there are, and if one reacts negatively, it could be that one is responding to *the counterpart within us* rather than the person sitting in the meeting. If that is the case, the new person presents both a challenge and an opportunity. The challenge is to overcome the initial reactive responses, but the opportunity is to actually start to work something through that is an urgent need of one's own biography.

One way to push back against the influence of the shadow, which seems to be stronger with those who are self-centered, self-seeking, is to awaken an ever-growing interest in the other person. This is especially hard when one tries it with people we do not really like, or at least think we do not like. If one works to develop interest in such people, that curiosity becomes a counterforce to the shadow influence. Interest could be as simple as beginning with: So, where did you grow up? What do you do on weekends? What is your favorite music? Over time, one can go further, but it really works in a socially proactive way. One feels gradually liberated from the narrow bonds of the self as one gradually opens up. Discovery of the other person makes us more accessible and that in turn leads to mutual interests. Interest in the other is thus a community-building exercise.

Then groups become a redemptive, transformative opportunity to do inner work that might otherwise lie dormant. When we encounter others we have a special opportunity to encounter ourselves.

As we begin to do this, the double, shadow, counterpart all start to shrink in the light of consciousness. As with ice melting in the sun, these apparitions cannot stand the light of day consciousness. The more we work on ourselves, the more they diminish in size and influence. They may never go away, but their influence grows weaker and weaker. With Michaelic strength, we become masters of our own destiny.

13

ORGANIZATIONAL TRAUMA

"The history of a people is found in its songs." —GEORGE JELLINEK

As part of my work for Antioch University I came across a colleague from the Seattle campus, Shana Hormann, who along with her coauthor Pat Vivian wrote an engaging book, *Organizational Trauma and Healing* (Vivian and Hormann 2013). Much to my delight, they take up a variety of themes that relate directly to the previous chapter and my interest in the double. In this section I would like to use a few of the clear, insightful charts and insights that they developed and discuss them from the point of view of Waldorf school administration.

One of the first aspects of consideration has to do with the basic shift from an individual focus to that of an organization. Often our groups are populated by people who bring their purely individual frame into aspects of dialogue and common tasks, with the result that it is hard to *shift consciousness* to the wider view needed by an organization. The table opposite shows some ways that the shift needs to occur.

There are a variety of activities in a Waldorf setting that help people shift from a purely individual frame to that of the whole organization: all school retreats, festival celebrations, class nights, long-range planning, work days etc. These activities all have a strong emphasis on dynamics of the heart (see *Organizational Integrity,* chap. 5). The heart is strengthened by healthy circulation and movement. When asked to help a group or organization that is stuck, I often have a simple answer: begin by bringing things into movement! This can be volleyball, singing, hiking and even painting the school. My favorite is eurythmy in the workplace (see part 2, chapter 2) as it brings a high level of intentionality and

INDIVIDUAL AND ORGANIZATIONAL FOCUS

Focus on Individual	Focus on Organization
Problem identification and problem-solving	Pattern identification and normalization
Individual responsibility	Collective responsibility
Limited impact on sustainability of the organization	Widespread impact on structures, systems and values
Acceptance of an individual's dysfunctional behavior by the organization	Aspiration to focus on organizational strengths and the central spirit of the work
Understanding the individual leads to the expectation that the individual needs to change	Understanding the whole leads to the expectation that system-wide dynamics need to change

(Vivian and Hormann 2013, p. 7)

reflection into the movement experiences. Yet whatever is selected, it is helpful to assume that people enter a room as individuals and that group consciousness has to be rebuilt again and again.

These considerations are especially important when an organization has suffered unusual stress or trauma, either first-hand or as a secondary experience.

Posttraumatic Stress Disorder

Posttraumatic Stress Disorder or PTSD is an anxiety disorder that individuals may develop after seeing or living through a dangerous event. These events include violent personal assaults, natural or human-caused disaster, accidents or military combat. Under usual circumstances as individual in danger has a healthy reaction meant to protect him or her from harm. This is a normal response to the kinds of dangerous events described above. Fear triggers split-second changes in his or her body to prepare to defend against the danger or to avoid it. The person experiences a heightened physical, emotional and mental state. After the danger has passed, the individual calms down and returns to normal functioning.

Some individuals, for a variety of reasons related to the effectiveness of their coping systems, remain in that heightened state for prolonged periods. This state begins to debilitate their abilities to cope. Individuals suffering from PTSD feel stressed or frightened even when they are not in danger. Many experience helplessness, feelings of confusion and isolation. They may be continuously hyper-vigilant, feel extremely anxious, and reexperience the event through nightmares or flashbacks. In an attempt to control their feelings of anxiety they narrow every aspect of their lives including relationships, thoughts and activities (Herman 1992).

Secondary Traumatic Stress

Secondary traumatic stress (STS) is a natural response of individuals to caring for or helping those who suffer from trauma. It refers to increased internal stress, negative emotions, distorted mental constructs and behavior changes that result from being exposed to others' trauma stories. Therapists, family members, first responders and others who learn about the suffering of clients and loved ones are highly susceptible to STS. The more intense and prolonged the period of exposure to the traumatization of others, the more deleterious are the effects. Compassion stress (Figley, 1995), which comes from using empathy in caring for others who have experienced trauma, ultimately results in the physical, mental and emotional exhaustion of compassion fatigue. Vicarious traumatization (VT) refers to identity alterations, negative shifts in worldview and other transformations that occur within therapists as the result of empathic engagement with clients' trauma experiences (Pearlman and Saakvitne 1995). VT includes strong reactions of grief, rage and outrage from repeatedly hearing stories of horror that accumulate and grow over time. VT ultimately includes feelings of sorrow, numbness, a deep sense of loss, loss of hope....

Anyone with unrecognized or unhealed traumas in their personal history may be especially vulnerable to secondary traumatic stress, vicarious traumatization or compassion fatigue. Individuals without health opportunities to recognize and address the impacts they are experiencing run the risk of persistent STS symptoms. For the professionals, education about the impact of exposure to others' trauma, clinical supervision, peer support, work–life balance and rejuvenating activities help mitigate the potentially long-term effects of doing trauma work. For the family and community members, a strong support system and specific education about trauma help to lessen negative impacts of being close to someone suffering from trauma.

Similarly at the organizational level, exacerbating and mitigating factors may also exist. Positive aspects of organizational culture, history, worldview and resources may mitigate any negative impact on the system, resulting in a fairly quick recovery for the system. Conversely, negative aspects of those factors may exacerbate the trauma's impact on the system and result in the system becoming traumatized. As with individuals who have a history of personal trauma that goes unrecognized and unhealed, organizations with a history of trauma that goes unrecognized and unhealed may be more susceptible to further traumatization." (Vivian and Hormann, pp. 16–20)

The authors go on to describe what they call "redemptive organizations," which have remarkable similarities to Waldorf schools, meaning the ideals are strong and many choose to serve despite the challenges. Why? Because there we find a higher social calling, a wish to educate our children in ways that support social renewal. In fact, when Rudolf Steiner was not able to effect his proposals around "the threefold social order" at the end of Word War I, he very deliberately stated that he would therefore turn his full attention to education. Indeed, every time a child is born in this world we have a new chance, an opportunity to help develop human beings who bring a greater sense of social justice and compassion to this world. Waldorf school communities are often filled with motivated people who are willing to change their lives based on deeply held values.

Redemptive Organizations

A redemptive organization is a type of entity established to benefit society or a disadvantaged or oppressed group. The culture of such organizations is centrally defined by this altruistic purpose. Redemptive organizations (Couto 1989), seek to redeem society from some evil as well as support the growth of their members, because of these dual purposes, redemptive organizations are vulnerable to becoming highly sensitized to the ills they are trying to address. Organizational insiders may become overly attentive to internal dynamics and judgmental of how peers live out the organization's values. (ibid., p. 21)

Distinguishing between organizational lifecycle transitions, organizational crisis, and organizational trauma is important. Most managers and leaders operate with a limited framework of ideas about organizational dynamics. They interpret what is going on as individual problems or issues or normal nonprofit functioning. Sometimes they recognize situations as organizational crises. Rarely do they see patterns related to organizational trauma. Managers' limited understanding means their inaction of choice of intervention may not fit the circumstances. Detrimental patterns continue.

Redemptive work can lead to trauma in another way. As noted before, the worldview of an organization is deeply affected by the response of the community to its work. Since the core identity of the organization focuses on changing societal norms and behaviors, a clash of values between the organization and wider society is commonplace. A gap between organizational members' belief in the importance of their work and society's ignorance or denigration of that work reinforces the separation and isolation of the organization in regard to its environment....

Organizational culture, an expression of the organization's consensual reality, emerges from a complex interplay of natural environment, physical realities and social interaction. (ibid., 2013)

Of course, much is affected by an organizations culture. In a Waldorf setting people often know the minute they walk into a school that they have entered a Waldorf school. It is not just the design of the buildings and the colors in the classrooms. In talking to teachers and parents, there is a distinct feeling for "Waldorf culture," a child-centered way of seeing the children and a curriculum that comes alive in the imaginative work of the teachers. Vivian and Hormann remind us of some of the key factors that shape the culture of an organization:

Founders' experiences and understandings
Organizational creation story
Organizational moral narrative
Values and standards inherent in the work
Boundary setting necessary for the work to be credible to its clients
    and its members
Identification with wider social change efforts (ibid., p. 38)

They then go on to identify factors that mitigate or enhance to possibility for organizational trauma:

Organizational characteristics and strengths can mitigate effects of trauma and enhance organizational health. Presence of these features needs to be visible, widespread, universally recognized, understood, and appreciated by the organization's members in order to be effective. These features include:

Strong core identity
Organizational self-esteem and self-efficacy
Facilitating structures and processes
Hopeful and energetic leadership
Positive connection to peer agencies (ibid., p. 52)

Factors exacerbating susceptibility
    We have seen several patterns that weaken an organization and increase its susceptibility to traumatization. When these patterns occur, an organization's culture is not as robust as it could be, and in some stressed circumstances these patterns compromise the organization's ability to make sense of its experiences and relate effectively to its environment. These patterns include:

Limiting attitudes and worldview set at the organization's creation
Unproductive relationships between organization and environment
Organizational amnesia
Unrecognized wounding from previous traumas (ibid., p. 55)

Then we come to the heart of the matter, the characteristics of organizational trauma, including a fascinating chart that compares strengths with shadows (below):

Organizational Traumatization Syndrome

The syndrome of a traumatized system is comprised of a multiple dynamic present in the organization. The existence of one dynamic does not mean the system is traumatized, but in a traumatized system a preponderance of these dynamics will be evident. We describe those dynamics separately but recognize that they mutually influence each other and together constitute the syndrome. These dynamics are:

Closed boundaries between organization and external environment
Centrality of insider relationships
Stress and anxiety contagion
Inadequate worldview and identity erosion
Depression expressed through fear or anger
Despair and loss of hope (ibid., p. 60)

How can we begin to work with organizational trauma?

Strategies

- Create processes for organization-wide dialogue and learning
- Remember organizational history and alleviate organizational amnesia
- Strengthen core identity and build organizational esteem
- Institute facilitating structures and process
- Open system to outside energy and information
- Institute ways to nurture organizational spirit and engage in renewal (ibid.)

And how can we identify organizational trauma in Waldorf schools? First of all, there are the tragic events that occur in the biography of a school. These might include a tragic fire, the death of a student, parent or teacher, a move of the school itself to a new site or the resignation of key personnel, to name but a few. I say "might," as I have known schools that pull through a tragic event stronger than they were to begin with, as well as schools that cannot seem to shake the tragedy. In the later case, the event becomes imbedded in the psyche of the school community, and one can say that organizational trauma has occurred.

PAIRED CHARACTERISTICS

Paired cultural aspects	Organizational strengths	Organizational shadows
Mission driven	Passion, commitment and excitement about helping women	Over-emphasis on self-empowerment
and	Philosophy of Choice	Expectation of interpersonal caring and support
Feminist	Empowerment for victims/survivors	Intense emotional atmosphere
Importance of relationships	Relationship-oriented	Confusion about power and authority
	Importance of friendships	
and	Inclusive, egalitarian and nonhierarchical	Distrust of leaders
Ambivalence about power and leadership	Participatory decision-making	Unconstructive ways of dealing with conflict
Institutional racism	Awareness of inequities	Emotional intensity
		Critique and self-consciousness
and	Commitment to diversity	
		Hurt and suspicion
Commitment to anti-oppression philosophy and work	Concern about racism	Abiding tension around issues of race and oppression

(ibid., p. 7)

In a secondary sense, there are schools that suffer from "stress and anxiety contagion" that continues year after year. I have known situations were the basic challenge of breaking even, paying teachers and end-of-year bills, becomes a yearly rite of hardship. One school I visited had to "borrow" tuition from parents, asking them to pay next year's fees in June instead of September because they could not make the last payroll of the school year. The following year they had to "borrow" already in May, as some of the funds that should have been in the operating budget for that year had been spent the previous year. When I arrived they were borrowing already in March. One can see how the story ends. This phenomenon becomes a kind of embedded trauma that is often harder to shake than the one-off tragedy. It takes extraordinary leadership to call the question, hold the required meetings and ask for a systemic solution instead of a series of tactical maneuvers. Often one needs outside help to break out of the pattern.

One way to help prevent organizational trauma is to do regular analysis of the present state of things, from budget to personnel to buildings. A hard look at present realities can spot things early on, and the sooner one starts to re-mediate, the better the chances are of full recovery. Thus I found the following strengths/shadows model developed by Vivian and Hormann very helpful:

Understanding the Strengths and Shadows Model

The Strengths and Shadows Model offers one way for organization members collectively to see patterns and describe their culture. Members identify organizational Strengths and Shadows and gain an understanding of the relationships between the two. These are depicted on a graphic template that spatially arranges Strengths in an inner circle and Shadows in an outer circle with arrows connecting the related Strengths and Shadows. These discoveries give organization members the opportunity both to accept the qualities of their organizational culture and to focus on aspects they want to change. In doing so, they gain ownership of their own change process.

Using the Strengths and Shadows Model

Identification and description can begin with either Strengths in the inner or Shadows in the outer one. The process is finished when each Strength and Shadow has at least one counterpart in the other circle...a single Strength might have several Shadows and vice versa. When the group has completed naming and connecting the Strengths and Shadows, it reflects on the overall image and shares insights and meaning. This is an opportunity for the group to accept this picture of itself; once that happens, they can discover and begin to name organizational patterns. Discovering and naming those patterns helps members to comprehend their organization as a system. Recognizing strengths and shadows as organizational characteristics interrupts the tendency mentioned earlier to see individuals as "troublesome" or the source of problems. Based on organizational context and need the group identifies three or four patterns to explore further. (ibid., p. 131)

Thus a school can engage early on, own the problems and build on strengths. Most of all, if parents, teachers, staff and board are all constructively engaged in regular review in this way, one can do much to strengthen the immune system of the school as a whole. No one can prevent tragedy, but we can all take steps to become resilient.

14

REFRAMING

"I can't understand why people are frightened of new ideas. I'm frightened of the old ones" —JOHN CAGE

If we take a minute to look around, we see frames all around us: window and door frames, spectacles, a wide variety on pictures that adorn our walls. They define and help identify one aspect of the world around us. Frames are like windows that let us see through an issue from a particular vantage point. They are also like lenses that help us focus. They filter out some things while letting other things pass through. How we see and understand the world is very much influenced by our preferences in framing issues and events.

This chapter is dedicated to the crucial leadership function we can call *framing*. Those who are bound to continually see the world through just one frame have limited vision and even fewer options. However, the most effective leaders often show a remarkable ability to reframe issues and at times exercise an ability to see through multiple frames. To do this, we need to use a certain amount of self-diagnosis to see ourselves and our preferred lenses. This creates the opportunity for "frame flipping" or reframing as needed. This in turn helps us decide as leaders what action should be taken.

Lee Bolman and Terrence Deal give a comprehensive overview of framing in their massive 526-page book, *Reframing Organizations: Artistry, Choice and Leadership*. For administrators and leaders who can devote the time to work with this book, it is filled with lively examples and scholarly contributions. As of this writing I have read it twice! Basically, they make the case for four major frames:

The structural frame sets goals and priorities, uses job descriptions reporting charts, emphasizes centralization and control from the top down or from the center outward, as well as organizational charts, and stresses efficiency.

The human-resource frame describes human needs, the fit between the individual and the organization in the belief that performance is enhanced when people are valued. The goal is to maximize human potential within the organization.

The political frame describes the competition around scarce resources and how people build coalitions and stakeholder groups that can exercise power. Decisions are held in the hands of designated groups, and many look forward to opportunities to bargain, negoiate or persuading.

The symbolic frame refers to the meaning of an organization. Leaders focus on collaboration among key people and groups to establish organizational culture and traditions. Symbols (McDonald's Golden Arches, for example) are used to convey meaning beyond words. In Waldorf schools much of this happens through festivals and assemblies.

As we all know, organizations are meant to help people get things done. Whether self-organized in the sense of Margaret Wheately or structured formally, they help people find each other through common interests and goals. We can do more good joining together in an organized way: a sports team, United Way, the Peace Corps or a community chamber orchestra to name a few. Organizations are made up of people, and individuals each have a particular way of processing information. How people respond to situations depends on both conscious and instantaneous unconscious responses, or "rapid cognition." *Reframing Organizations* cites a 2007 study that describes four characteristics of this intuitive "blink" process: "It is non-conscious—you can do it without thinking about it and without knowing how you did it. It is very fast—the process often occurs almost instantly. It is holistic—you see a coherent, meaningful pattern. It results in 'affective judgments'—thought and feeling work together so you are confident that you know what is going on and what needs to be done" (p. 11).

Some chess masters are said to recognize instantly more than 50,000 possible configurations on a board or play several games at once, spending only a few seconds moves. In Waldorf high school science classes, students are asked to apprehend phenomena as a clear reality that speaks without preconceived "framing." Only afterward does one take time to process and integrate. "The essence of this process is matching situational cues with a well-learned mental framework—a deeply held, nonconscious category or pattern" (ibid, p. 11).

In everyday life, we usually make decisions based on how they are framed and our tendencies to see the world in a particular way—perhaps from a human resources perspective (people interacting) or from a structural, political or symbolic frame. We are often "frame-bound" instead of reality-bound, and as the old saying goes, "To a hammer all problems look like nails." Wise administrators or leaders have a whole box of tools (part of the rationale for this book) and use skills and capacities according to needs instead of pre-framed approaches to issues. We want to move beyond mechanical, rote responses to multi-frame thinking that adapts with flexibility to any situation in the organization or workplace.

In a Waldorf school, time constraints and limited resources often seem to compel us into an "only-way" mentality, seeing all situations as nails because all we have is a hammer. It helps to devote energy and attention to the whole toolbox to have options outside our preferred frame of reference. In organizations based on an anthroposophic worldview, I have found a tendency to see everything developmentally. This is especially true of teachers. But some issues really do not fall into the human-resource frame. Often the structural frame is neglected; instead of looking at systems and structures, people will use a tremendous amount of human energy working through the same issues again and again. Generally, I find the structural and political/economic frames under-utilized or misused, while many repeatedly to human-resource or symbolic frames of reference.

A helpful chart adapted from *Reframing Organizations* summarizes these concepts:

Overview of the Four-frame Model				
	Structural	Human-resources	Political	Symbolic
Organizational metaphor	Factory or machine	Family	Jungle	Carnival, temple, Theater
Central concepts	Roles, goals, policies, technology, environment	Needs, skills, relationships	Power, con-flict, competi-tion, politics	Culture, mean-ing, metaphor, rituals, cer-emony, stories, Heros
Leadership image	Social architecture	Empowerment	Advocacy and political savvy	Inspiration
Basic leadership challenge	Attune struc-ture to task, technology, environment	Align organization and human needs	Develop agenda and power base	Create faith, Beauty, meaning

(p. 19)

Learning multiple perspectives, or frames, is a defense against thrash-ing around without a clue about what you are doing or why. Frames serve multiple functions. They are filters for sorting essence from trivia, maps that aid navigation, and tools for solving problems and getting things done.... The structural approach focuses on the archi-tecture of organization—the design of units and subunits, rules and roles, goals and policies. The human resource lens emphasizes under-standing people—their strengths and foibles, reason and emotion, desires and fears. The political view sees organizations as competi-tive arenas of scarce resources, competing interests, and struggles for power and advantage. Finally, the symbolic frame focuses on issues of meaning and faith. It puts ritual, ceremony, story, play, and culture at the heart of organizational life. (pp. 21–22)

The authors describe four key characteristics of most organizations, which I feel apply especially well to non profits such as Waldorf schools, Camphill communities:

First, *organizations are complex*. People, whose behavior is notori-ously hard to predict, populate them. Large organizations in particu-lar include a bewildering array of people, departments, technologies and goals. Moreover, organizations are open systems dealing with a changing, challenging and erratic environment. Things can get even more knotty across multiple organizations. The 9/11 disaster resulted from a chain of events that involved several separate systems. Almost anything can affect everything else in collective activity, generating causal knots that are hard to untangle. For example, after an exhaustive investigation, our picture of 9/11 is woven from sundry evidence, conflicting testimony, and conjecture.

Second, *organizations are surprising.* What you expect is often not what you get; imagine the shock of Enron's executives when things fell apart. Until shortly before the bottom fell out, the company's leadership team appeared confident they were building a pioneering model of corporate success. Many analysts and management professors shared their optimism.

Third, *organizations are deceptive.* They camouflage mistakes and surprises. After 9/11, America's homeland defense organizations tried to conceal their lack of preparedness and confusion for fear of revealing strategic weaknesses.

Fourth, *organizations are ambiguous.* Complexity, unpredictability and deception generate rampant ambiguity, a defense for that shrouds what happens from day to day. Figuring out what is really going on in business, hospitals, schools or public agencies is not easy. It is hard to get the facts and, if you pin them down, even harder to know what they mean or what to do about them. As the 9/11 incident illustrates, when you incorporate additional organizations into the human equation, uncertainty mushrooms. (ibid., pp. 30–31).

Many of us may be reluctant to admit it, but we often don't know what we are doing, in part because of so much uncertainty around us. We rarely have all the facts we need, and it is hard at times to get the right people together at the right time to sort out the issues. As administrators and leaders we continually piece together elements of a solution, even adapting and changing our response from hour to hour. We live in a time a continuous uncertainty. A good start might be to acknowledge the most common sources of this uncertainty:

- We are not sure what the problem is.
- We are not sure what is really happening.
- We are not sure what we want.
- We do not have the resources we need.
- We are not sure who is supposed to do what.
- We are not sure how to get what we want.
- We are not sure how to determine if we have succeeded. (ibid., p. 32)

Although human beings have a great capacity to learn from experiences, we often fail to see all the consequences of our decisions, making our "learning" incomplete. In Waldorf settings this may happen because of the rapid turnover of administrators. Good things may be launched, but then people move on and there is little attention to a mid-course correction, let alone any evaluation of the consequences. Consequently, projects are often abandoned before there is time to reap positive results, while "organizational churn" produces a continuous stream of new plans and personnel, with little institutional memory or harvests of past efforts. There are ways to mitigate these tendencies. In my administration course at Antioch University, I often use four simple words: *investigate, communicate, decide, communicate.*

We need to start by determining, as much as possible, what is taking place. This can take time, and we need to communicate our findings, even if preliminary, before too much time passes. Otherwise the rest of the organization or community is left in the dark or rumor mills fill the vacuum. Leaders often want to make decisions before communicating, but I have found that early communication can draw out information that improves the eventual decision. Of course, we have to follow up with further communication after a decision. If we maintain an attitude of research and investigation, it tends to involve others and lessen outside criticism.

> Because organizations are complex, surprisingly, deceptive and ambiguous, they are formidably difficult to comprehend and manage. Our preconceived theories, models and images determine what we see, what we do and how we judge what we accomplish. Narrow, oversimplified mental models become fallacies that cloud rather than illuminate managerial action. The world of most managers and administrators is a world of messes: complexity, ambiguity, values dilemmas, political pressures and multiple constituencies. For managers whose images blind them to important parts of this messy reality, it is a world of frustration and failure. For those with better theories and the intuitive capacity to use them with skill and grace, it is a world of excitement and possibility. A mess can be defined as both a troublesome situation and a group of people who eat together. The core challenge of leadership is to

move an organization from the former to something more like the latter. (ibid., pp. 39–40)

The Structural Frame

Can we do things more efficiently by dividing work into separate tasks and coordinating functions as smoothly as possible? (A supreme example of this is Amazon.com and how they separate each function and goal, reportedly into 500 separate steps, with most of them geared toward constantly improving consumer service. Their growth is a testament to mastery of the structural frame.) Several key assumptions are support the structural frame:

- Organizations exist to achieve established goals and objectives.
- Organizations increase efficiency and enhance performance through specialization and appropriate division of labor.
- Suitable forms of coordination and control ensure that diverse efforts of individuals and units mesh.
- Organizations work best when rationality prevails over personal agendas and extraneous pressures.
- Effective structures fit an organization's current circumstances (including its goals, technology, workforce, and environment).
- Troubles arise and performance suffers from structural deficits, remedied through problem solving and restructuring. (ibid., p. 45)

I have found in working with Waldorf schools that there is often a reluctance to address structural issues owing in part to fear of centralized authority (see the chapter on authority in this book). People fear that things will become rigid and dehumanized, and of course that potential exists. Yet, in many cases, organizations that have established clear roles, authority and structure tend to experience more creativity and higher morale. People want to know the "rules of the game," how things work and how to get things done. Uncertainty, as mentioned, drains human resources, forcing people to spend too much time figuring out how to navigate an issue or where to go with a question. There is real merit in establishing clear procedures and a reliable structure. The structure of an organization is like the skeleton in the human body. We cannot function without it. Rather than inhibiting initiative, when there is certainty it releases capacity and the potential for greater initiative. These statements support the main thrust of our earlier chapter on role clarity; it is possible to have a high level of freedom in the classroom *and* clarity of structure and roles (though the latter is often neglected).

Two issues are central to structural design: how to allocate work (*differentiation*) and how to coordinate diverse efforts after assigning responsibilities *(integration)*. Even in a group as small and intimate as a family, it is important to settle issues involving who does what, when the "what" gets done, and how individual efforts mesh to ensure harmony. Every family will find an arrangement of roles and synchronization that works—or suffer the fallout. Division of labor, or allocating tasks, is a keystone of structure. Every living system needs to create specialized roles to do important work.

The Human-Resource Frame

Ultimately, the most important reason to exist as a school or nonprofit is the people. They are the reason we come together in service to a mission and why so many sacrifice time, energy and resources to serve. We always need to ask: How will this decision or action affect the children, parents and community members associated with our enterprise?

In working with the human-resource frame we always need to look at the needs of human beings and their interrelationships. When the fit is good, people can contribute according to their individual abilities. When the fit is poor between individuals and the "system" or organization there may be a danger of exploitation. People and human resources are consumed and individuals may become victims. The human-resource frame is essential for organizational health.

> In Maslow's view, basic needs for physical wellbeing and safety are "prepotent," meaning they have to be satisfied first. Once the lower needs are fulfilled, individuals move up to social needs (belonging, love, and inclusion) and ego needs (esteem, respect, and recognition). At the top of the hierarchy is self-actualization, or developing to one's fullest and actualizing one's ultimate potential. The order is not ironclad. Parents may sacrifice themselves for their children, and martyrs

sometimes give their lives for a cause. Maslow believed that such reversals occur when lower needs are so well satisfied early in life that they recede into the background later on. (ibid., p. 121).

To get to the stage of what I call *released capacities*—whereby people can contribute their very best—we must continuously remind ourselves of the following:

- Hire the right people and develop policies and practices to retain employees.
- Emphasize common goals and shared interests.
- Communicate openly and frequently.
- Publicly test assumptions and beliefs.
- Practice inquiry before advocacy.
- Develop an organizational culture that both allows for risk-taking/ initiative and protects individuals from hurt or embarrassment.
- Act with consideration and compassion in human situations.
- Continuously work on self-awareness, interpersonal skills and emotional intelligence.

Bolman and Deal cite four dimensions of emotional intelligence:

> Two are internal (self-awareness and self-management), and two are external (social awareness and relationship management). Self-awareness includes awareness of one's feelings and one's impact on others. Self-management includes a number of positive psychological characteristics, among them emotional self-control, authenticity, adaptability, drive for achievement, initiative, and optimism. Social awareness includes empathy (attunement to the thoughts and feelings of others), organizational awareness (sensitivity to the importance of relationships and networks), and commitment to service. The fourth characteristic, relationship management, includes inspiration, influence, developing others, catalyzing change, managing conflict, and teamwork. (ibid., pp. 171–172).

If we want to work successfully with the human-resource frame, we need to attend to both tasks and processes. The former is often overt and front and center in our consciousness; the latter is often neglected and under-utilized. We need to get things done but also *do things in a way that attends to the needs of the people involved and recognizes the importance of healthy interpersonal dynamics.*

The Political Frame

Of the four, this might be the most difficult frame to associate with Waldorf schools and anthroposophic initiatives, largely because of the very term *political*. Even in the general public, politics often has a bad reputation. Yet for the purposes of this book, this frame of reference also has considerable value for administrators and leaders. Here are a few key aspects:

- Most nonprofit organizations know how hard it can be to cope with a scarcity of resources and divergent interests in allocating funds in a budget. The back-and-forth around these issues often involves at least a low level of jockeying for influence, which falls in the political frame.
- To exercise influence over decision-making, people tend to form coalitions and find allies to help steer a decision to an outcome considered favorable.
- Within organizations there are often divergent perceptions of reality and needs.
- Although high ideals may guide a school or nonprofit, deciding who gets what in budget deliberations can involve bargaining and negoiation among groups lobbying for scarce resources
- Conflict is part of any organization when real interests and people are involved. It is a natural part of working together and can, when managed well, contribute to outcomes that benefit the core mission of the organization

How can we navigate the political mine fields and find the right ways of working with the competing interests inherent in organizations? In his book *Intuitive Thinking as a Spiritual Path: A Philosophy of Freedom*, Rudolf Steiner describes a quality called "moral technique," the art and practice of making decisions and taking action. Bolman and Deal cite these thoughts on moral reasoning:

> At the lowest, "pre-conventional" level, moral judgment rests primarily on perceived consequences: an action is right if you are rewarded and wrong if you are punished. In the intermediate or "conventional" level, the emphasis is on conforming to authority and following the rules. At the highest, "postconventional" level, ethical judgment rests on general principles: the greatest good for the greatest number, or universal moral principles....

These questions embody four important principles of moral judgment:

Mutuality: Are all parties to a relationship operating under the same understanding about the rules of the game? Enron's Ken Ley was talking up the company's stock to analysts and employees even as he and others were selling their shares. In the period when WorldCom improved its profits by cooking the books, it made its competitors look bad. Top executives at competing firms such as AT&T and Sprint felt the heat from analysts and shareholders and wondered, "Why can't we get the results they're getting?" Only later did they learn the answer: "They're cheating, and we're not."

Generality: Does a specific action follow a principle of moral conduct applicable to comparable situations? When Enron and WorldCom violated accounting principles to inflate their results, they were secretly breaking the rules, not adhering to a broadly applicable rule of conduct.

Openness: Are we willing to make our thinking and decisions public and confrontable? As Justice Oliver Wendell Holmes observed many years ago, "Sunlight is the best disinfectant."

Caring: Does this action show concern for the legitimate interests and feelings of others? (Bolman and Deal, pp. 221–222)

The Symbolic Frame

Waldorf schools are rich in the use of the symbolic frame, from the rose ceremony at the beginning of the school year, to festivals, graduations and recognition of rites of passage. The symbols and imagery speak both to the ideals and the hearts of those involved, and help members of the community reaffirm their choices and commitments to each other and the school. In a world that is often chaotic and confused, the symbolic frame helps give meaning and purpose. As with the rose ceremony welcoming a new class or first graders or saying goodbye to eighth- or twelfth-graders, a message is conveyed that is larger than the moment. The use of symbols and imagery speak to the eternal within each one of us. They also give us hope and a sense of purpose in living.

The symbolic frame has a way of distilling things to the "essence" in the following ways:

- What is most important is not what happens but what it means.

- Activity and meaning are loosely coupled; events and actions have multiple interpretations as people experience situations differently.
- Facing uncertainty and ambiguity, people create symbols to resolve confusion, find direction and anchor hope and faith.
- Events and processes are often more important for what is expressed than for what is produced. Their emblematic form weaves a tapestry of secular myths, heroes and heroines, rituals, ceremonies and stories to help people find purpose and passion.
- Culture forms the Super Glue that bonds an organization, unites people and helps an enterprise to accomplish desired ends." (ibid., p. 248)

Waldorf schools love stories and storytelling throughout the grades, and symbols remind us of stories that rest deep within human consciousness. More than entertainment, stories give even adults great comfort, direction and hope in the process of transformation. Tensions are released and new beginnings are possible. This is possible through the use of metaphor, humor, play and rich imagery.

It is tremendously important that administrators and leaders attend to organizational culture and the atmosphere in which people come together. We can say that an organizational culture speaks to the way things are done, both in the actual events and in the *way people interact*. It is the product of accumulated wisdom and shared practices over time.

Even in our everyday life such as shopping, we know the difference between shopping at Nordstrom, Macy's or Walmart. It is not just the products sold but also the ambiance, the feel of the place. The cynic might say it is all about price, and that customers at Nordstrom can afford more and therefore the atmosphere is more upscale (more of a political frame approach, which also has validity). But if I were to argue the symbolic frame here in this section I could retort: Okay, lets drive a fleet of trucks to a Nordstrom, fill them with their products, and put it all on the shelves at Walmart. Would the store now have the culture of Nordstrom? My point is that it is more than price and product...the symbolic frame communicates the consciousness of those who work on the displays, the style, the ways of interacting with people and the culture. Successful retailers are masters at the symbolic frame. The golden arches of McDonalds communicate volumes.

An administrator or leader is well advised to use the symbolic frame as part of the "tools" available in the workplace. Here are a few tips:

- Attend to the openings: school year, first sentences in letters, first faculty meeting...they set a tone and communicate ever so much
- Appearances matter: clothing, entryway of building, offices, display cabinets in the halls etc.
- Look to defining moments as opportunities to use the symbolic frame, such as a crisis or accident within the community. How one handles the death of a parent or child in the school community....
- Attend to closings: end of year assembly, reports, conclusions to speeches etc. The images and experiences in closings walk out the door with the participants and stay with them even over long vacations....
- Look for simplicity in messaging and communications. Do not confuse. Keep things straightforward. Apple has done wonders with the lower case *i*.
- Remember that all leaders symbolize the intent and mission of and organization. What you do *represents the organization*, and *much can rise or fall on the how and not just the "what" of your actions*....

We all work with time, so lets use it well! This applies not only to conventional aspects of time management, but also to the symbolic frame; our symbols and images, stories and speeches link the present with the past and the past with the future. Help people "make sense" of the flow of events; give them a context and help them see the larger meaning and purpose behind current concerns. Expand, give context and help folks conceptualize the larger framework.

> Symbolic perspectives question the traditional view that building a team mainly entails putting the right people in the right structure. The essence of high performance is spirit. If we were to banish play, ritual, ceremony and myth from the workplace, we would destroy teamwork, not enhance it. There are many signs that contemporary organizations are at a critical junction because of a crisis of meaning and faith. Managers wonder how to build team spirit when turnover is high, resources are tight, and people worry about losing their jobs. Such questions are important, but by themselves, they limit imagination and divert attention from deeper issues of faith and purpose. Managers are inescapably accountable for budget and bottom line; they have to respond to individual needs, legal function if they recognize that team building at its heart is a spiritual undertaking. It is both a search for the spirit within and

creation of a community of believers united by shared faith and shared culture. Peak performance emerges as a team discovers its soul. (ibid., pp. 283–284)

How can administrators and leaders decide which frame to use and when? Bolman and Deal offer a few sample questions for choosing a frame:

Choosing a Frame		
Question	If Yes:	If No:
Are individual commitment and motivation essential to success?	Human resource Symbolic	Structural Political
Is the technical quality of the decision important?	Structural	Human resource Political Symbolic
Are there high levels of ambiguity and uncertainty?	Political Symbolic	Structural Human Resource
Are conflict and scarce resources significant?	Political Symbolic	Structural Human resource
Are you working from the bottom up?	Political	Structural Human resource Symbolic

(ibid., p. 311)

The goal is to use a multi-frame approach in which one can move back and forth depending on the evolving situation and the changing players. Those who can do this skillfully tend to be more successful. We need to know our preferred frame, let go of it when needed, and reframe according to the situation at hand.

The essence of reframing is examining the same situation from multiple vantage points. The effective leader changes lenses when things don't make sense or aren't working. Reframing offers the promise of powerful new options, but it cannot guarantee that every new strategy will be successful. Each lens offers distinctive advantages, but each has its blind spots and shortcomings.

The structural frame risks ignoring everything outside the rational scope of tasks, procedures, policies and organizational charts. Structural thinking can overestimate the power of authority and underestimate the authority of power. Paradoxically, overreliance on structural assumptions and a narrow emphasis on rationality can lead to an irrational neglect of human, political, and cultural variables crucial to effective action.

Adherents of the human-resource frame sometimes cling to a romanticized view of human nature in which everyone hungers for growth and collaboration. When they are too optimistic about integrating individual an organizational needs, they may neglect structure and the stubborn realities of conflict and scarcity.

The political frame captures dynamics that other frames miss, but it has its own limits. A fixation on politics easily becomes a cynical self-fulfilling prophecy, reinforcing conflict and mistrust while sacrificing opportunities for rational discourse, collaboration, and hope. Political action too often is interpreted as amoral, scheming, and oblivious to the common good.

They symbolic frame offers powerful insight into fundamental issues of meaning and beliefs, as well as possibilities for bonding people into a cohesive group with a shared mission. But its concepts are subtle and elusive; effectiveness depends on the artistry of the user. Symbols are sometimes mere fluff or camouflage, the tools of a scoundrel who seeks to manipulate the unsuspecting or awkward gimmicks that embarrass more than energize people at work. But in the aura of an authentic leader, symbols bring magic to the workplace. (ibid., pp. 333–334)

Study questions for administrators in Camphill communities, Waldorf schools, and other initiatives based on anthroposophic insights:

- Which frame do you tend to use most frequently?
- Have you observed others around you using the different frames of reference?
- Is there are frame used most often by the faculty? By the board? By parents when they meet in groups?
- How can an administrator or leader encourage others to look at perspectives other than their preferred point of reference?
- Has you organization changed its way of working over the years? Has there been a migration from one from to the other?
- How have key leaders affected the framing of issues for your organization?

- How can we learn to use a variety of frames depending on the needs of a particular situation?
- How do the indications in anthroposophic self-development, such as the basic exercises found in my book, *Guided Self-Study,* intersect with the topics of this chapter?

15

HUMOR

"Without music, life is a journey through a desert." —PAT CONROY

I have always wanted to write something about a few of the more (or less) humorous experiences I have had on the road by way of illustrating how important it is to develop the right perspective toward events beyond our control. Administrators and school leaders may not travel as much as I have these past years, but I hope they can relate to some of the stories that although painful at first, have provided me with perspective when viewed in hindsight.

Leaving aside the many mishaps that can occur when flying, eating out or visiting friends, I would like to focus on one aspect, namely lodging. It might seem like a simple affair, and it often is just that in the form of a Holiday Inn. But every once in a while I have been persuaded to stay with a family, and that is where the stories get interesting.

A. Idyllic cabin: A family offered to put me up in their backyard in what was described as an idyllic cabin, complete with surrounding flower beds, the songs of birds and a peaceful nature environment. After a day of airports I thought this would be wonderful. And in many ways it was, at least the nature part of the story. It turns out the cabin was actually the children's play house, and the bed inside was better suited for dolls than a six-foot man! I calmly explained the problem, and they obliged with a room in their house.

B. Room with a view: So, avoiding cabins from then on, I was invited to stay in a large house with a guest room overlooking the valley. They asked if I like cats, and I said I did (that should have been a giveaway). They told me it even had its own bathroom down the hall. What they did not mention was that they had a dozen house cats. In order to get to the bathroom I had to navigate down a long hall filled with cat litter boxes in various stages of use. I managed to do so for my pre-sleep washing up, but much to my horror found out (in the middle of the night) that the hall light bulb was gone. Finding my way down that hall in the dark became my worst ever obstacle course, and I had to do some serious decontamination upon arrival in the bathroom.

C. The pull-out sofa: Regarding cats, early in my travels I was often offered a pull-out sofa with phrases such as "It is very comfortable, we all sleep there occasionally." Again, one learns to listen for what Sylvia Ashton Warner calls "key words," in this case "we all sleep there." My heart sank when I found that the sofa was in the middle of a fairly chaotic living room. Yet they kindly set it up for me and I settled in. (What can one do at 11 p.m.?) Soon, other living things started to settle in as well...I counted at least two cats and a dog who were delighted to share their quarters with me.

D. The guest cottage: So of course, one gradually learns to avoid certain situations. By now my list included: cabin, room with a view, pull-out sofas and was about to include the phrase "guest cottage." At first I thought my luck had changed. The cottage in question was truly beautiful. It had a spacious living room, kitchen, bathroom, all recently remodeled and tiled in an attractive style and an adult size bed! When I arrived late at night I could smell the sweet scent of flowers growing on the veranda outside, and someone had thoughtfully set out materials for breakfast. So I settled in for what I hoped would be a peaceful night's sleep. But that was not to be. In the middle of the night I woke up itching all over. When did I last shower? I decided to shower first thing in the morning and tried to go back to sleep, but could not because of the constant itching. Finally I sat up and turned on the bedside light. The bed was covered with an army of red ants, hundreds of them. I ran in to the bathroom, passing the kitchen on the way only to see them all over the breakfast makings, and ran into the shower. With streaming hot water I managed to wash them first off the shower and then myself. I remained there for some time. As dawn broke I gingerly exited the shower and called my hosts. I was transferred to the nearby Hilton.

E. A roommate: Most of the time I travel on business alone, but once in a while a colleague joins me for the flight. Some years ago I attended a workshop in Holland with a well-known colleague from another university. They picked us up at the airport, took us to a restaurant and then to the bed and breakfast place for the overnight. Doing all these things with the colleague was fine, and we had many good conversations. Yet all that abruptly stopped when our hosts led us into our room (again, key word: "our") consisting of one smallish bed. We both stood there, too astonished to say anything at first. Luckily I got my voice back in time to run after our hosts and insist on a separate room. There are limitations to colleagueship.

F. The reader can see my membership in the Holiday Inn Frequent Guest program was gradually growing in value and points. Yet not all hotels are safe, either. Once I was dropped off at a little place in the middle of what seemed to be a desert in the southwestern part of the U.S. It had been one of those horrible days of several short connections with nothing but pretzels and peanuts. I was famished, but also really tired. So I went to bed promising myself a hearty breakfast at the hotel restaurant early the next morning. A little weight loss would do me no harm (it is amazing how we try to find virtue in necessity). The next morning I was up early and ran out of the room and headed for the restaurant, hoping it was open that early. It was not. It fact, there was no restaurant, not even sad donuts or raisin bran trying to pass as a continental breakfast…nothing. So I left the motel and walked out into the street, only to find that it was not a street but a deserted highway in the middle of nowhere. I gladly agreed to be picked up at noon, thinking I would have a peaceful morning to prepare, but my host had not left a number, and I was now stranded. In the end, all I found was an old candy machine. Not exactly what the doctor had ordered for breakfast.

G. Holiday Inn: For a while after that, I adopted a new faith that had certain key words: Holiday, Best Western, Hilton etc. But even in these cases, things can go wrong. Once after a lecture in a distant city my host came up to me and introduced the "driver" who would take me to my Holiday Inn. It was very late at night and we did not talk much. I never even discovered his name, nor would my tired brain have remembered it. He dropped me off at 11 p.m. at a Holiday Inn and sped off. I walked in only to find that it was full and they had no record of my name or that of my host (a frequent confusion). It turns out it was one of four Holiday Inns in that city! However, the manager kindly phoned around, located the correct one and called a taxi. I hit the bed around 1 a.m., knowing the workshop would begin early the next morning and everyone would expect a rested leader.

One of the lessons learned from these experiences is that expectations play a key role in our feelings of how things turn out. The above were all the more challenging because at some point or another I had let myself imagine comfortable lodging. In contrast, I have stayed in very simple rooms in China, India and Nepal but since my expectations were lower I was relatively happy. The work for those who travel is to manage expectations ahead of time and to ask enough questions to become informed (inquiry before advocacy). It has also gradually become apparent to me that the position of the host—i.e., board president, and the tone of voice and friendliness when the invitation is issued have little to do with the actual lodging. Living styles and descriptions vary considerably.

But most of all I have learned to place these experiences in "the humor box" rather than just get aggravated. They make for good dinnertime stories (always omitting names and locations), and actually end up providing a rich context for future experiences. "I've seen worse" is a line I have had to use more than once. I continually need to remember that even the hard knocks of life end up giving us perspective and inner strength.

16

A Number Exercise

"Get people to sing together and they'll act together, too."
—Pete Seeger

This can be done in a group or as an individual: take a clean piece of paper and in the left margin write the numbers one to seven. Then take some time to quietly write next to each number a personal reflection or context in relation to self-awareness in organizational life. The following are considerations, but one need not read them to do the exercise. The point is to look at oneself in relation to group size and organizational dynamics. These can then be shared voluntarily and can lead to fruitful discussion with colleagues.

One

This number is often seen as a negative: being "alone," solitary, isolated, the only child or the exception to the rule. Yet this number when it pertains to self can have vast potential. Who am I? What is my journey on this Earth? What are my tasks in this lifetime? These questions alone are worth many hours of quiet reflection.

But one can also look at the rhythm of the day and see if there are in fact any times when I am really just with myself, or am I always over-run by the needs of the periphery? What is it like to be in a room just by myself? Why do some of us avoid times of solitude? If I need such time, can I build it into each day?

There are so many things in life we cannot control, and yet we continue to stress over them. Again and again I have found that some time each day for meditation (in my family I call it "alone time") can make a big difference. People may have one type or meditative practice or another (and mine is routed in practices arising out of Anthroposophy), but for the purposes of the sanctity of the "one," I simply urge administrators and leaders to simply *do meditation*, even if it is as simple as sitting quietly and attending to breathing. There are so many options available to us in mindfulness practices, so it is not so important where one starts but that one actually starts.

In terms of work, which tasks are best for me to do on my own and which ones need others? I have found that as one gets older, one can find more and more opportunities for initiative and individual decision-making independent of others. One cannot defer everything to the views of people around us. There are times when we have to simply decide some things on our own, especially in regard to personal conduct.

Also in regard to organizational life, there is a need for unilateral decision-making and the delegation of tasks to individuals who have the qualifications and experience. A mature organization often has a lot of strong people doing work in collaboration with each other, but along the way making a host of individual decisions and taking responsibility for completion of tasks. If the mission and vision re clear to all, individuals are freed to work out of their own initiative.

The experience of being a "one" is a vertical relation to the spiritual worlds and can open the floodgates for inspiration and intuition. Let there be times for the "one"! (see bibliography for the source of the drawings).

Two

Again, this number can at first be seen in a negative light: just two of us, or "polarity" or "where is everyone else?," a feeling of being a distinct minority. There is also the danger that the issues be two dimensional, either/or, and that other perspectives are not considered. Yet if one spends

some time with the number two, one can again increase understanding of the potential that lives in this dynamic:

First: "How glad I am to have a speaking partner! Before you came along, I just conversed with myself, now we can share!" This potential for dialogue is a tremendous gift, and every one of us deserves at least one speaking partner in our workplaces, someone who is there for us as a person, not just because we serve on the same committee. I urge all leaders to ask for a speaking partner, and the organization should sanction the time spent each week (an hour can work) in conversation. Many larger problems can be avoided if one has a place to vent, share and process. There is much literature on the value of dialogue, and most of it points to the growth and mutuality of learning through conversation.

We can also look at our daily rhythm in relation to the number two: It had been a busy day, but I was really happy my wife and I had a chance to take a long walk around the local park and see the otter emerge from his hole in the ice (although that may have made the experience a "three"). Along the way we talked, caught up on many things, and "tuned in" again to each other. This tuning in is as vital to relationship as is water and food for nutrition. Relationships needs friendship time, just as plants need water. In my experience, most relationship building happens in dialogue.

In the workplace, we have many opportunities to work in tandem with others. It is really great to share a task, do a project, or present together. One has to plan and prepare, and yet there is often something really spontaneous that occurs in the process. I often end of saying aloud or to myself afterward: I did not know that about you! Places of work benefit from work teams of two.

In the context of the larger organization, it is vital that before any decision or action, at least the pros and cons are considered, if not a variety of other perspectives. One can have one person play one role, say advocate, while the other takes the opposite view. Many times a community disaster could have been avoided if the organization had had the internal resources to play out the "two" of a decision or action ahead of time.

Spiritually, we need the dichotomy, "the two," to give birth to something new: mother and father, light and dark giving birth to color, yin and yang, warmth and cold that allows the seasons. Sometimes the very discomfort of the "two," such as the interval of the second played together in music, can create a longing for resolution and new beginnings.

Is there enough of the "two" in my life? Too much? How do I experience myself when I am with one other person in contrast to a larger group? What happens to my sense of "one" when I am part of a "two"? As in the diagram opposite, what is my relationship to both the "above" and the "below"? And I have known some people who so heavily favor the "two" that they continuously call on someone to talk privately about issues that should have been brought to the whole group. In those cases, the world of two can divide rather than stimulate.

THREE

What happens when I find myself as part of a trio, a committee or group of three? It is a very different experience from the above reflections. Now there is the possibility of three different perspectives. In my experience, a group of three can easily settle into a work assignment, and the skills, capacities and experiences often balance one another in a helpful way. It is my preferred configuration for a leadership team. Why?

It can have a balance of skills, capacities and experience, and yet a group of three is small enough to take action. When my leadership groups have had proper orientation and are working collaboratively, it has been possible to have "stand-up meetings" of 10 to 15 minutes in which decisions can be made and action taken. I am sometimes viewed as being on the aggressive side when it comes to moving forward with issues, but that is because I feel that it is far better to make a decision and adjust with time than to live continuously in a state of uncertainty. Leaders are role models and usually serve in highly visible roles. Not deciding or procrastinating or making excuses ("We are lacking some needed financial information.") can send the wrong message to the larger community. Once confidence is lost, it is hard to regain. People usually understand that "to err is human," but not to act is a terrible price to pay for safety (not deciding is also a decision).

One can imagine a triangle or a pyramid, and see that if it is well proportioned, it can be quite reliable. If one person is more reticent, the group is small enough that the two others will notice and do what they can to draw a person out.

My experience of myself in a group of three is usually a "wakeful," or highly conscious experience. One cannot drift…one has to stay fully attentive in the conversation or meeting. A group of three calls on me to be active and awake. Some of the best executive committees I have been part of have consisted of three people.

FOUR

Four was an important number for Native Americans, as it represents the four directions of the earth: north, south, east and west. It is a stable group, solid and reliable. A standing committee, such as one involving finances, is well served with four. Something about this configuration has to do with earthly matters. From the point of view of group dynamics, four lends itself to practical tasks.

As for my own experience in groups of four...well, they are mixed. I have sometimes had to help them navigate away from two "pairs" within the four, especially when gender or more political aspects come to the fore. Personally, I am often somewhat on edge in a group of four, but that may not be true for others, thus the exercise of writing down one's own experiences mentioned at the beginning of this chapter.

FIVE

Here we have the possibility for full harmony as in the pentagon or pentagram. Five points of view bring wonderful perspective, even wisdom. I have grown fond of this group size when it comes time to convene a council or circle of "elders," as even with only five people in the room, many insights can be gathered. It is a cosmic constellation

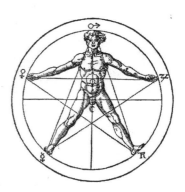

and can portray the complete human being in balance.

With six and seven one can also make note of personal experiences. There are also groups that are much larger, such as twelve or fifteen or more. It is also helpful for the leader to become aware of his or her interactions with these configurations. How do I relate to the group when it is a certain size, and what can be accomplished when groups are configured in certain ways? The answers to these questions can help us bring more intentionality to our working groups and ultimately get more done.

Finally, a footnote: our relationship to groups and their size can change over time. As we grow older, our ability and comfort level may evolve, and that is also worth noting. Some may revel in larger groups in their twenties only to go for the more sedate threes and fives later on. Others may have more of a singular bent early in life and then long for companionship later on.... Again, there are no "rules" that need to be followed, only opportunities for professional and personal growth. One just has to learn to observe oneself in groups and read the interactions the way one used to be able to read the weather. Much organizational stress would be avoided if we could just learn to see what is around us.

17

OUR KARMIC COMPANIONS

"To send light into the darkness of men's hearts—such is the duty of the artist." —ROBERT SCHUMANN

Think back to a time when you went on a trip with friends, perhaps a multi-day hike, a visit to Mexico, or a retreat or training program. By the end of the experience there might have been a level of familiarity with the other participants that was not there at the beginning. You may not "like" everyone equally, some you may have even learned to avoid, but overall there is often a feeling of warmth and camaraderie at the end of the trip or event. You know each other out of shared experiences, and in many cases friendships have arisen. These new friends will henceforth be in your life, often despite miles of separation in the years to come. When you take up a conversation again, it will be like picking up the thread rather than beginning anew. On a trip or retreat you built a foundation of shared experience, you "bonded" and that has now become a wonderful new reality in your life.

This common experience gives one a taste of a larger version of bonding we can call karma and reincarnation. One may not be at first comfortable with the idea, but if one can entertain some of the aspects I plan to introduce below it can prove helpful to administrators and leaders in the workplace. For karma is a longer version of the multi-day hike on the Appalachian Trail; it is a journey over several lifetimes. Along the way one makes connections that carry over into subsequent lives, and their influence can be felt and experienced especially when one is in a close working situation with others.

It is one of the pleasures and challenges of working in a Waldorf school that we are united with others who share similar values. We are drawn by a mutual attraction to the mission and vision of the school, the philosophy and way of working with children. People find each other in common purpose and intention, and those who have been drawn together more often than not have connections that go far back.

This may not be visible at first, because after all each family is different, our children have different needs, and some of us as parents may spend just a few minutes a day at the school. But the more involved we become, and especially if one takes up work with real responsibilities as the school, the connections tend to surface more readily. At first it may be a matter of mutual interest: "Oh, you love good jazz too!" Or, "Yes, I have always have an herb garden." When these mutual interests become known it is like fireflies lighting up the night. The many points of discovery bring great joy. We realize the school is not just for our children; we, too, have many wonderful reasons to associate with the other families.

These connections can intensify over time to the point at which some of the other adults at the school become best friends. These are the people you invite to a family celebration; these are the ones you choose to take to a concert or a local restaurant. These friendships can become so strong that they endure even after the children have graduated.

But even on the friendship level some complexity can arise. What if you are a parent who is asked to serve on the board of trustees and one of your best friends is the board president? Roles have a way of changing, and there may be times when you see things differently from your friend on the board. Or you may be a faculty member who is asked to serve a term on the board, and suddenly the relationship with some of your "friends" changes due to positions you take on certain issues. In most cases, these things can be worked through with good conversation and dialogue, but one needs to attend to the dynamic of changing roles.

When patterns of interaction emerge, either positive or negative, one has a first glimpse of a larger dynamic (perhaps karma) at work. By *patterns* I mean things such as repeated outcomes of discussions in which two members are often on the same "side" or opposed to each other, even though the issue may be different each time. Behaviors, especially those that are more instinctive, show a connection to the will forces in the human being. And the will is a cosmic thread that connects our lives on Earth.

Briefly stated, when we die, we soon discard all our clever thoughts and gradually even our feelings leave the soul. But as the journey of life after death unfolds, the will forces that a person had in life are carried forward, according to Rudolf Steiner. In many cases we "will ourselves" into a new birth situation so that we have an opportunity to take on tasks that will assist us in our further development. We return to Earth with intentionality and a wish to develop ourselves further and to work with certain others, especially those with whom there are unresolved tasks. We seek out the people we need to work with.

OPPORTUNITIES

We often find many of our karmic companions in and around a Waldorf school. This can be a joyous discovery. Here are people for whom I feel great kinship! We quickly become friends, have great fun, and enjoy doing things together. When this happens with a whole group of people, we form a kind of karmic cluster of like-minded people who have much in common, coming as a kind of unexpected "grace." Of course, we have to work very hard with some friendships one really has to work toward a connection, but our "karmic companions" often seem to be thrust into our lives by external forces.

This affords us many opportunities. Countless Waldorf schools and indeed other ventures such as tech companies have been established by karmic companions, sometimes even working in a garage (Apple and Microsoft). There is no end to what these folks can do—invent software, construct buildings, raise funds, host potlucks, or recruit new families and teachers. In South Korea, a karmic group gathered every Monday evening for a year to translate my book *School as a*

Journey into Korean. The familiar ground of friendship can help people accomplish much with relative ease. During the early stages, we do not need policies and procedures (or so it seems); people simply in trust and mutual knowledge of one another. There is strength and vitality to working with karmic companions.

Such karmic groups often continue long into the biography of a Waldorf school or Camphill community. The original founders may change roles—become teachers or connect themselves with the board— but for them the school is about more than educating children; it is a social opportunity to reconnect with one another. This last statement points to a highly potent spiritual force.

We tend to think we are the only ones who "build" our schools and teach and administer them in the years that follow. In fact, however, we are a small piece of the cosmic action. Finding karmic companions unleashes tremendous creative forces in the world around us, as in the Titans of ancient Greece, involving beings who use our activity as an opportunity to lend themselves to our intentions.

Schools are built spiritually, not just physically. When we find our karmic companions and we pull together we are sending forth a mighty invitation to the spiritual worlds to invest in our endeavors. Especially in the age of Michael, this dynamic of human and cosmic collaboration is an ever-present reality for schools and other organizations founded on a spiritual view of the human being. We, and our karmic companions, do the inviting; the children and their friends respond on many levels. The cosmos also responds with unexpected resources and often surprising support that makes the impossible possible.

This makes it possible for many of us to get up in the morning, and to do things again and again that we did not even think we could face, let alone accomplish. Our limbs move, our feelings are stirred, insights flash into our consciousness, all because we are swimming in a spiritual ocean far greater than we imagined. Let us never forget these intangible resources.

CHALLENGES

Finding our karmic companions also presents challenges. We bring unresolved issues with us, even past conflicts. A school now becomes our opportunity either to resolve matters or to perpetuate them. In my experience, it is often a bit of both. Rudolf Steiner gives us an example of this in a lecture on February 20, 1912:

> The acquaintances we make somewhere around the age of thirty in one incarnation may have been, or will be, persons related to us by blood in a previous or subsequent incarnation. It is therefore useful to say to oneself: The personalities with whom life brings you into contact in your thirties were once around you as parents or brothers and sisters, or you can anticipate that in one of your next incarnations they will have this relationship with you. The reverse also holds true. (*Reincarnation and Karma*, p. 56)

Thus, some karmic companions we find in a school may have been our siblings or parents in a past life. Alternatively, people with whom we work closely during midlife may become tied to us by blood in a future life. This sheds new light on colleagueship. With family members there might be deep connections while much is unspoken, and the same happens with karmic companions in community settings. We sometimes find a kind of sibling rivalry that is unexplained by the flow of the day-to-day agenda. Why does Jim always seem to counter what Charles says in a meeting? Such instinctive and reoccurring responses often indicate deep pools of karma.

There is also a phenomenon I call a "karmic knot." For example, a couple of people become so tied up in conflict there seems to be no resolution. Just as a knot gets increasingly difficult to untie when repeatedly dipped in water and dried, similarly multiple earthly lives can give rise to karmic knots that cannot be unraveled in a single lifetime. I have seen a teacher in a karmic knot finally give up and leave, only to do very well at another school. It is a deeply humbling experience to learn that not everything can be resolved now. Time is a great healer, but we cannot control the clock. Time has its own wisdom.

The negative side of karmic companionship is that the administration of a school can be held hostage to one or two well-placed karmic knots. When this happens, progress is impeded and people start to walk in circles around the problem. We have to make every attempt to resolve the issue (this is why John Cunningham's "Dialogue and Restorative Circles" is a chapter in this book). Given healthy process and facilitation, much can be resolved, and when it is all concerned reach a new level of work that is no longer instinctive but born from the trials of fire and water. The best antidote to the negative working of karma is hard-earned consciousness. When one is aware of one's own role in a situation, and can see the larger dimensions of biography and karma at work, then the knots of life start to relax. Sometimes one can only go so far, and then one has to decide: can I now live with the situation? Has the healing gone far enough, or do I need to express my gratitude for the learning made possible in these circumstances and now move on?

Finally, a few words about moving on (my father touches on this again in his letter at the end of the book): I used to think that to leave a school was a sign of failure. But as with many things in life, my views have evolved. Of course there is great value in perseverance and continuity, and many of our schools would not be where they are had some karmic companions not stuck to it over time. But for others, moving on can be a fresh start, a new beginning. Schools need new blood, new human impulses, and moving to another school can promote "beginner's mind" for teachers, parents, and board members. As in nature, movement promotes life, and it is better to go with life than to stagnate.

Of course, it is possible to enhance movement while staying with the same job; changing roles is one example, which I have done several times at Antioch University. We can strive to become different persons and bring inner movement to refresh and enliven our outer circumstances. However, this depends on the free resolve of everyone involved.

✥

Postscript

I shared this short chapter with my father, Siegfried Finser, who has lived with and studied karma for many years. He sent the following:

> An executive at Microsoft who had his children in the Seattle Waldorf School asked me, "What good is it to know about Karma? How does it help me lead my life?"
>
> He and I worked together on his question. We realized that Karma cannot be used as a guide to behavior or decision-making. It can be useful only in deepening our understanding, enriching our awareness, enlightening our empathy. Every time someone explains their behavior by saying they have a karmic relationship, it is a red flag, a kind of untruth. The only explanation for one's actual decisions or behaviors that holds water in our time is the self-directed, truthful reason for the action. Karma is part of the "world of necessity" that meets us out of the unknown. What we do should no longer be part of that. What we do should more and more be done out of the realm of freedom, our spiritual activity.

I myself am almost always aware of the karmic overtones and undertones. It's like the piano accompaniment to one's personal melody, part of the spiritual architecture around us. I try to act mindfully with this awareness of the larger dimensions, while trying not to use it as a motive or reason for making one decision or another. It is far too complicated for simplistic application.

18

Role-Plays and Adult Learning

"Without craftsmanship, inspiration is a mere reed shaken in the wind." —Johannes Brahms

It is important to work with adults differently from the way we do with children. Those of us who have done some of both have learned to differentiate not only in terms of content but also teaching style. The didactic approach often used with children can appear condescending and archaic to adults. An adjunct in the Waldorf program at Antioch University who tries to do with adults what was done with children soon fades, for the learning needs of adults and children are so different.

Children want to see teachers who personify the historical characters in the curriculum and serve as catalysts of curiosity and discovery. They want to look up to their teachers as role models. Many classrooms are deeply influenced by the personality and style of the teacher, and children often extend themselves because of their love and respect for their teachers.

One unique aspect of Waldorf education is the educator's use of imitation in the early years (ages one to nine). As a former foreign language teacher, imitation was my tried and true friend. All I had to do was speak with lively gestures or sing a song and they followed along. They learned to sing, play games and carry a dialogue without translation. They did not know word for word what they were saying, yet they knew. Young children can learn foreign languages as they learned their mother tongue, through listening and imitation.

Yet as the students get older, the imitation game is fraught with peril. In high school, a totally different approach is needed, in which we challenge observation skills and a growing capacity to think. Simply doing as another teachers have don can be the worst way to go.

Likewise, so many teaching interns will see someone teach a math lesson and then think that is the way to go. Far more important is the ability to understand the needs of children at a certain age level, such as their ability to process math, as well as the whys and wherefores of a math lesson. Beginning teachers also need to think for themselves, wake up, so to speak, and ask critical questions so that their teaching is consciously embraced and not done in a rote fashion. I ask beginning teachers not to imitate me or any other adult, but to challenge and explore things for themselves.

Thus with adults, the didactic "I will tell you what to do" approach does not work for more than brief periods of time. If the instructor is too directive, after a while adults will naturally start to question and even rebel. They want to be involved in the generation of ideas and learn through conversation and experimentation. Sitting and taking notes also does not work for long. When too passive the material is often not internalized and has minimal lasting value.

Conversation groups tend to get energy flowing and help prepare the foundation for a new presentation. So I have found that in teaching adults it is very helpful to articulate a few key themes and then set up small conversation groups around a focusing question. So if the topic is leadership, one might remind folks of their various experiences in life regarding leadership that worked or did not, and then ask them to talk with each other in small groups on the question: What are the key components of successful leadership based on your life experience? Depending on the size of the groups (size does matter; see chapter 16), we can then return to the large group after a while and ask for a few gems from the discussion groups. After this has transpired, I give a brief twenty- to thirty-minute presentation on leadership styles, followed by questions and comments. This format has worked in countless settings, and seems to validate adult learning needs.

Another way to work with adults is to do a role-play on a selected theme. Again, it is helpful to set the stage otherwise they will enter into the activity "cold" and take too much group time to "warm up the topic." So I often do some warming ahead of time with a few introductory comments, especially on the issue of why the topic is so important. Adults like to see context and practical reasons for doing something (whereas children will often suspend disbelief for considerable periods of time and go along with an exciting presentation with amazing open-mindedness). After an introduction, it is important to adhere to a few clear steps when doing any role-play:

1. Set up the practical aspects, such as how many chairs in which configuration, and give a time frame for the entire experience.
2. Clarify the topic and the goal of the exercise.
3. Either assign roles or ask that they attend to that first thing, as well as any expectations regarding minute taking or reporting out afterward.
4. Let them know you will serve as coach and consultant if they need help during the role play.
5. Do the role-play.
6. Give them a time to reflect with each other as a small group.
7. Debrief as a large group. I prefer to ask process questions first, such as "How was that for you?" Then go into content reflections as time allows.
8. The next day or next session it is helpful if one allows a few minutes to reflect back on the role-play experience. Often people will say that it was an artificial situation, that some were not emotionally invested because it was a fictional narrative etc. Then often the comments go to the realization that unless one has some practice, say in conflict resolution, it is hard to deal with the issues when they arise in the workplace.

Role-plays are of course staged events, and some people really get into them and others may stay more aloof. Yet I have found that in working with adults, role-plays get us closer to real-life situations than just a lot of theory. *People today have an infinite capacity to say things that sound good, and even act as if they know it all, only to fall flat on their faces when similar challenges come up in real life. The best way to prepare is to practice and reflect on practice.*

Conversely, if one just does practice without reflection the learning might not be fully assimilated, and people can be carried away in the joys or struggles of the role play, treating them even as a form of entertainment. When well done, role-plays can assist adult learning by promoting real-life experience and practical learning by reflecting back on what happened. The reflections can then be used to raise the next role-play to a higher level.

In the following pages I have chosen a few role-plays that I have used in administration and leadership development courses over the past years. Some were written by my father who helped many schools as a consultant over the years, others were suggested by my students or came from my own experience in the field. I ask the reader not to get hung up on the details or specifics, but to read them over to get a sense for how role-plays might assist in collaborative leadership training.

1. *The Unexpected Gift*

Narrative: The local children's museum has just received word that a long-time patron and friend will donate one million dollars as an unrestricted gift next year.

The Challenge: You, as the board, have now been asked by the executive director to give guidance as to how the money should be spent or not: form an endowment, lower admissions fees, buy new materials for exhibits, add a wing for a parent/toddler program, start a visiting teacher program for instructors to go into schools and so on? As a group you have many differing ideas as to how to spend the money. Your assignment is to come up with a plan.

The Players: Seven board members from various socioeconomic, cultural, racial and professional backgrounds. Assign your own role before beginning the role-play.

2. *What Does "Waldorf" Mean?*

Narrative: The Green Valley Charter School is Waldorf-inspired but has not yet been fully recognized, which means it uses Waldorf methods but cannot use the word Waldorf in its name. The school is now three years old and has been located in a reclaimed public school building in a suburban neighborhood. Most of the teachers have Waldorf training from an accredited Waldorf teacher education program. The board is made up of parents who like the idea of an alternative education for their children and are happy to mix Waldorf pedagogy with other contemporary trends in education. Their view could be summed up with the phrase, "use what works."

The Challenge: The school relies on state funding that is based on a head count of children enrolled each year as well as results from standardized testing. The faculty, staff and parents have to fund raise for any "extras," which in the past two years included a eurythmist. Now the state has launched a new reading program that requires hiring several teaching aids. To make room for that in the budget, the board has proposed to cut the eurythmy position. When the faculty strenuously objected, a parent offered to do folk dancing instead. A meeting has been called to resolve their differences.

The Players: Two experienced Waldorf teachers, two board members and the school administrator.

3. Alleged Harassment

The Narrative: The Evergreen Waldorf School is a full member of the Association of Waldorf Schools and has been in existence for thirty years. It is considered by many to be a successful K–12 school, and their graduates have done well in college and beyond. The teachers have known one another for many years, and although administrators and staff have come and gone, most of the faculty members are seasoned pedagogues.

The Challenge: A rumor has spread that one of the girls in the high school told her friends that one of the high school teachers has been increasingly inappropriate with her. Various stories are living in the student body, but it has now come to the attention of the faculty leadership group. They have called an emergency meeting to deal with the issue. Their first question is how to proceed/what to do.

The Players: The faculty chair, administrator, school counselor, a senior faculty member and the board president.

4. Dwarfs vs. Elves

Narrative: Two very experienced kindergarten teachers had a falling out. They seemed to have different interpretations of the curriculum, how to celebrate festivals and how to work with parents. Over time, their differences became so entrenched that they had marked off separate play areas for their children, and all festivals and special events had to be held twice, much to the consternation of parents and other faculty members. Each kindergarten teacher had a loyal following of former students, parents and even teachers within the school. Yet they could not work together.

The Challenge: When a new board president was selected, she decided enough was enough. She called together a group of teachers and staff, and brought in a consultant to help resolve the problem. This is the consultant's first meeting. What questions need to be asked? What strategy should they use?

The Players: Two teachers, two administrators, the board president and a consultant.

5. *The Move*

The Narrative: After many years of existence, the Tall Oak Waldorf School had outgrown its building. Enrollment was limited by classroom size, and many teachers complained of facilities that were no longer adequate. They had formed a building committee to look at expansion, but their options were limited due to zoning issues. A few days before the new school year, word came to the Administrator that an old public school building was available on a rent-to-own basis. She called the board president, and together with a small group of teachers who happened to be around, they went over to inspect the building. They were pleasantly surprised to find the facility in relatively good shape, so they convened a board meeting that night and authorized an offer. It was accepted! With great joy the administrator, faculty chair and board president wrote a letter informing the parents of the good news.

The Challenge: With so little time, no one had done a demographic study of the parent body. It now turned out that about one third of the students would have to commute more than an hour each way. Those parents were in an uproar. They demanded an all-school meeting. The administrator wisely called a few of them in to meet for a "planning session" first.

The Players: The administrator, the board president, a teacher, and several parents.

It was difficult just to get the meeting going, owing to the high level of emotions.

6. *Living Waldorf School*

The Living Waldorf School has been in existence for fifteen years as of this writing. The K–8 school has attracted excellent teachers, dedicated parents and many children. Enrollment has held steady at 215 to 220 students for the last three years. The buildings have been well maintained, and parents have begun to ask about the possibility of starting a high school.

It is now August 15, and the Living Waldorf School has just learned that a Waldorf charter school is in the planning stage and will open eight miles away. Parents, teachers and board members are in a state of shock. Why didn't they know about this potential competitor sooner? How will they respond to this challenge?

The leadership of the school has called a meeting to address the issue. Participating in the meeting are the faculty and college chairs, the board president, treasurer, the parent–teacher organization (PTO) chair and the development director. This is their first meeting session. How will you proceed?

7. *Energetic Board Member*

Joan, a parent with a strong business background, was recently elected to serve on the board. She is joining a board composed largely of faculty members, founders, and adoring parents. After several meetings, it has become very apparent to Joan that the school is inefficiently run and could probably break even, or perhaps show a surplus, if fiscal matters were reformed by a competent manager.

After several unsuccessful attempts by Joan to gain support from the board to "personally" take charge of the situation, she has now turned her attention to persuading the school to obtain a computer and install "Penny Saver" software with the assistance of an outside accountant to set up the management control systems.

There are several factions within the school community who are resistant to Joan's plans, perhaps partially due to their perception that Joan is abrasive. The school bookkeeper, who has not been consulted in this process, feels particularly vulnerable by Joan's proposed changes. The bookkeeper has always used a manual system to chart the accounts.

After some initial enthusiasm to reconcile this matter at a previous meeting, the board has started to factionalize and there is a growing sense of conflict about how to resolve this issue. A special meeting of the board has been called to address this issue. Present at the meeting are six regular board members (including Joan, the college chair, a faculty member and an additional faculty member). The school bookkeeper has been asked to attend this portion of the meeting.

8. *Administrative Conflict*

A new administrator, Kathy Power, was recently hired for the Winding Brook Waldorf School. She replaced a long-time parent and friend of the school. Kathy was hired to bring a new level of professionalism to the school administrative function, but this change has raised some concerns. The use of the administrative space seems to be at the forefront of the current crisis. The administrative space is a large room separated by partitions at one end for administrative offices and at the other end there is an open area, where the receptionist sits and the office mechanics are located. The open area under the previous administrator was a gathering and meeting place for parents. Kathy claims the administrative space needs to be quieter to provide clearer thinking, more confidentiality in conversations, and fewer distractions at work. Her needs represent a significant cultural change. A space committee consisting of a Faculty representative, the college, a board member, the administrator, and a parent (who frequently uses the space) has been formed to try to address the space issue. The board president has agreed to facilitate the meetings. The group has met with little success to this point except acknowledging their individual wants and differences.

A recent crisis has occurred over the use of the copy machine. The administrator has issued a directive insisting that teachers and parents who want something copied should place the material in a specific box with a short note detailing the copy instructions. A minimum lead-time of six hours was requested. A teacher needed a quick copy for class he was teaching and went in to do it. The administrator announced that this was the sixth exception that day and she would not tolerate it and threatened to resign if more consideration were not given to her directives. An emergency meeting with the space committee was called by the board president to resolve the issues.

Roles (using your names with the exception of Kathy):

- Kathy, the Administrator
- The Board President
- A Board Member
- Parent
- Faculty Member
- College Chair

9. Parent Initiative

The school is struggling to maintain its financial health. The decision was made by the finance committee to conduct an Annual Appeal to try to raise $20,000 to meet a possible short fall for the year.

A parent, not on the committee, proposed that the school consider joining three other reputable organizations in sponsoring a Bingo game. It requires that each organization furnish three volunteers on the same night each week to assist the conduct of the games.

The proceeds, after expenses to the Bingo operator, are divided evenly among the four sponsoring organizations. The numbers look good. Based on similar Bingo projects the school could net as much as $30,000 in a year. The parent advocating this approach to fund-raising has no financial stake in the project. There is a groundswell of support from a lot of the parents because of the fact that many would find it difficult to contribute to the annual appeal.

The College of Teachers has asked to meet with the parent and review all elements of the Bingo proposal and communicate some of their concerns. The College has a pre-meeting get-together to discuss the situation and the financial situation in general. The group wants to select a spokesperson to present their concerns. There are six teachers present. How will they work the issue?

10. *The Four Seasons Waldorf School*

In its twentieth year, the Four Seasons Waldorf School has experienced a surge in enrollment, and in the recent past the construction of a new gymnasium and a building for grades five to eight.

Both the parents and faculty were optimistic for the future of the school. Several families had made substantial donations toward the school's development.

As usual in spring before the end of the school year, faculty met for several planning sessions to map out programming and staffing needs for the fall. Enrollment projections were optimistic given that the school had experienced unprecedented growth.

In anticipation of yet another generous donation from a board member, the summer management team made a decision to move forward with the building of a new eurythmy hall. This approval was gained over the summer months while many teachers were away. However, it did receive board approval.

When faculty reconvened at summer's end they were met with the news that construction of a new eurythmy hall would soon begin. Tenders had gone out and a contractor was hired. Site preparation and construction of the hall began in early fall.

Early into October news came that the anticipated donation would no longer be available and was, in fact, a misunderstanding. To make matters worse the optimistic enrollment projections were way off the mark and now the school had hired its faculty for programs. The school was facing a huge deficit. The summer management team was accused of faulty decision-making that excluded the full faculty circle. There was a feeling that the administrator and eurythmist who were part of the summer management team were looking out for their own interests. However, they pointed out that faculty had made budgetary decisions in the spring regarding programming and enrolled projections. Now, the board was calling for the restructuring of administration. There was much division among faculty, board and administration. A meeting had been called. In attendance: the administrator, eurythmist, board president, a faculty member who was away over the summer and another board member.

11. *The Shinun Breakfast Waldorf School*

The Shinun Breakfast Waldorf School is hiring for first-grade position. Two candidates have applied: one is fully trained and has taught one class up to sixth grade. The other is a spouse of the college chair and still in training. School is about to start in two weeks.

The college is pressured to make this decision because the first-grade teacher, hired from within, left abruptly after having an affair with a college member. The affair is undisclosed to the public, but two college members know the real reason for her sudden departure.

Two members of the college are hiding this secret, and the college is splintered for a while over whom they will hire. The candidate with experience has references, which reveal questionable but vague behavior in the past. The other is only one year into her training and is the wife of the college chair. Please conduct the college meeting to decide what to do. All seven members are present.

Please note that the names of schools and individuals are invented for the role-plays and do not represent actual situations. If some of the situations sound familiar it is purely a coincidence. In each case, players are encouraged to use their own names in the role-play unless otherwise indicated. After each role-play, participants are expected to debrief as a group and then report out to the larger group. These steps need to be facilitated by someone not involved in the role-plays. Issues of confidentiality and safety need to be addressed from time to time, and participants are encouraged not to continue the conversations outside of the class setting.

19

Human Resource Management

"As every wind draws music out of the Aeolian harp, so doth every object in Nature draw music out of his mind." —Ralph Waldo Emerson

Perhaps no other area occupies the attention of top leadership and nonprofit boards than does HR. Issues such as how to conduct a search, manage benefits and compensation, supervision, termination, evaluation and mentoring are all top of the list. Many small nonprofits fly by the "seat of the pants," making decisions as they go. Gradually over time policies are developed and things can become more stable. But even in an organization that has been around for a long time, HR issues have a way of popping up, and because they involve people and real tasks, they can move to front and center of attention.

In Waldorf schools, many of the teachers involved in making personnel decisions have little or no background in HR. Over time, senior faculty and staff begin to accumulate collective experiences that can be valuable, and sensible organizations will write down their policies. But along the way many mistakes are often made, some of which can expose the organization to litigation. Fortunately, this seldom happens as there is much goodwill among the key players. But to serve as a wake-up call, here are a few examples of serious breeches of what should be covered and communicated in standard HR hiring policy:

1. During an interview for a job, a young female teacher was asked about her plans for having children.
2. In another school, a teacher announced that she was expecting and asked for maternity leave beginning March 1. The senior faculty met without her and came back with the response that her maternity leave would start January 1 instead as that would be "better for the baby."

3. A young male teacher who had a slight speech impediment was hired by a school. Some time before school started, he met some of the parents in a social gathering and afterward a board member called to ask him to withdraw because they did not like the way he spoke.
4. A school had a deficit and decided to reduce the number of work hours for some teachers from twenty to nineteen per week, putting them below the minimum hours needed to receive benefits.
5. When faced with two qualified candidates for an administrative position, a school hired one of them because they wanted to "support" one of their families. The person in question was the wife of a teacher.

Many of these incidents could have been prevented if the schools involved had required all employees to do some basic training in sexual harassment, ethics training and other courses that are often available online and do not take much time to complete. If the teachers and administrators had done so in the above cases, they would have known that issues of gender, race, pregnancy etc. are considered protected categories and need to be treated with knowledge and skill.

Sometimes a school has to go through a "shock" incident or even a series of them before they collectively "wake up" to the need for greater HR expertise. I recently visited a Waldorf school that has a top rung HR committee made up of qualified staff and a couple of board members with expertise in this area. They told me it is one of their best functioning committees. They also have a clear policy manual, including matters pertaining to employment.

This chapter seeks to draw attention to the need for professionalism in HR. It cannot be a comprehensive manual on HR. Yet I would like to go into some detail on one aspect by way of illustrating the depth of understanding needed. The topic I have chosen is "doing a search." Out of many years of experience and readings on the subject, here are a few key themes:

1. To search or not to search? Many a time I have been in a meeting in which someone says, "so and so would be good for the job" or, "let's ask so and so to move up to a new position." Not only do comments like these circumvent a search, but they immediately color the whole discussion with a specific name that is placed on the table. From that point on, anyone participating is perceived as

either being in favor or not supportive of the person mentioned. It is hard to go back to due process once personalities enter the equation. Thus I have found that it is best to follow common HR practices and do a search.

2. National or not? In some cases it might make sense to just post the position in a common area, on the web and perhaps in the local media. In other cases, certainly with full-time positions, it is best to extend the reach to the national scene and find a wide variety of venues to advertise. In the case of Waldorf positions, the larger organizations such as DANA, AWSNA, TEN are most helpful. The point is to give all potential applicants a fair chance to apply through equal access, and if they don't know the position is open, they cannot.

3. Composition of the search committee. The group that conducts the search and does the initial screening is crucial, in that we all see with different eyes, and one needs a good cross section of the organization either represented or understood within the group. In Waldorf schools, that means some teachers, administrators, and if it is a school-wide position such as director, a board member or two. The search committee is responsible for shepherding a smooth process that is transparent to the community, even if the contents of the search are confidential. They also need to do a thorough check of references. With school-wide or leadership positions it may be helpful to have pairs of two doing the reference checks, so one person does not become the repository of all the information about a particular candidate.

4. Phone or Skype interviews? Yes, by all means, as these are low cost ways to see how a candidate responds to a set of prearranged questions (the committee needs to ask the same questions of all candidates, so that has to be agreed upon ahead of time). After the phone or Skype interviews, the committee needs to leave itself enough time to process and share impressions. Although first reactions can be off base, they are often an indication of what might come later should the candidate be a finalist or even hired. Finalists need to be identified and the questions modified for the face-to-face interviews.

5. Who sits at the table? For face-to-face interviews, I have come to like the idea of an hour glass, namely expose the candidate to larger groups first, such as a meet and greet, and then key constituencies, and then finally a session with the search committee. This way the search committee can benefit from any learning, perceptions and experiences gleaned along the way and focus more clearly on key issues in the final interview.

6. Follow up? Even unsuccessful candidates deserve a follow up conversation, and if it is done well, they may become future "friends" of the organization or school. Certainly the successful candidate will need a specific, detailed and clear communication by someone who stands in a position of respect and authority. How the job is offered often affects future attitudes. From many experiences, I have truly learned to respect human freedom, and if one needs to "persuade" a candidate it often means future trouble (persuasion is not the same as negoiation, which is justified within certain boundaries).

So what are we really doing when we conduct a search? One might say the goal is to find the right person for the organization with the skills, capacities and experiences needed. Thus one needs competencies and congruencies. Some organizations tend to favor the one more than the other, so here is a checklist that might prompt balance in the search process:

Quest for Competence

- rational
- objective
- normative

Primary Interests

- prior experience
- skills
- training

Predominant Frames

- structural
- human resource needs

Tools

- job descriptions
- search committees
- interviews

Quest for Congruence

- subjective
- ritualistic
- opportunistic

Primary Interests

- values
- style
- prestige
- fit

Predominant Frames

- political
- symbolic

Tools

- social matching
- norms of organizations
- civil discourse

The role of the search committee might also vary depending if the emphasis is on the quest for competence or the quest for congruence. Do we want the most experienced, skilled person or do we want a good fit? These goals are not mutually exclusive, but they tend to bring out some push and pull in searches, especially when there are internal and external candidates.

Internal vs. external candidates. Of all the issues that have most perplexed me in hiring, it is the handling of internal candidates. To use the language of the above chart, the congruence or fit is often good, or presumed good. They are known quantities, and some have a wealth of understanding of the culture of the organization. I have seen some get undue scrutiny, and it can be hard to compete when so much is known about you. Why is it so hard to see someone with fresh eyes when they have been around for a while?

If nothing else, a search process, with the application of some external candidates, can help objectify the process with an internal applicant. They need and deserve the same process as anyone else, and one really has to work hard to objectify perceptions and screen needed from extraneous information. At the same time, it is a disservice to have a shoo-in candidate, because that undervalues the applicant who may be left feeling, "I was hired because I was already there." Whenever there is a significant change in responsibilities, there needs to be a threshold moment in which the candidate and the organization can change their thinking and orientation. Asking for an application from an internal candidate can be a chance to validate and recognize achievement and, if successful, to celebrate the outcome. The world works in cycles, seasons if you will, and people also need to see the life cycle changes that occur when personnel changes are made. I am in favor of working with internal and external candidates on an equal basis so that the organization and the community can later say, They found the very best person available for the job.

Bolman and Deal in *Reframing Organizations*, make the case that many for profit companies pride themselves in promoting from within:

Costco promotes at least eighty percent of its managers from inside the company. Similarly, ninety percent of managers at FedEx started in a nonmanagerial job. Promoting from within offers several advantages:

- It encourages both management and employees to invest time and resources in upgrading skills.
- It is a powerful performance incentive.
- It fosters trust and loyalty.
- It capitalizes on knowledge and skills of veteran employees.
- It avoids errors by newcomers unfamiliar with the company's history and proven ways.
- It increases the likelihood that employees will think for the longer term and avoid impetuous, shortsighted decisions. Highly successful corporations rarely hire a chief executive from the outside; less effective companies do so regularly." (Bolman and Deal, pp. 144–145)

My only caveat to the above points is that a small nonprofit often operates more like a family in the early days, and one needs clear policies around searches and hiring to make up for a bias toward informality. In a situation in which everyone knows almost everyone, it is all too easy to promote and hire based on subjective feelings and neglect to follow objective procedures. At the very least one needs:

1. A clear job description agreed to by all decision makers.
2. An understanding of the skills, capacities and experience needed.
3. A job posting so others have a chance to apply.
4. Careful screening and checking of references.
5. Clearly defined interview questions.
6. Interviews that are consistent and formal.
7. Clarity around decision-making and hiring of the new person.

Thanks to online resources available these days, as well as best practices of professional organizations such as AWSNA and DANA, it is now possible to do a much better job with HR with less expenditure of time and money. But one has to have the will to do so as well as organizational follow through so that stated policies are actually followed.

20

TIME

"There are two golden rules for an orchestra: start together and finish together. The public doesn't give a damn what goes on in between."
—SIR THOMAS BEECHAM

"How much time do we have left?" This question was one of the last things Georg Locher said to me when on his deathbed in December 2014. As with many contributions of this wise teacher and mentor, those words have stayed with me, following me as a constant reminder to focus on the essentials in life. The passing of a good friend and colleague gives one ample opportunity to reflect on the passage of time.

This chapter takes a short journey through various considerations of time and ends with some applications to the tasks of leaders and administrators.

Time and Organizational Culture

Many of us these days spend a great deal of time in airports and airplanes. When we do so, it quickly becomes clear that time is the ultimate ruler of the aviation industry. Flights arrive and take off according to a precise network of traffic controls, and airports feature giant displays with exact arrival and departure times. If a flight is delayed, it might move from 9:22 to a 9:37 departure, as every minute counts to the harried traveler. If we were to remove all watches, clocks and references to time, airports would fall into chaos within minutes. The culture of aviation is based on hairsplitting attention to precise measurements of time.

By contrast, having recently spent twenty-four hours in a hospital, I was amazed at the very different relationship there to time. When I signed into the ER, they took all my information but would not give me even an approximation of when I might be seen. Indeed, there were some who had already waited for four hours. The next morning, after a sleepless night caused by the coming and going of nurses and a complete disregard for quiet time, I asked when my MRI would happen. The nurse looked at me as if I had asked to go to the moon. I repeated that I just wanted to know the approximate time of the test, and when she had recovered she responded that it would happen when they sent up the stretcher. Persistent as ever, I asked another orderly for a time orientation, and the most I got was "sometime this morning." Here, as in most hospitals, I discovered a whole different relationship to time.

This got me thinking that in fact our relationship to time varies in different organizations. A day in a public school might have a fairly strict observance of periods and time increments, whereas a summer camp might not. One can make one's own list of known organizations and their relationship to time. But if I am correct in my observation that time is influenced by organizational culture, what does that mean for us as participants and leaders?

Alignment of the Inner and Outer Clocks

Just as some of us are morning people and some function better in the evening, so we all have inner clocks. There are a variety of factors that make up the springs and coils of those inner clocks: our rate of metabolism, our processing of ideas, whether we are rested or tired, our personality type etc. We are who we are, and many of my books are dedicated to the proposition that we need to practice self-awareness so that we can take charge of personal change when needed. But we all have inner clocks.

Then there are the outer clocks, the ones we find in airports and on the walls of schools. They measure what most people like to think of as objective criteria. We might say that the outer clocks are like the beat in music, and the inner clocks are more like the melody line, with dotted quarter notes or triplets, depending on the particular constitution of each individual. The interesting part is when one starts to align the inner clocks with the outer ones…is there a fit or not? I have known teachers who make great camp counselors, but some who do not measure up to regular classroom teaching. We all know doctors who cannot keep to a schedule. If our doctors were in charge of air traffic controls our aviation system would be even more fragile than they are. In other words, if we are to be successful in a chosen career path, a certain degree of harmonization is needed between the inner and outer clocks of our life. Too often those with creative inner clocks are forced to adapt to the rigidity of outer clocks, and our world then suffers from a lack of creativity, innovation and real solutions to intractable problems. Did Leonardo paint the *Mona Lisa* according to forty-five-minute periods in a school day? Does the tech wiz in the garage turn off the lights when the clock strikes ten?

Who Is in the Drivers' Seat?

I have spent most of my adult life trying to do more in less time. In my remaining years I now hope to do less with more time. How did I get to this place? The world, including family, work, technology, aspirations etc. all conspired to urge me on to do more and more. As one takes on more responsibility, one either flounders or one gradually learns to become more efficient. Although there is a debate as to whether there really is such a thing as multitasking (or just split attention), many of us have learned to accomplish more in each day than we used to in the past. Thanks to my iPhone, tablet and laptop, I can communicate in all sorts of ways at relatively high speed. Skype and conference calling has replaced many face–to-face meetings, reducing travel (at least for those meetings). I have learned to squeeze things in between appointments, such as texting while at the doctor's office (instead of looking at a magazine). Many people walk around the streets with barely visible earphones talking to invisible persons. Appointments are in shorter increments, and everything seems to be in constant motion.

What has happened to the quality of our time on Earth? Are we happier and healthier? We may be living longer, but those I know in their advanced years are not always thrilled by their longevity. Many people today feel they have become slaves of time, that the clock is in the driver's seat, and that we are merely passengers being whisked from one place to another. There are no ready solutions to this riddle of time, but I urge you to reflect each day on your use of time. When have I been in charge, and when have I been subject to the tyranny of schedules? Do my choices even matter anymore? Can I make a few choices out of respect to my inner clock?

Shortly after writing the above lines I received an email from my brother Mark, who often shows his care and thoughtfulness by sharing something such as the following passages.

ψ

Thoughts for the Week: What Do You Want from Life? (Mike, Scott, and Zack, March 27, 2015)

Time and meaning have been on our minds of late. We recently received an invitation to a client's seventieth birthday celebration, a daughter turned thirteen, a twentieth wedding anniversary is around the corner. Time marches on and we are reminded that everything we do professionally—the money we manage, our investment philosophy, our financial planning process and the relationships we build with our clients—are ultimately in the service of helping clients create the lives that they want.

We consider ourselves guides for the journeys of our clients. The dictionary defines "guide" as "to assist (a person) to travel through, or reach a destination in an unfamiliar area, as by accompanying or giving directions to the person." By definition to be a successful guide we must first have some sense of what the client's desired destination is—what kind of life they want to live. Which is why an article by Jonathan Clements, writing in the Wall Street Journal, "Three Questions to Help Set Your Financial Priorities," caught our eye.

At its heart the article touches on the connection between people's satisfaction with their financial situation and their overall happiness, and the notion that their finances should be geared toward helping them lead the lives they want. This simple notion is at the heart of so called "life planning," and one of the pioneers of the life planning movement.

> George Kinder, founder of the Kinder Institute of Life Planning—which trains financial advisers in life planning—and author of *The Seven Stages of Money Maturity,* has developed three questions to try to elicit what people want from their lives.

> Question No. 1: Imagine you have enough money to satisfy all of your needs, now and in the future. Would you change your life and, if so, how would you change it?

> "It's the winning-the-lottery question," Mr. Kinder says. "What we're trying to get at is, what do you care about the most?" (Clements).

Kinder's experience is that people often mention hobbies they wish they had more time for, things they would like to buy, and trips they would like to take. Interestingly less than ten percent say they'd quit their job, but forty percent or so say they would work less. For founders who are selling a business we often ask "What would your perfect calendar look like"?

> Question No. 2: This time, assume you are in your current financial situation. Your doctor tells you that you only have five to 10 years to live, but that you will feel fine up until the end. Would you change your life and, if so, how would you change it? (ibid.)

The magic of this question is that narrowing your framework for life's accomplishments to ten years or less forces you to consider what is most important. Kinder calls it a search: "What are you going to deliver?" "What is your sense of mission?" (ibid.). You may discover that what is important to you is an orientation to family, to travel, or to doing something creative. People often mention projects they want to accomplish like writing an autobiography or a virtue they want to pursue like being kinder. Pull out a white board or a blank sheet of paper and brainstorm. What words and ideas resonate for you?

> Question No. 3: Your doctor tells you that you have just one day to live. You look back at your life. What did you miss out on? Who did you not get to be? What did you fail to do? (ibid.)

What do you consider most important? This question deals with basic issues—an unresolved family conflict or an unfulfilled creative pursuit. What issues and preoccupations wash away for you when push comes to shove, and what remains?

Jonathan Clements concludes:

> If you can figure out what you are passionate about, that can provide a road map for retirement—and the motivation to save. But also consider how you can find extra time today for the things you care about. You might work fewer hours, swap to a less-demanding job, pay others to do household chores or shorten your commute. (ibid.)

The three questions are a reminder to spend time thinking about what we *really* want and what we *really* value, and trying to make conscious decisions about aligning how we spend our priceless time and valuable treasure.

The three key questions for self-reflection were brought to my attention in an email by three gentlemen who introduce the idea of "guides," in their case in regard to their clients. But that notion got me going: What if each of us were to find our own guide, or inner voice, to accompany and assist us in navigating the unchartered waters of time? We could access this "guide" in moments of silence, when we are alone or otherwise undisturbed. The guide might be seen as a dialogue partner, unseen to the rest of the world but a potent companion. In moments of decision (Do I stay in this meeting that is running an hour late or go home to my son's birthday celebration?), we could ask for help. Of course, the very asking already tips the scales, as the guide will not care much about a business meeting and will most often come down in favor of those aspects of our lives that we hold close to the heart. In the above case, I wager the guide sides with the birthday celebration. But is that not precisely what we need? Someone who advocates for the very things that often get overrun by the pressures of living and working? Our guide could become our unseen advocate, and cheerleader for the inner clock mentioned above, a person who helps us live as if we had only five to ten years more. I urge my readers to adopt a guide, today.

Time and Human Biography

I would like to suggest that time varies in relation to our stage in life. Most of this is well known, so I will just give a few indications.

A young child at play can seem totally oblivious to time. The sandbox is the world, and the stories that unfold have a fascination that cannot be measured. All of my children spent hours at play, either with blocks, dolls, imaginary friends and in making crafts. When we had to call them to supper, it was often as if we were waking them out of a sleep, a play world that existed on a distant planet.

The adolescent seems to struggle with a reorientation to time. As they are now older, they can do many things more quickly, sometimes too quickly. But then they have a remarkable ability to stop the hands of the clock, such as when standing in front of a mirror arranging hair even if we are all waiting in the car ready to depart. Time at this age is subjective. A few minutes of adult conversation can be an eternity (and we hear about it afterward) or they have "just started" their latest game four hours ago. Our youngest has a favorite phrase he used at age 13 and 14: "almost done." It was quite remarkable as it expressed the adolescent wish to keep things undefined, yet not be too abrasive if possible, and at the same time it avoids the expenditure of verbal energy with a longer explanation. How much in life is "almost done...?"

Then there are the years of midlife, in which there is never enough time. Work, children, relationships, friends, managing a home...it seems that one could literally run all day long and not keep up. It seems that as one enters the thirties, one accumulates more and more. In the forties, there is often a break, a crisis that serves as a wake-up call. Yet for many, life takes over again and it takes the maturing inner life to start addressing things that are out of balance. One also becomes more aware of health issues, and that can serve as an inner guide when all else fails.

Finally, for those fortunate to reach old age, there is a kind of return to the timelessness of childhood. My mother has spent much time in her eighties remembering her life, reliving times with the family, thinking of each of her children. Often when I call she would say something that came out of that reflective place, and sometimes I would need to reassure her that she had been a great Mom and that I am indeed so grateful for all my parents did for me. Just doing simple things, such as preparing to go out for lunch, can take up to an hour if it involves a wheelchair and other complications. One has to slow down with old age. Time lengthens out again.

So as mentioned, these aspects of time in relation to human biography are not new to most readers. But this leads me to my essential question: To what degree are we willing to live all seasons of our lives at will, rather than just according to plan? Can I choose, even in my fifties, to go outside and garden with the absorption of a young child at play? Can I choose to juggle five things at once for a few days in the midst of a convention and then in turn select an "old age" tempo for a day or two afterward to regroup and slow down? In short, am I willing to take charge of time in my life?

Waldorf Johannes Stein, a founding teacher at the first Waldorf school in 1919, used to say, "There is the time of your birth...and the time of your death. In between, you have the time of your life." That second sentence leaves a lot of space for self-selection.

Leaders and administrators who serve for many years in one organization can feel less and less free in regard to the allocation of time. It is as if an organization starts to consume our life forces and our use of time. We are amazing at adapting, even shaping ourselves to the needs of an organization. The classic solution is to leave a job and adopt a new organization. That works for many people, as it gives at least the illusion of a clean slate.

I would like to suggest, as also indicated in the email from my brother, that we need to quit our jobs on a daily basis. What does this mean...no paycheck, health insurance? But, but.... No, that is not what I mean. In fact, in most cases our coworkers will never know what happened. I am talking about an inner deed, a resignation that occurs as part of "letting go" of each day. Am I willing to walk away from this job, or does it have me by the neck? Are my priorities clear and am I acting out of them?

When I have tried this, and it works well as part of a review at the end of the day, I have found that I end up with mostly small adjustments. The next day I may visit the gym in the early afternoon instead of hoping to get to it at the end of the day. I may remember to call a friend. The point is that we reestablish our ownership of living and choice setting on a daily basis.

When one does that, a kind of clearing occurs. It is much like when my wife grabs my reading glasses and cleans them for me because she just can't stand how they look. After a clearing, we see better. Leaders and administrators need good vision. If they are able to spend some time (a precious commodity indeed) and once in a while lift their heads above the piles of "commitments," one can start to see the forest again. The landscape opens up, and we are able to move with greater ease. And in the greatest irony of all, spending some time on the reflections described in this chapter might actually make us more effective after all. When we slow down we can achieve more.

21

Your Deficit Can Become Your Abundance

"All my concerts had no sounds in them; they were completely silent. People had to make up their own music in their minds!" —Yoko Ono

First, a word of warning to all the business managers who have eagerly turned to this chapter in the hopes that I will announce some new accounting technique that will magically balance all budgets. That is not what this section is about, although whenever one talks about personal change it has the potential to change the financial dynamics as well. For people make things happen, and activity is almost always reflected in the movement of money. Yet the focus of this chapter is on human change and some of the struggles we all experience today. First, I would like to take up the theme of change from the point of view of biography, followed by teaching and then end up with administration and leadership.

When I was in eighth grade, my father was suddenly transferred from New York City to Brussels, and the family found itself moving in January. I had been with one class of students at a Waldorf school for eight years and was looking forward to the culminating play, trip and graduation. Instead I missed it all, and was thrown into a large class speaking a foreign language I did not at all understand. As my friends of eight years celebrated, I sat in total incomprehension trying to stay awake or pick up a few clues from blackboard sketches or facial expressions. But honestly, I was utterly alone all day in an unfamiliar setting. So I never had an eighth-grade graduation or usual culmination to the elementary-school years.

By the time twelfth grade graduation came around, I was back in the U.S. attending a large public school in suburban New York State. I sat through a long ceremony with 350 others, most of whom I did not know.

Your Deficit Can Become Your Abundance

I cannot remember if any family members attended. I was just a number lost in the crowd.

After three wonderful years at Bowdoin College I had enough credits to graduate early, so I walked down the aisle, not with friends I had known since freshman year but with mostly unfamiliar students of a different class. I believe my parents came for the day, but otherwise there was no time for a party or anything special. A year later I graduated from Adelphi University with my MEd, and graduation consisted of a diploma sent in the mail. The same happened many years later with the PhD from Union. To draw this melancholy story to an end, I never really had any graduations or their respective celebrations afterward.

Many of us have such stories that describe some deficit arising from school, home or friendships. These things happen in life. Despite all parental efforts, one cannot totally "protect" children from unfortunate experiences, and things happen in ways that we cannot avoid. The question always is: What do we do about it?

Most of the change later in life comes from intentional practices that can be described more fully in other settings (see my book *Finding Your Self*). But sometimes what life taketh it also giveth, to sound biblical. In the case of graduations, this is what happened.

After several great years of teaching children, I found myself in a leadership role at Antioch University New England. Much to my joy, each summer at the end of July we graduate another group of Waldorf teachers in a festive celebration at the Pine Hill School in Wilton, New Hampshire. The ceremony consists of much singing, an instrumental solo or duet, speeches, diplomas and presentations from each group of graduates. The Pine Hill building is ideal for the display of artwork and other student achievements throughout the hallways and adjoining classrooms. Afterward we cross the street to High Mowing School where we have a splendid graduation dinner with the graduates, their families, friends, faculty and other students in the program. It is always a high point of our academic year.

Recently I realized that I have had twenty-five graduations in twenty-five years, surrounded by the people I care about most in life, my large

Antioch family. The connections with students are deep and last years after that graduation. No matter how hard we work during the summer session, I always come away feeling nourished. I leave the graduation happily tired and deeply fulfilled. Life has brought me abundance exactly where I needed it most, around "graduations."

If one stops to look squarely at some of the deficits in life, I suspect one can find many instances such as the above. How does this happen? As usual, I am not sure I have the whole picture, but for starters I can suggest that the deficit, if real, creates a kind of soul longing. In my case it was for a sense of festive completion. That longing works from within in powerful ways, generating a search for fulfillment. We then guide ourselves, often unconsciously to seek a resolution of that wish. One might even say that we each have within us a "cleverer self" that guides us in ways we cannot fully appreciate at first.

In our conscious life our thoughts move from moment to moment, often around the ordinary occupations of living and working. But under the surface, a wish acts as a great locomotive, chugging along in the soul, pushing us to meet people and engage in activities that could lead to fulfillment. Sometimes the realization of a wish is not as obvious as it was with my graduation experience. The results can be more subtle, and one does not always realize the fulfillment until some time has passed. The moment of fulfillment is often clothed in different colors, and may not correspond to the exact image we had in the first place. But I am convinced that more often than not life directs us to opportunities for resolution.

So the key is to recognize the deficit, work with it and then let oneself move into life experiences that may not always make sense at first glance. It is like paddling a canoe in a river: we can give some direction to things, but much movement comes from the current. The "flow" of life is what has real genius, that aspect that can help us find fulfillment.

This also applies to administrators and leaders, and not just because they are people too! When one steps up to a specific role or task it can serve as a kind of catharsis, a make-or-break opportunity. The stakes become higher. In that new setting, biography becomes an even greater undertone of daily living. Patterns from childhood, events long forgotten, can suddenly loom up again. They are either put to good use or they hold us hostage. The difference lies in the level of conscious engagement. Thus it is absolutely crucial for those in leadership positions that they practice self-awareness. We need to look at our deficits and our joys, see them again and again with new eyes, and then let the stream of life guide us to resolution. This may seem a bit passive, but again to use the canoe analogy, if one tries to "think" one's way around rapids on a river it does not work. One has to feel, sense, let go and trust in order to let that movement work in the way described in this chapter. Letting go can be the best way to find something anew.

This process can be assisted by periodically asking oneself questions that lead to inner movement. They might include:

- Can I remember as vividly as possible a scene from my life at age seven, twelve, fifteen etc.?
- Who are the people who have most influenced me in my life?
- Can I picture again the houses I have lived in during my life?
- Looking at my friends, when and how did I meet them?
- What were some of the most painful experiences I have had in my life?
- Which experiences have brought me the most joy?

This is only a short list. There are many possibilities, but it is best for us find our own questions to work with, ones that really matter.

Speaking of joys and sorrows, Rudolf Steiner says it is important that we develop a good attitude toward them. Rather than "poor me" in regard to pain and suffering, it is better to look at these trials as things we have wanted, things we sought after as an opportunity to grow. And regarding joy, rather than thinking "what a great person am I to have this happen," it is better to see joy as a blessing that is bestowed upon us. We do not earn our joy; it is a gift (various places in Steiner, *Reincarnation and Karma*).

So a deficit can become an abundance if we are prepared to do the inner "turning," the pivot that can turn straw into gold. We can influence more than we think in life, and for the self-aware leader much is possible.

22

EMAIL AND TIME MANAGEMENT

"There's nothing remarkable about it. All one has to do is hit the right keys at the right time and the instrument plays itself."
—JOHANN SEBASTIAN BACH

Some time ago I read an article in the *Wall Street Journal* (December 3, 2014) with the eye-catching title "Stop Wasting Everyone's Time." The focus was on meetings and emails: "In studying more that twenty-five companies, VoloMetrix has found executives who consume more than 400 house a week of colleagues' time, 'the equivalent of 10 people working full-time every week just to read one manager's email and attend his or her meetings,' she says." The article goes on: "Many employees spend a lot of time writing responses because they fear failing to answer will offend colleagues or hamper their work. However, many emails don't require a response" (p. D3). Some habits are so deeply rooted that it is hard to make changes, such as using email "Cc" unnecessarily or writing a lengthy response to seem polite when a simple yes or no would do.

Some managers are now using project-management applications that can store project files in one place online (such as Google docs) which all who need to can see, update and comment on. This is particularly helpful in limiting one of my problems—namely, a long string of emails that I erase because most of it is obsolete only to find that there was one piece of information buried long ago that I need again. Many times, I have had to ask a colleague to resend something, because I was trigger-happy with the "delete" key. Others react by storing far too many emails, and then it is hard to find what is needed.

Besides time efficiencies, email raises many other workplace issues. Over the years I have found that otherwise polite people will say things on an email that they afterward regret. It is so easy to press "send" as part of emotional processing rather than waiting a few hours or even a day. Or I have been interrupted in the middle of an email and then return without rereading what was said, or doing an inappropriate cc or bcc (sometimes I even hit the wrong button). Emails are often written on the fly yet have a permanent quality, and they have a way of reappearing at the darndest times.

There are some matters that are still best handled in face-to-face conversation. The big question is how to discern those issues before it is too late. Often the face-to-face comes about as a "make up" session rather than having the original conversation. So I have started my own tentative list of "face-to-face preferreds," which now include evaluative issues, program changes, anything major to do with employment, life crisis issues or matters that are really personal. On the other side of the coin I am trying to use emails mostly for short communications, reports, planning and routine business. It is not easy, as so many things are shades of grey, but one litmus test is that if the person on the other side starts sending me a lot of emails on an issue, it may be time to pick up the phone, Skype or arrange a face-to-face.

Use of email also has much to do with work hygiene. So many people today spend far too much time in front of a screen, with resulting issues from back and neck pain to carpel tunnel and vision issues. I now try to self-manage with a one hour rule: I get up and deliver the next message or response in person if there is a reasonable chance someone is available. People are often so glad to see someone stop by their place of work, for they too are sitting far too much. My iPhone is always in my pocket, but once in a while I need reminders that a ping of an arriving email is not in charge, I am.

Waldorf schools intend to foster deep human connections: teacher to child, parent to teacher etc. I have found that other than communication through email, real relationship building happens best when one meets in person. I enjoy taking one of my graduate students for a walk on the bike trail, or sitting over a cup of something good in a local café. One usually comes away from those interactions with a feeling of warmth and connection, even if the conversation is intense at times.

For many people today in all sorts of work settings, the day is packed with emails and conference calls. Various studies have found over the years that all too often people call a meeting, and at the risk of offending someone, to many people are included. In fact, the greater the number of participants the greater the chance time will be wasted. All too often one sees folks multitasking with laptops in front of them or smart phones just under the table. Attendance and "attending" can be too different things, and often we are physically but not otherwise present. After ninety minutes most meetings become suspect, and any agenda needs to take into account participant needs as well as those of the organization.

I am a great fan of poetic meetings. This is not about reading poems, although once in a while I think that would be more useful than the items under discussion. Rather, by poetic I refer to the use of meter or rhythm such as short/long or long/short/short. So in regard to the later one has famous examples of hexameter, such a Henry Wadsworth Longfellow's *Evangeline:* "This is the forest primeval..." (long–short–short–long–short–short). Even reciting hexameter can be health-giving, though I suggest closing the office door first. But in regard to meeting structure, I urge administrators and facilitators to work with meter: alternate short and long items to promote meeting hygiene. So for instance, one might structure a meeting as follows:

1. a short moment of recognition for a participant's achievement
2. an announcement of an upcoming event
3. an in-depth discussion on a policy
4. two brief reports
5. another longer discussion on a future festival and so on

The point is to treat an agenda much like a musical score or a piece of poetry. By alternating meter or beat one promotes breathing and change. People tend to wake up when there is change and fall asleep when things drone on. Facilitation is an artistic endeavor, and if done well, participants will stay awake and be more productive. If they are, then more will be accomplished and people will be willing to contribute and attend future meetings. One can actually build real positive momentum through how we all conduct ourselves in our meetings. When minutes can flow out in email form afterward and reports reach participants ahead of time, we have a real chance of saving time and getting something done. With the time saved, the hope is that we attend to work/life balance and the renewal that is needed to continue to serve.

23

LEADERS AS SPEAKERS

LEADERS NEED TO SPEAK

"The high note is not the only thing." —PLACIDO DOMINGO

Although there is a great deal of literature available today on how leaders need to motivate employees and articulate the mission and vision of the organization, much less is presented about the use of language and speech as leadership practice. We all know that leaders need to be good communicators, but what about how we use language and speech itself? As we have seen, all it takes is one misplaced phrase or inappropriate expression and an entire career can unravel. CNN and other media outlets regularly feature these bloopers of politicians, business leaders and others who use a few words with less-than-usual consciousness. Words can make or break a leader. So what should we know about the use of language?

One has only to listen to speech being used around us to realize that language has become less conscious. People are often not awake to the meaning and use of the words they use in speaking and merely repeat what they have heard but did not understand themselves. Poor grammar, colloquial expressions and misapplication of phrases occur all the time. Rote memorization in schools fosters poor speech, as language becomes abstract and divorced from life. Media sound bites and texting have not helped. There are times when I hear people in public places doing little more than exchange monosyllabic sounds and short phrases. Speech seems to have been degraded.

It is no wonder then that it is hard for people today to really understand each other. For along with the loss of sensitivity around language one can observe a lessening of listening skills. People repeat themselves again and again because many of their listeners have just "tuned out." It seems that the range and complexity of sounds accessible to the human ear have diminished. Our hearing has become sclerotic. Rudolf Steiner once said:

> The worst thing you can do is select a theme, master the material by memorizing every word, and then give the same speech over and over again. That is the worst method you can select. One can only cultivate the right sense of responsibility toward that which is carried in one's speaking when every address, subjectively speaking, is personally experienced as something new. Even if the same theme is treated thirty times, it is necessary that for the speaker there is always something new." (Werner Glas, quoted in Sussman, pp. 170–173)

I have had an opportunity to experiment with this while on book tours. The audience of course expects a talk on aspects of the newly published book, but what makes an event interesting is to first take in who is in the audience, make eye contact and focus a few anecdotes to people who are known to me. Then, I start to reshape inwardly the "standard talk" and adapt it to the audience. Sometimes I skip over things covered elsewhere, or go into more detail when I sense interest or audience response. After a few minutes one starts to "breathe with the audience," and the talk starts to flow creatively. Only when I am very tired or jet-lagged do I fail to pick up on audience clues, and then I am disappointed. Fortunately, far more often I feel energized and refreshed after giving a talk, and that is due to the participation of the audience and their encouragement for me to be fully present with them. The speech then comes alive, and I am renewed as a result.

What can we collectively do to renew language? Marie Steiner and others have developed speech courses for the renewal of speech that can involve many years of study (four is the common minimum). Acting groups can work intensively with the renewal of speech in a dramatic context. But for leaders working with a full-time day job, there are a few basic steps that can help us begin to turn the corner:

Foster good conversation. This can happen in small groups or one-on-one, but a real conversation is more than a mere exchange of information. When we converse, ideas and feelings come together in a conscious encounter.

One way to improve awareness of the potential in conversation is to practice Goethean conversation, a step-by-step group process that can lead to both better listening and speaking. In her pamphlet *The Art of Goethean Conversation,* Marjorie Spock speaks of the importance of "attentive listening" and creating a "receptive openness to the life of thought" (Spock, p. 3). To do this it is best to have a theme set ahead of time so members can live with it and bring forethought to the meeting. Then when one enters the room, Marjorie urges us to refrain from idle chatter as that can dissipate the atmosphere. When the facilitator opens the conversation on the agreed-upon theme, participants are asked to "build" on the thoughts of one another. After one person speaks, the next tries to reference or incorporate the essence of what has already been said before moving to a new idea. Conversation thus gradually becomes a kind of tapestry that grows in complexity but is interconnected. A good summation at the end also helps bring a sense of completion to the experience.

My friend and former colleague from Great Barrington, Massachusetts, days, Joseph Savage, drew up a sequence for use in a Goethean conversation, which I have found very helpful:

> Our attempt is to weave together our thoughts and ideas through conscious listening and expression of thoughts that build on a theme or idea to achieve a deeper and clearer understanding together. This is not just another discussion group in which each person expresses his or her opinion. There is rigor in genuine conversation—an attempt to unearth the matters at hand, to reveal the hidden, to understand ourselves and the other, to explore the inner nature of the thing at hand, to articulate understanding, and so enable new understanding. Conversation enables polarities, mired in their own assumptions, to speak to each other, so that a third, and new, reality is able to emerge.

Rules of conduct

1. Speak from experience not opinion, or identify what you have to say as opinion.
2. Identify any sources of your information.
3. Listen carefully to the previous speaker's ideas.
4. You may ask questions to clarify ideas.
5. Build on the previous speaker's thought.
6. Limit each comment or question to one thought or idea.
7. Try to keep each comment under a minute.
8. Give everyone else a chance to speak.
9. Try not to judge (agree or disagree with) another's comment but remain open to new possibilities, thoughts and ideas.

The best way to understand this process is to try it. In most cases, when I have brought this to a group, the participants are surprised at the depth and atmosphere created by using such an intentional exercise. Give it a try.

Poetry and verses can help humanity rediscover the genius in language. We all have our favorites, from Robert Frost to Maya Angelou, and favorites can change over time. The important thing is to live with some of the great works of art these amazing people have composed and let the language sink in over time. One can return to a good poem again and again as it educates the soul and refines our feelings. There is an entire chapter in this book with some of my favorite poems and verses that are directed in particular to those in leadership roles.

A further heightening of speech occurs in the use of a mantra for meditative purposes. Here one is working with words that have been carefully chosen by a "wise one" to help us reconnect with the spiritual worlds. Working rhythmically and with full inner focus, it is possible to build an active inner life through the use of key words and phrases in a mantra. Rudolf Steiner contributed much material for the aspiring meditant (see Steiner, *Verses and Meditations*). For more advanced work, one can contact members of the School of Spiritual Science through the Anthroposophical Society in Ann Arbor, Michigan, or the Goetheanum in Dornach, Switzerland.

In a short section between leading thought 111 and 112, Rudolf Steiner speaks of another level of reconnection:

In ancient times, this harmony existed as a matter of course, because the Divine-spiritual was active in the stars, where human life, too, had its source. But today, when the course of the stars in only a continuation of the way in which the Divine-spiritual worked in the past, this harmony could not exist unless man sought it. Human beings bring their Divine-spiritual portion—which they preserved from the past—into relation with the stars, which now bear only their Divine-spiritual nature as an aftereffect from an earlier time....

Anthroposophy truly values what the natural-scientific way of thinking has learned to say about the world during the last four or five centuries. But in addition to this language it speaks another, about the nature of human beings, about their evolution and that of the cosmos; it would fain speak the language of Christ and Michael. (Steiner, 1973, p. 84)

So what is the language of Christ and Michael? This question deserves much inner contemplation and struggle. I urge readers to take it up with sincere focus. All I can do here is to hint at a few aspects that have surfaced in my own struggle to understand. Here are possible characteristics of Christ–Michael language:

When we strive to become truly alive in our thinking, as Steiner described many times, it is possible for our language to receive a fresh impulse. Inner picturing through active imagination is a step in this process. *See* the thoughts and the words will change.

Whenever we take an old form or habit and bring about change, something starts to readjust in our language, as well. For example, a teacher who does research and makes new discoveries ends up speaking very differently than those who deliver the same lessons again and again, year after year.

Similarly, words can become enchanted. Like snow white in her glass coffin, they can fall asleep. This often happens with conventions of speech and idioms that are passed on unconsciously. In contrast, if we listen to young children learning to speak their mother tongue, or listen to a person from a foreign country learning a new language, things are often said in unusual ways. The listener is forced to wake up a bit, and in that waking, I feel something new can enter. Steiner himself used syntax and word combinations in very unusual ways— we do not fall asleep as easily when we pay attention.

The gesture of Michael is all-encompassing, but is directed especially toward human striving on Earth and our earthly callings and professions. He is very interested in the specializations and development of skills that help us fashion will deeds, tools for living. With Christ one associates with a being who is eternal, timeless and cosmic. Thus, Christ–Michael language will have a quality of reuniting the cosmic with the earthly.

This new kind of language feeds on inspiration. When I saw the movie *Selma,* I was again impressed with the power of Martin Luther King Jr.'s language. It was both lofty and passionate, inspiring and practical. All kinds of people, from many different professions and backgrounds, could relate to his words. His speeches stand for me as examples of Christ–Michael language.

When aspire to leadership, or if we already carry such responsibilities, I suggest directing attention to the development of speech. Anthroposophically inspired speech artists around the world work from indications that Marie Steiner gave for the creative art of speech formation. The few lessons I have had over the years have helped tremendously in developing my thinking, as well as learning how to connect with others through language. Speech formation is an ideal artistic path for leadership development.

24

BETRAYAL AND FORGIVENESS

"Jazz came to America three hundred years ago in chains."
—PAUL WHITEMAN

These are strong words, and any reader might wonder what they have to do with the theme of this book. Yet they represent two mighty spiritual forces that can work within any social organism, and some consideration of them may bring perspective, and even healing, to difficult situations.

I begin with a reminder of some of the social challenges that surface in the workplace, challenges that may not reach the level of betrayal, but nevertheless fall on that side of the social spectrum. I will then hint at a few of the larger, spiritual dimensions involved.

On an everyday level many of us have experiences that deflate or pull us down. We all know that sinking feeling after an unfortunate interaction, sometimes overt and sometimes not. Here are a few examples:

You share something with a friend or colleague in confidence, only to discover later that it was passed on to others.

There is a moment in a meeting when you needed a word of encouragement or recognition and nothing happens.

The "silent treatment" might continue for days; people sometimes go to great lengths to avoid one another.

There is a person you have looked up to and respected, and now you discover that he or she has done something wrong.

As the result of a series of unfortunate instances, one loses trust.

There are times when someone says one thing to your face and another behind closed doors.

At other times a person just evades the truth.

In any workplace, there is the potential for gossip and its consequences.

It is more serious when a good friend or colleague turns on you,
and you may not know the reason.

Any one of these experiences can be addressed if not healed by straightforward conversation. But all too often, such situations are not addressed but allowed to fester and grow. Over time, particularly if the players are the same, one can develop a real sense of betrayal. One can say inwardly: you do not see me for who I am. You have created an image of me that is not true. I am living with a lie. This state of being can be very destructive to ones physical and mental health, and if not addressed, can hinder any productive work with the others concerned.

Before moving on to some of the causes and the opportunity for forgiveness, I turned to the 2,515-page *Oxford Universal Dictionary on Historical Principles* that my father passed on to me and looked up *betrayal*. I found some very interesting definitions:

to give up to, or place in the power of the enemy by treachery;
to be or prove false; to disappoint the hopes or expectations;
to disappoint;
to lead astray, as a false guide; to mislead, deduce, deceive;
to reveal with breach of faith;
to reveal against one's will the existence, identity, real character of
a person"...and so on.

It ends with the biblical "Verily I say unto you, that one of you shall betray me," and ends with the notion of a temple that was betrayed in ancient times (p. 173).

The configuration of betrayal includes everything from disappointment to being false or deceiving someone. In their book *Trust and Betrayal in the Workplace,* Dennis and Michelle Reina describe a spectrum from major intentional betrayals to minor unintentional betrayals:

Major intentional betrayals are carried out to hurt and harm. We feel them in our deepest core. Unintentional minor betrayals are incidental to other actions. We may not pay much attention to them initially— but they do add up! When they do, they may have the same impact and cost as major intentional betrayals. Regardless of the nature of the betrayal, it erodes trust, compromises or even ends relationships, and certainly damages performance." (p 110)

The authors go on to say that betrayals are often the by-product of fear and self-interest.

Most acts of betrayal are minor in nature, a slip of the tongue, careless comment or misunderstanding. Yet if not addressed, over time these minor instances can take on the full weight of a major betrayal. Gradually the social fabric of an organization is worn thin, even torn apart, and people distance themselves from each other. Once trust is lost, it is hard to regain. And this can go right into the health and well being of all concerned: "Trust is energy producing; betrayal is energy depleting. Trust feeds performance; betrayal eats away at it" (ibid., p. 113).

The good news is that it is possible, over time to work through the experience of a betrayal and then rebuild relationships. Dennis and Michelle Reina offer a seven-step process:

1. Observe and acknowledge what has happened.
2. Allow feelings to surface.
3. Get support.
4. Reframe the experience.
5. Take responsibility.
6. Forgive yourself and others.
7. Let go and move on (ibid., p. 129).

This seven steps sound so simple and straightforward, yet they require considerable inner fortitude and commitment. In my experience, many people stay at the first three stages for a long time, observing, commenting, feeling and trying to get others to support. One cannot wallow in the experience too long, otherwise it becomes a kind of emotional addiction. There is a real need to do the inner work of reframing, taking responsibility for one's part in the experience, forgiving and moving on. Sometimes one party to the incident does the inner work and the other does not. All of us need to attend to these healing pathways.

The notion of breach of faith is particularly relevant in a school community where one assumes people have gathered out of common values and ideals. In these circumstances it is particularly challenging when one finds out the true character of another person is less worthy than one imagined earlier. The fall from a high place is much greater than from a low one, and intentional communities need to be particularly aware of betrayal and the need for forgiveness.

One more consideration: The betrayal of Christ brings to consciousness the role of Judas and those that can at times play that role. Judas as one of the twelve was part of the company of disciples and even accepted as one who could minister unto others. Yet for thirty pieces of silver he was willing to betray his teacher and master. This is not the place to go into depth on this subject, but the story of Judas brings to mind the role of money around issues of trust and betrayal. We have come so far in our pedagogical understanding of children, of the importance of meditation, nutrition and so on, but have advanced only in small steps in our relationship to money. Often a wonderful child-centered discussion in a faculty meeting can give way, minutes later, to a most dismal discussion of budgets and salaries. Our consciousness around money and its role in the world today has yet to evolve (see *Money Can Heal*).

In the meantime, money often takes a place onstage when betrayal is afoot. People will do the strangest things when their livelihood or salary is at stake. Sometimes even the perception that one's livelihood is threatened can become corrosive. There are deep mysteries here. For instance, it was only after he dipped the bread in the bowel that Judas was able to betray Christ. Why is that? These are questions that have no easy answer, but they can give us perspective the next time we have to take up financial matters. Beware of how we treat one another, especially around issues of money.

After some time of contemplation, the issue of betrayal was still tugging at me, like a young child pulling at my clothes wanting attention as I stood in a store. What makes a person betray another? It is especially puzzling when it comes from a friend. What can cause a betrayal? My search is still in progress, but I recently found a hint. As many of us will recall, Cain and Abel each made a sacrifice to God. Abel's sacrifice was accepted, but Cain's was not. The story usually rushes on to the idea of fratricide, but let's pause for a moment at the first stage. What was Cain's inner experience when he discovered his sacrifice was rejected? It is not as if he had done anything wrong or made a mistake. The sacrifice was simply rejected. The higher beings did not want it; they relinquished it. Yet, through this refusal, a kind of opposition was created in Cain's soul. How would you feel? He must have had mix of feelings over the rejection, such as bitterness and pain, but also longing for acceptance. Injustice always leaves a mark on people. Some are able to overcome feelings of rejection, pain and bitterness and for others it festers.

I suggest that these feelings are connected to root causes of betrayal. When we are personally disappointed, it can lead to a perverse wish to harm another, even those who are close to us. At the same time, there remains a "longing" for redemption and to *move through* the betrayal to rediscover each other on a new level. This is why both parties need to be involved inwardly rather than staying with a you-versus-me dichotomy. Betrayal, though wrong by any measure, is also an unmistakable call for help. Standing behind it is a longing for a breakthrough and a chance to overcome a particular obstacle.

I have learned to watch for polarity, for it has within it the seeds of innate tension which, if not worked with creatively, can lead to conflict or betrayal. The above- mentioned polarity of Cain and Abel is one such polarity, not just of two brothers but what they represented. Cain was the farmer, the "earth person," the masculine element in our human nature that wants to work with external materials and conquer the outer world. Abel was the herder, who tends and nurtures life, the feminine within us that seeks intuition and the divine life of wisdom (Steiner, 1997, lect. 2).

We all have a Cain and an Abel within us: let's do things in the world, build, overcome, "get things done today" vs. go with the flow, let things happen as the sheep graze, have some time to reflect and ponder what lies on the heart, for after all, one needs inner direction in order to make sense of life. Every day in the life of an administrator is a balancing act between the Cain and Abel in us. If we totally neglect one or the other brother we are at risk. With one extreme one could eventually loose a job if things were not accomplished, if we had nothing to show for all our work. One the other hand, one could lose ones heart, and then where would we be?

Turning to forgiveness, I have always wondered about how Christ could forgive Judas *before* the betrayal. To *for-give* means to give in abundance before it is asked for. What inner resources are needed for such a deed? In his book *The Occult Significance of Forgiveness*, Sergei O. Prokofieff cites Rudolf Steiner describing a soul quality referred in German to as *Milde:* kindness or gentleness. This is described as a moral instrument that can help in the battle with evil on Earth. Through it's etymological roots, *Milde* is related to the word *forgiveness* and those who have the capacity for forgiveness. Rather than a sign of soul weakness (as often portrayed today), gentleness is capable of transforming a one's etheric body and enhancing the life forces.

On the way to initiation, the medieval hero Parsifal had to develop *Milde,* and in his version of the story Wolfram von Eschenbach also uses the word *saelde,* which is related to the Gothic *selei,* meaning goodness, gentleness and blessed. Developing these soul qualities in oneself means creating conditions that allow the cosmic spirit to descend into our "I" as spirit self, or spirit with whom the Christ prophetically endows his Apostles when he sends them into the world to *forgive* others in his *name* and cancel out their sins (Prokofieff, p. 117). This leads to a transition in human culture and the possibility of *Philadelphia,* or brotherly love.

All around us we find opportunities to forgive, from the simplest instance of a missed appointment to the loss of trust in another person. As on a playground seesaw, sometimes we are up and other times down. The question of free choice for each of us is this: How do we deal with these dynamics? The fulcrum, the crucial point in the middle, is our "I"-being. What sort of intentionality do we bring to the situation? How do we choose to stand in the center of the balance of life events?

Lately I have pondered the connection of two lines from the New Testament: "Forgive us our trespasses as we forgive those who trespass against us," and "Love one another as I have loved you" It seems that both call for an inner path of transformation. The German verb *erkennen* has aspects of recognizing, perceiving and knowing. All three are needed. We have to discover and recognize our trespass, our guilt toward the other before we can know it and begin the process of forgiveness. We need to perceive our own wrongdoing, as it is often connected to the wrongdoing of the other. Separateness and self-ness prevent us from forgiving; connection enhances it, which requires a gesture of humility.

Along this path we can develop what Georg Kühlewind calls "mirrored consciousness":

> In meditative consciousness, however, we must experience the becoming-with, the transformation "into" what is cognized. There is no other way. It is self-surrender, self-extinguishing—pain. It is joy: the coming-into-being in the other: realization, accomplishment.... Today's misfortune can prove to be a blessing; the joy of today can prove to be a tragic error. (1981, p. 5)

We learn as we transform, and this act of forgiveness can become love, love of human beings *how they are, not as we want them to be.*

The inner path of metamorphosis is the decisive element. When we are able to work out of creative soul forces, out of our sun nature, then we are able to "give gently" and help in a given situation. Gentleness and forgiveness do not need to manifest outwardly. We need to learn to be gentle within ourselves, to accept all that the world offers. It is okay to drop the ball once in a while; it is okay to make a mistake. As administrators and leaders we need to learn to forgive both others and ourselves. Recently, my motto has been: Look at it, learn from it and move on. Life usually gives us opportunities to do better next time.

25

Working with a Board

"I used to be shy—You made me sing.
I used to refuse things at the table—Now I shout for more wine."
—Rumi

Most administrators and school leaders sit in on board meetings, reporting and making contributions to the discussions. Some have done this for years at other nonprofits, for others joining a Waldorf board can be a new experience. When I visit schools one of the most frequent questions I get is: How can we improve the consistency and productivity or our board? So this chapter will begin with some of the basics that can be found in most board-development workshops, and then continue on to the particular anthroposophic challenges of having a board work for a Waldorf school.

There is much literature available on the Internet and elsewhere regarding best practices, and most of it is a matter of sound common sense. These include:

1. Make sure your board has a shared *vision* as expressed in your literature, minutes, presentations and especially the strategic plan. You need to know where you are going so you can all pull together. Just having a vague purpose such as Waldorf education is not enough; the goals need to be specific, understandable to outside audiences and actionable/achievable.
2. A board needs to develop clear *expectations* of individual board members, and they need to be enforced and evaluated. Just feeling

good about someone is not enough. Membership on a board is a leadership role and those on a board need to perform. The most common complaint I get when traveling is irregular attendance and failure to follow through on tasks freely agreed to. When some underperform it leaves others to do more, and an inside vs. outside group can develop consisting of the "doers" and the "commentators." There are other places in an organization for panel discussions and philosophical debate, but when you are flying the plane you need to keep your hands on the controls. Mixed performance of board members is one of the key causes of turbulence in an organization.

3. Board *recruitment* need to be done strategically and on a regular basis, not just at the end of the year when someone is stepping down. This can mean looking at potential people to join a board committee (these can be seen as the "farm team," asking the talented ones to step up and chair the committee the next year, and then ideally the person would be known and available to be considered for board membership in the third year. Terms need to be clear ahead of time. I am in favor of three-year renewal terms with term limits after six to nine years. No one is so precious that they cannot be replaced, and boards also need new energy from time to time.

4. Boards need to *self-assess* regularly. I like the method used at one of the boards I attended in which the chair handed out paper for goal setting at the first meeting of the new year (somehow emails still result in lower response rates). Each trustee, in the meeting (otherwise they don't all come back) fills out two sections: personal goals and goals for the group as a whole. These are then returned to the chair who can reference the group goals occasionally throughout the year. Then at the last meeting, the sheets are handed back, and each member is asked to do a self-assessment based on the individual goals set in the fall and then the group has a discussion on the group goals around the question: How have we been doing? Then one can even end the process by articulating some new goals for the next cycle. Thus a board can become a learning organization.

5. Boards need orientation for new members and on going *education* for all. This helps a board stay current with best practices in governance, finance and educational trends. It is also an opportunity for faculty to share some aspects of Waldorf education so there is the best possible alignment between the leadership of the faculty, administration and board.

6. Just when everything is going well, it is a good reminder that *change* is always needed. Can we do things better next time? Who else do we need on this board? How have our committees been performing? Are we sticking to our mission and our strategic plan?

7. It is vital for the success of the entire organization that *staff* are valued and appreciated. To this end, it is in the interest of the board to be sure staff roles are clearly delineated, especially in regard to interactions with faculty and parents. *A board should not run the school, but should instead make sure that roles are clear, systems in place to deliver the programs and that everyone is evaluated regularly.*

8. Sometimes boards get so involved down in the weeds managing day to day matters arising from a school that they forget one of their primary tasks: *resource development*. This is a matter for the whole board not just the development committee of the board. To be blunt, I have seen a lot of "hand-washing" on fund-raising—board members blaming their development committee, the staff at the school or the parent body. This is a good area to post the sign: *The buck stops here as far as institutional advancement.* A high performing board is only minimally involved with the internal affairs of the school but super involved in community relations, finding "friends" and identifying potential donors. Most nontuition money that comes into a nonprofit comes from major donors rather than events. Teachers often advocate for events as they see the social value of holding them, but in fact donor cultivation has a much higher yield. Donors need to be cultivated and engaged. Board members can play a large role in this, especially if it is guided, supported and directed by a capable development officer on staff.

9. A board meeting is not a social gathering, although I have met with boards in pubs, restaurants and all sorts of unlikely places. There is nothing wrong with this social aspect, and I have been able to get to know people much better as a result of them. But the work of the board needs to be taken seriously. This means also doing some things that may not be fun, such as attending to policies, seeking relevant documents, checking up on legal matters, attending to accountability all around and upholding established policies and procedures. Someone has to be the keeper of records, and there needs to be enough continuity on a board so that there is some institutional memory and the school does not have to reinvent the wheel each year.

10. Many board meetings begin with snacks or even a potluck. There is a lot to be said for warmth and relationship building. Yet there needs to be a point at each meeting in which the group gets down to business and is able to *focus* on critical issues. I once sat on a board where one member continually went "global." Anytime we were about to make a crucial decision, the person would lift off with a questions such as: How does this fit into our future plans for a high school? Where do we stand with teacher evaluation? On the surface, these questions were always well-intentioned and needed, but *not at that place in the decision-making process*. There is a time to decide, and the chair needs to be able to rally the group to focus on the decision at hand and not take up tangents (which I find is often a subtle way of avoiding making difficult decisions)

11. And despite all the work mentioned above, it is important that from time to time board members have *fun* together so that they get to know one another and find serving to be rewarding.

12. Finally, and this is not an exhaustive list, a board needs to value leadership and create the conditions for risk taking and initiative. Creating such a culture is not easy and does not happen automatically. One place to start is with the question: What can we do to support leadership and initiative?

Given this backdrop, we can ask a question one of my administration students recently asked me: How can we get our board interested in the study of Waldorf and the anthroposophic basis of this education? By asking more about the person's particular school, it turns out it has occasionally had an "anthroposophist" on the board with mixed success. Sometimes the person was unable to communicate well or did not have the skills and experience needed to contribute when financial matters came up. If we bring in a "token" anthroposophist, we also run the risk of overlooking other criteria that board membership requires (more on that later), and the group can become less cohesive. As we had that conversation, I suggested possible approaches:

1. Listen carefully to what is on the minds of board members and see if you can identify a theme that could be met through a study. For example, if board members are concerned about parent attitudes toward money and what "they get" for the tuition, one might want to suggest a study of an article involving social finance, or even the book *Money Can Heal*. The point is to start with an evident interest and build upon it.

2. In planning the study, teachers should not do it alone but ask another board member out for coffee and a conversation. Plan how you will do the study together, and if the other person shows interest in some aspect, he or she can lead that part of the board discussion. Board members will listen differently to other board members who are also new to the concepts.

3. Hold regular retreats with the entire board, faculty and staff. There is something magical about a large group, especially if there is good food and time for fun. The people who need to meet each other do, and sometimes a new teacher who is also searching for anthroposophic understanding can actually take a few steps forward in talking to new board members. The unplanned encounters are worth planning.

4. Work artistically together. In our Western culture especially, we learn by getting our hands dirty, whether by clay, paints or beeswax.

Make something and then have one of your senior teachers lead a brief discussion starting with: "What did you experience?" That sharing can be easily connected in a light way (no lectures here) with some of the fundamentals of Waldorf education, such as the education of the will, leaving time for questions and discussion. Then board members can walk away with a real experience and *context for the concepts.*

5. Avoid any proselytizing or anything that stands in the way of human freedom. Waldorf is an education toward freedom, and we need to leave each person free to develop and grow as needed in this lifetime. If a board member is exposed to some aspects of Anthroposophy and then feels it is too overwhelming and leaves the board, that is ok, but we need to respect the individual decisions each person makes in a lifetime.

6. Having said that, I am also called on frequently to say to the relativists: But you know, this is a Waldorf school, striving to achieve the ideals articulated by Rudolf Steiner and his worldview we call Anthroposophy. If you are uncomfortable with that, it is okay to seek an alternative school. We are here for those who wish to take up the work with us.

This brings me to identify the key factors that I feel are requirements for board membership:

1. Skills, capacities and experience that will help the board function efficiently. (These often include finance, organizational work, administration, community relations and fund-raising.)

2. Support for Waldorf education and sympathy for those in the board and the faculty who are striving to work out of Anthroposophy. Note the word *sympathy* as opposed to *antipathy.* To get people under criteria number one, we need to set the part at sympathy rather than look for true believers. Sometimes they come in the same package, but more often than not sympathy (which usually means an openness to learn more) as well as some of the above skill sets is good enough.

3. Willingness to work energetically as a group. We once had an accountant on a board I served on and he thought each meeting was an accounting class. Eventually we had to ask him to leave since he was not willing to work with others. It is always good to look at the whole constellation of members before inviting someone new. What is needed in terms of human capacities at this time in our biography as an organization?

4. Willingness to do the work. Some schools have advisory boards that meet once a year. Those who can only commit that sort of time should join such boards. But in most cases, schools and non-profits need people who are willing to serve on a committee, read the minutes, follow up on tasks and get the work done. We need worker bees!

Those are my basic criteria, but of course one wants to look at balance in the group: age, gender, race, local community history versus new arrivals and so on. These things are more intuitive, and can be discussed in a nominating committee when seeking new members.

Schools have boards that can be as small as seven or eight or as large as eighteen to twenty. There are many pros and cons to each extreme, but in most cases a group of twelve to fifteen can serve well together. It is very helpful if the composition of the board reflects the community it tries to serve, namely parents, teachers and members of the community who are not parents or teachers. This last group is the hardest to find, but their perspective can be well worth the effort. Sometimes an alum parent can be in that position. In general, I like the idea of thirds in board composition: no more than one-third teachers/staff, one-third parents and one-third community. Some boards have had "representatives" from the PTO, faculty or from an alum association. I have a personal aversion to the notion of representatives on a board. First of all, how can one really "represent" all the parents? Does one have a referendum each time there is an issue at hand? In practice what most often happens is the representative ends up expressing a personal opinion or those of a few close friends. Instead, I feel that each person who has a vote on the board should satisfy the criteria for membership established by the school and be willing to make decisions as trustees of the whole. Membership on a board also requires doing work for the board, such as fund-raising. Those teachers and parents selected to serve should be willing to think and act like a trustee, even when some decisions are difficult or go against the will of close colleagues and friends. Good school governance requires people who are willing to act in the best interests of the *whole school*. After a decision is made, even those trustees on the "losing side" of the vote must support the decision and defend and articulate it to the best of their ability (and not merely represent it back to another group).

This then brings us to the issue of board leadership. Schools usually give a lot of thought to the hiring of an administrator or the selection of a faculty chair. That is good as these are crucial roles. Yet the selection of a board president is also important, and that often receives less attention. Whereas most board members want to be involved in say the selection of the administrator, rarely are faculty consulted sufficiently in regard to board leadership. One might say: Well that is the business of the board. Of course it is, but in practice a board president often becomes a school leader, speaking up at all school meetings, leading community sessions on budget discussions and writing letters to parents and staff. The tone and style of a board president makes a big difference. Too often schools rise and fall, move left or right due less to intentional policy changes or strategic plans but more so through the vagaries of individual leaders. Each board president I have met has a particular set of skills and experiences, many of which are put to good use on behalf of the school. But it needs to be intentional and not reactive. Rather than veering off to become a "Hollywood school" or "bankers' school" because of the person in a leadership role, it should always remain the Waldorf school dedicated first and foremost to the children's needs. We need strong personalities to get jobs done, but we should not be ruled by personality— thus the need for vision, goal-setting and strategic planning.

I have also become a big believer in vice presidents, treasurers and recording secretaries to help balance the team. And the board leadership should meet regularly (monthly) with the faculty/admin team to coordinate agendas and communicate. With these things in place one begins to approach the necessary conditions for collaborative leadership.

In recent years I have more calls than ever from schools that have gone through a series of action/reaction steps in regard to leadership. Each case varies somewhat in detail but here is the general pattern:

1. The founding leaders step back to retire or as the result of exhaustion. The school starts to drift, and decisions are not made in a timely or effective manner.
2. In frustration, the board demands changes and hires professionals from outside the Waldorf movement "to straighten things out."
3. Although those administrators sometimes adjust to a new way of working, they often become frustrated and feel that they are misunderstood and their authority not respected. Often teachers start to resent being directed by people who do not have a connection to their pedagogy or philosophy and protest to the board.
4. If the cultural disconnect becomes too great, the faculty demands change and the board may either dig in and resist, or reluctantly agree that some of the recent hires are not working. Everyone is then left with the question: So, what do we do now?

We are left with a singular challenge in our anthroposophically based organizations: How can we enlist the professional expertise needed for raising funds, communications, admissions and so on, while remaining true to the mission of the organization? I feel the solution in most instances is for the organization to seek the best people available and hire them on the condition of continued professional development. That means that professionals from outside the Waldorf community need to go to summer courses offered at various sites around the country that are based on an anthroposophic view of the human being. Even a week each summer can make a big difference. This also means that teachers who are selected for leadership roles but are lacking in certain skill sets need to go to summer or weekend training in areas such as communication, conflict resolution, HR and so on. The best of both worlds occurs when teachers and administrators train together in programs such as in the Antioch Administrator Training. In such a setting, participants can learn from one another, share common concerns and model collaboration that can then be transferred into real-life situations when they return their schools.

Most of all, boards need to invest in leadership development and send their leaders to the training programs, fund them and provide mentorship when they return. A small investment in this way can yield many positive results. In the end, what board members most want is to see their school function smoothly without their constant intervention. Strong pedagogical and administrative leadership can allow a board to step out of the daily monitoring of activities and focus on fund development, outreach and strategic goals.

26

SEEK AND YOU WILL FIND

"There is no feeling, except the extremes of fear and grief, that does not find relief in music." —GEORGE ELIOT

Some time ago I was sorting out old files in a box of long-forgotten materials when I came across a thirty-year-old Christmas card from Lisa Monges. On the right side was her Christmas greeting signed simply "L. D. Monges" and on the left was a portrait of Rudolf Steiner standing behind a sofa. In addition to the well-known black outfit and white collar, one cannot but help notice his strong hands and expressive fingers, the serious, well formed facial contours that are filled with light, and of course the eyes that look outward and inward at the same time. On the top left hand corner one finds a four-line verse, followed by Steiner's signature and date February 17, 1924, and the two words: *"am Goetheanum."*

Of course one always has to wonder why such a card finds its way into the reader's hands just as the Anthroposophical Society leadership at the Goetheanum has introduced a very particular theme for the year ahead (see the newsletter *Anthroposophy Worldwide* for more on the theme of the year). I decided that, since very few things in life are really an accident, it was the right time to take up this gift from Lisa Monges and work with the verse in a renewed way. By the way, Lisa was a pioneer eurythmist in the U.S., helped start the Spring Valley School of Eurythmy, and taught eurythmy to a group of community children once a week in her living room. I was one of those children. Later, after years of mowing her lawn as a teenager, I turned to Lisa Monges when, at the age of eighteen, I heard about an exciting conference for members, and I asked her to sponsor me.

There in my hands was the Christmas card with her signature and a verse in Rudolf Steiner's own hand. It begins with the line *"Suche in der Welt nach allen Seiten"* (to seek in the world on all sides, in all dimensions), a challenge these days. Recently I have encountered more people than ever who deliberately tune out—turn off the radio, TV news, internet news feeds, newspapers and so on, because current events are so "depressing." How many stories of ISEL (or ISIS) can we read? When will the random acts of violence in schools and places of work stop? How many natural catastrophes do we have to ingest? I understand this point of view, and yet I continue to read parts of *The Wall Street Journal* most days, occasionally catch the evening news, and have give some thought to world events. I respect those who need to create islands of sanity, but I still feel an inner obligation to stay engaged in world events. Why?

In another context (the founding of the first Goetheanum) Rudolf Steiner used the word *Weltbejahung,* one of the words he coined that is nearly impossible to translate. The closest I have come is "affirmation of the world," one's willingness to say "yes" and not reject what the world offers. This is a high order. How can we do that? It may be only part of the story, but my approach is to see it not as agreement with all that is happening but a "living in presence," or awareness, of what the world offers us today. It is possible to witness, to be aware, and not immediately rush to judgment, acceptance or rejection as so many are apt to do. There are days, even months, when it is terribly cold in New Hampshire, and there are the warm summer days, and of course we all have preferences. But can I learn to practice *Weltbejahung* to all kinds of weather, as well as the news stories that enter my consciousness?

Some might ask: What is the point of doing this? Along with being overwhelmed, many feel helpless in the face of world events. What can I do as one solitary person? The second line of the verse has a clue that helps us with this riddle: *Und du findest dich* (You will find yourself). What? I can find myself in another atrocious story on CNN? Isn't that the last place I would want to find myself? On one level, of course. But if we actually take a few minutes to think (something we cannot take for granted these days), the percepts from world phenomena start to work on the soul, and concepts start to arise. For instance, after a series of stories from the Middle East recently, I spent time thinking about the root causes of fundamentalism: What makes people fanatics? Why do those who seem to be on a religious path (with all the teachings of peace) turn a corner and become fundamentalists? There are many in our circles who could help with this question (Christopher Bamford comes to mind), but my purpose is not to answer it here. I just want to point out a series of steps:

1. We seek to know the world in all dimensions.
2. This leads to new experiences that can take shape in new thoughts.
3. If we have done the thinking, we have to own our own concepts.
4. By owning our thoughts, as well as the soul depths from which they arise, we can experience ourselves in a new way.

Thus the world leads to self.

Then we move to the third and fourth lines of the verse: *"Suche in dir nach allen Tiefen / Und du findest die Welt."* Here we have the reverse process. If we are willing to seek in the depth of the soul and delve into our innermost being, we can find the world in a new way. There are many ways in which this can happen, but one has to do with meditation and reflective practices in general. When we do the inner work, we find our center, our essential Self. One can emerge from strenuous inner work with a heightened sense of integrity, authenticity and groundedness. Like the violinist who practices for hours before giving a concert, when one has done the inner work then one meets the world/audience on a different level. What a difference it makes if one has prepared a presentation or simply tries to wing it. When one is rooted in the depth of soul experience, one can then stand in a different relation to the theme or task at hand. And when one does so, one meets others and the world in a new way. So again we have a sequence:

1. Seek inwardly in all possible depths of inner experience.
2. Let the research and soul exploration give rise to new experiences.
3. These experiences become the ground of authenticity.
4. When we are authentic in relation to others and the world, we will rediscover the "world" on a new basis.

This little verse actually contains all of Anthroposophy, the meditative path, self-knowledge and so on, as well as all the initiatives, schools and farms that have grown from authentic deeds of sacrifice. If there is any need for final proof, we have only to talk with a seasoned biodynamic farmer or Camphill community coworker, a veteran Waldorf teacher or a doctor practicing anthroposophically extended medicine. Nowhere could we find such depth, insight and wisdom as we do from such people. They know the world not only from working in the world, but also by having worked on themselves. Their inner work has led to new achievements in their fields and professional lives.

In my travels I have met many people who have spent their lives working with Anthroposophy in this way. There really is no better evidence of the fruitfulness of Anthroposophy than to experience such remarkable people. They are outwardly successful, but after just a few minutes one finds that they are also remarkable human beings inwardly. Their humanity and work success seem to go hand in hand.

The inscription on that old Christmas card ends with the two words *am Goetheanum:* at the Goetheanum. These words should not be overlooked. It is not just about the historical Steiner, but also about the Goetheanum impulse that continues to work around the world in so many ways. We need to be willing, as he was, to identify ourselves and our work as coming from that impulse. Our future success depends on the authenticity of our inner work and the integrity that arises from compassionate engagement with the world. We do not reject; we embrace. We do not criticize; we suggest. We are here not to judge but to help—servants of all that is good, kind and just.

Our Anthroposophical Society is dedicated to these goals. May we find the strength and the friends to help us realize our aims.

27

Administrators as Knights Templar of the Twenty-first Century

"I think my fans will follow me into our combined old age. Real musicians and real fans stay together for a long, long time." —Bonnie Raitt

Most readers will remember the Templars for their leadership on the Crusades and their striking white banners featuring a red cross at the center. Others might know of their relationship to money and their eventual betrayal and execution. For the purposes of this book, I would like to highlight a few aspects that pertain especially to administrators and leaders in the organizations of today:

The Templars were known for their simple lives on a personal level. They did not have possessions, houses, land and such but pooled their resources for the sake of their order, the greater whole. We could say that they lived in the spirit of brotherhood (as far as I know, they were all men) and practiced this aspect of threefolding in regard to their personal lives. Although the order accumulated tremendous wealth, the individual knights took nothing for themselves.

This spirit of brotherhood/sisterhood in the modern sense lives strongly in the case of many administrators in our not for profit organizations of today. Many in these leadership roles could indeed earn much higher salaries in business, have the qualifications for a variety of other jobs, but instead choose to work in a Waldorf school or Camphill community out of idealism. Some speak quite eloquently about career changes and conscious decisions to do what is best for family and quality of life issues over compensation. I am continuously impressed with the degree of altruism in today's administrators.

The Templars were the first bankers, not just in the sense of accumulated wealth but also in terms of the circulation of money. They established a credit system encompassing most of the Western world, in which people could leave funds at one location and withdraw them from another when, say, traveling. This was an entirely new way of working with money. It embodied the notion of "good-faith credit" based on a network of trust.

Our administrators today of course work with money in a variety of ways, from fees and tuition to development and maintenance of buildings. Most administrators cultivate active relationships with vendors, local contractors and community leaders as part of just getting the job done. They bring the mission of their school into a kind of circulation that goes far beyond the walls of any one institution. Those that have been with a school or organization for a period of time often earn the trust and confidence of community members in a way that supports the future growth far beyond financing. Administrators end up knowing a great deal about circulation.

The Templars worked in groups, yet adhered to a clear leadership hierarchy. The Grand Master was both a spiritual and an earthly leader. There was a strong sense of individual leadership and a need for belonging to a group, or order. Administrators in most organizations I know have a healthy respect for authority and leadership, yet know how to develop teams in the workplace. Moving from directing to supporting roles comes easily for many, and they are often less conflicted than others when it comes to the need to support strong leadership. In this sense they model some of the things discussed in the chapter on agreements, especially the balance of group and individual.

The Templars paid the ultimate price for their service, when mostly out of jealousy and greed, they were betrayed and on one fateful night, were rounded up all over Europe and imprisoned. Many were eventually burned at the stake.

Fortunately this has not happened to our faithful administrators in our modern times, but many a person has had to move on, sometimes on the heels of considerable frustration. Now as my father mentions, changing schools or jobs is not always a bad thing, but I do feel that many administrators are so to speak sacrificed on the alter of organizational dysfunction. They can so easily become the lightning rods, the visible "face" of any difficulty, and they do not always have a band of loyal followers, as do many class teachers. A facet of this phenomena is the Development and Administrative Network of the Association (DANA) Survey some years ago indicating a turnover rate of 2.5 years. As one of my students recently pointed out, the second digit (.5) also speaks volumes.

↓

My hope is that through this book and the discussions that it evokes, schools and other nonprofits who use it as a study will wake up to some of the issues that need work. I cannot possibly cover all the topics needed, nor can our Waldorf administrative training program through Antioch University New England adequately prepare administrators for the challenges they face and will encounter in the years ahead. But we can wake up to the needs at hand. I call upon teachers, board members and parents of our Camphill communities, clinics, retirement communities and especially our Waldorf schools to find new ways to support their administrators and school leaders. A teacher who steps up to the plate to serve as faculty chair often does so with tremendous heart forces and goodwill, leaving the purely pedagogical realm with considerable reluctance. Many of our faculty leaders are in fact reluctant leaders who need our full support. These administrators and faculty leaders are our modern Knights Templar. Let us wake up to organizational dynamics and to our roles as followers. Our future depends on our collective response to this wake-up call.

The Sleep of Prisoners

By Christopher Frye

The human heart can go to the lengths of God.
Dark and cold we may be, but this
Is no winter now. The frozen misery
Of centuries cracks, begins to move;
The thunder is the thunder of the floes,
The thaw, the flood, the upstart Spring.

Thank God our time is now when wrong
Comes up to face us everywhere,
Never to leave us till we take
The longest stride of soul men ever took.

Affairs are now soul size
The enterprise
Is exploration into God.

Where are you making for?
It takes so many thousand years to wake
But will you wake for pity's sake?

PART TWO

VOICES FROM THE FIELD

In part two, the reader will find articles by a variety of authors spanning both pedagogical and leadership perspectives that are helpful for effecting change. Many of the authors are themselves respected leaders in a variety of organizations around the world. These articles are meant to serve as separate study texts, and could be taken up in any order as the need arises. Some might be more suitable for a board study, others for faculty or parents. The hope is to encourage reflective practices and support leadership development.

THE ARTISTIC MEETING: CREATING SPACE FOR SPIRIT

BY HOLLY KOTEEN-SOULE

When Rudolf Steiner brought together the individuals who would become the teachers of the first Waldorf school, he asked them to work in a new way, not only with the children, but also with one another. He asked them to work together in such as way as to invite the interest and guidance of spiritual beings into their endeavor.

The challenge of creating and maintaining a connection with the spiritual world, as difficult as it was then, may be even more intense in the present time. Materialism has grown considerably stronger in the twenty-first century, and with it has come an increasing need to bring a balancing, healing and renewing element to daily life.

The Waldorf classroom is a place where this renewing spiritual element can be found. It arises from the children themselves and from how we work with them. It can also be found in the meeting life of the school, in how the teachers and other adults work together. There are many resources available today on conducting effective meetings in the workplace. This article will focus on how we can create a space for spirit in meetings, and how this endeavor can support us in our individual development, in our encounters with colleagues and in strengthening our groups and communities.

Meetings as an artistic activity will be a second focus. Understanding meetings as an art form and using an artistic approach when planning and carrying out a meeting can allow participants to be refreshed and inspired at the meeting's conclusion. While including an artistic activity in the agenda can be helpful, it is more critical that the meeting itself be artistic and display the wholeness, drama, and dynamics of any other artistic creation. Artistic activity can often be a doorway to the recognition of spiritual archetypes and the building of spiritual understanding. A meeting that is conducted as a form of art greatly enhances this possibility for the participants.

Meetings as Spiritual Practice: Waking up in the Other

Near the end of his life, after the burning of the first Goetheanum and during a period of upheaval within the Anthroposophical Society, Rudolf Steiner began to speak urgently about the need to build communities based on a shared spiritual purpose that extends beyond our cultural or hereditary ties. He described physical waking as a response to the stimuli of the natural world in our surroundings. Our waking up at a higher level happens when we encounter the soul-spirit of other human beings. He went so far as to say:

We are also unable to understand the spiritual world, no matter how many beautiful ideas we may have garnered from Anthroposophy or how much we may have grasped theoretically about such matters as etheric and astral bodies. We begin to develop an understanding for the spiritual world only when we wake up in the encounter with the soul-spiritual in our fellow human beings.[1]

On other occasions, Steiner also spoke about a need in our age (the fifth post-Atlantean epoch) that can only be fulfilled in groups. He referred specifically to the spirit of brother/sisterhood hovering above us in the realm of the higher hierarchies, which needs to be consciously cultivated so that it can flow into human souls in the future. These statements constitute a strong call for us to create opportunities for more, rather than fewer, encounters with our colleagues, despite the inevitable challenges with which we are all familiar.

The Reverse Ritual

In considering meetings as spiritual practice, it may be helpful to recall our understanding from Anthroposophy that at a certain point in the course of the evolution of the cosmos and humanity, the higher creative beings drew back from the sphere of the Earth. This withdrawal was necessary in order for human beings to develop in freedom. As a result, the physical Earth is in the process of dying. The human being, having been given freedom and the possibility of spiritual consciousness, has become an increasingly decisive factor in the future of the Earth.

One of our tasks is to help reenliven the Earth. We do that with the substance of our human thinking—not our ordinary thoughts and reflections, but spiritual thoughts arising from creative Imaginations, Inspirations and Intuitions. These creative thoughts represented for Steiner a new spiritual form of communion for humanity. He gave many indications how both individuals and groups could work with creative, enlivening thoughts for their own benefit and for the benefit of humanity as a whole.

It was Steiner's deep conviction that the appropriate form for community-building in our time is what he called the reverse ritual. He distinguished this ritual from a traditional religious ritual, in which a mediator is charged with drawing the spiritual hierarchies down to a particular place. "The anthroposophic community seeks to lift up the human souls into supersensible worlds so that they may enter into the company of angels."

We must do more than talk about spiritual beings; we must look for opportunities nearest at hand to enter their company. The work of an anthroposophic group does not consist in a number of people merely discussing anthroposophic ideas. Its members should feel so linked with one another that human soul wakes up in the encounter with human soul and all are lifted up into the spiritual world, into the company of spiritual beings, though it need not be a question of beholding them. We do not have to see them to have this experience. [2]

The "College Imagination" (also known as the "Teachers' Imagination") that Steiner gave to the first group of teachers is an example of such a reverse ritual, in which a group working with a common meditative picture creates the possibility of connecting with specific spiritual beings and bringing back creative impulses for their earthly work.[3]

If Waldorf teachers wish to work with these ideas and with the example of the "Teachers Imagination," how can we form and conduct faculty and college meetings in this light? How can our meeting life be spiritually sustaining for individuals and build a vital sense of community in our schools?

Space for Spirit

We know what it feels like to have participated in a successful meeting. We are enlivened at the meeting's end. We also know that what occurred could not have been achieved by any individual member of the group. These are indicators of spirit presence. It is possible to learn how to create such meetings—ones that lift us out of our ordinary awareness and allow us the possibility of working more consciously with the spiritual world. We can create more space for spirit in our meeting life in the following ways.

I. Imbue the meeting place with a sense of conscious care. It is often the case that certain individuals have a natural feeling for the need to prepare the room where a meeting will occur. When we prepare a space with care, we are working with the elementals, spiritual beings that, according to Rudolf Steiner, are detachments from the higher hierarchies, sacrificing themselves for the creation of the material world. They have a great deal to do with the physical setting, and also with our individual physical well-being, our thinking, feeling, and willing, and our communications.

In my own experience, how the room is prepared can have as significant an effect on a meeting as it does on what happens in our classrooms when we make sure that they are clean, orderly, and beautiful. Imagine how the arrangement of the furniture could enhance the quality of the group's interaction. Consider the effect of having as a centerpiece a seasonal bouquet gathered by a member of the group, rather than one that was purchased at the florist shop. It is especially helpful if all members of a faculty take a turn at preparing the setting, so that more members of the group carry the importance of this aspect of the meeting.

II. Create a threshold mood. Meetings that begin with a moment of silence and a mood of reverence allow participants to be aware of stepping across a kind of threshold, out of their everyday consciousness into a heightened sense of presence. An explicit acknowledgment of our spiritual helpers, the spirit of the school, and those persons who have been connected to our institution and are now in the spiritual world, can also shift the group's awareness. A conscious effort to begin on time helps create the sense of going through a doorway together. A verse can also represent a threshold and, when brought in the right mood, offer a kind of protective sheath for whatever may happen in the meeting.

III. Reestablish the sense of the group. This activity has two parts. The first is the recognition of individuals and the second is an affirmation of the purpose of the group. A key to the first part is the interest that we take in one another. Listening to colleagues share something out of their lives or an aspect of their work with students can wake us up to one another in a potent way. The sharing can be brief and, in the case of a large faculty, may involve only a portion of the group each week. Sharing can also be connected to the season; for example, at Michaelmas the focus could be, "What in your life is requiring a fresh burst of courage and will?"

This part of the meeting can deepen our understanding of our colleagues and build the level of trust that we need to work together on spiritual matters. Movement or artistic activity can also serve to strengthen the group's capacity to work together on issues that require sensitivity to one another. At this stage of the meeting the "I" of each individual is acknowledged as he or she steps into the work with the group, or the "We."

The second part of establishing the sense of the group requires an affirmation of the group's purpose or task. A verse or reading can be helpful but must be relevant and alive for the group. For some groups, it may be important to choose a new opening for each year or to work with festival themes in order to strengthen the sense of community and purpose at this stage of the meeting. For other groups, choosing to work consciously with the same verse for many years may actually bring them to an ever-deepening understanding of its meaning and effect. Although study is often used to bring a group to a common focus, this is successful only if everyone is actively engaged.

IV. Practice conscious listening and speaking. We know that listening perceptively to another person requires letting go of our sympathies and antipathies and our own preconceived ideas; in fact, we must momentarily let go of our own I to experience the "I" of the other as he or she speaks. Marjorie Spock wrote most poetically about the effects of perceptive listening:

> First, there is what it does to the soul of the listener. A miracle of self-overcoming takes place within him whenever he really lends an ear to others. If he is to understand the person speaking, he must draw his attention from his own concerns and make a present of it to a listener; he clears his inner scene like one who for a time gives up his home for others' use while himself remaining only in the role of servant. Listeners quite literally entertain a speaker's thought. "Not I, but the Christ in me" is made real in every such act of genuine listening.
>
> Second, there is what happens to the speaker when he is fortunate to be listened to perceptively. Another kind of miracle takes place in him, perhaps best described as a springtime burgeoning. Before his idea was expressed to a listener, it lived in his soul as potential only; it resembles a seed force lying fallow in the winter earth. To be listened to with real interest acts upon this seed like Sun and warmth and rain and other cosmic elements that provide growth-impetus; the soul ground in which the idea is embedded comes magically alive. Under such benign influence, thoughts grow full cycle and fulfill their promise. Moreover they confer fertility upon the ground through the simple fact of having lived there. Further ideas will be the more readily received into such a soil and spring more vigorously for its life-attunement. And the soul that harbors them begins to be the creative force in evolution for which it was intended by the gods.[4]

Brief spaces of silence can also allow thoughts and insights to ripen and fall into the conversation. Can we provide for the seed thoughts of our colleagues, out of our own souls, what the Sun and rain provide for the sprouting plant? It is a rare group that does not need to recommit regularly to practicing this kind of listening and speaking.

V. Work with imaginative pictures over time. Imagination is a language that can bear fruit in the spiritual world. Translating the group's questions and issues into stories and pictures can enhance the group's meditative work during the meeting or individual work during the course of the week.

Look for an archetype, myth, or fairy tale that can reveal new aspects of the matter under consideration. Taking time over two or three meetings to explore major questions invites the possibility of richer insights. Colleagues will want to hold back from building support for one or another course of action and to be open to new information as it emerges during this phase. Having worked successfully with imaginative pictures in the child study process can help trust their use in other situations as well.

VI. Share responsibility. Individuals who are able to carry the consciousness for a group have certain capacities that are usually recognized by the other members of the group. Not everyone has these in the same measure, but it is important to recognize talents among colleagues and give one another opportunities and support to develop latent capacities. Different individuals can lead various parts of a meeting. A group of two or three people can plan the agenda. Incorporate means of regular review for those taking responsibility for the yearly schedule.

It is clear that a group is healthiest when individuals are continuing to grow and develop. Even the most competent facilitator needs to step back or work with a new colleague in order to gain fresh perspective. Rotating leadership and having several individuals carry one or another aspect of the meeting facilitation make it more likely that all members will feel involved. All members are responsible to bring to the group the results of their individual meditative life. Spiritual leadership requires learning how to create the conditions for meaningful conversations and then helping the group follow up on what arises out of those conversations.

VII. Let the meeting breathe. In the work of the classroom we need to prepare carefully and be ready to respond to what comes from our students. A meeting that has a compelling wholeness and feeling of flow is probably the result of a well-crafted agenda along with some adjustments made during the meeting to an emerging sense of clarity and direction. Having prior agreements about how to deal with new information or agenda changes is helpful. A rhythmic relation to time in a meeting creates more of an opening for spiritual insights than either an overstuffed agenda or a formless one.

There are a number of simple possibilities for making a meeting more rhythmic. For example, honor the times on the agenda, but not so rigidly that people feel cut off or topics are truncated. Vary the conversation from full-group sharing to small-group work and individual reports. Create a balance between pedagogical and other topics, looking back and looking ahead, exploring new questions and making decisions. When the group is not moving physically, make sure there is plenty of inner movement. Remember to invite the spirit of Play and the spirit of Humor into the meeting.

VIII. Expect to be surprised. There is nothing more uninviting than a completely predictable meeting. On the other hand, a meeting in which the group is pulled this way and that by personal agendas is equally frustrating. We must stay awake to the influences of Ahriman (too much form) and Lucifer (too much impulsiveness) as they work in individuals and in our groups.

To stay the course in the creative spiritual stream, we need to ask real questions; practice positivity and open-mindedness; be comfortable with not knowing; and expect answers and solutions to come from unexpected places.

IX. Review. During meeting review, we reflect on what went well and what could have been better, so that we can improve our work together. Review serves another important purpose as well. Just as our nightly review is a conversation starter for the work with our own angel during sleep, our meeting review serves as a seed for the continuing conversation with the spiritual world between meetings.

Running late in a meeting is sometimes the reason that groups neglect review, but review can often capture essential aspects of a meeting in a brief and economical way. In this regard, poetry is more useful than prose. Brief characterizations, even one-word or one-image offerings, can illuminate hidden gems. Hearing individual voices during the review can be a supportive bookend to the work, like the personal sharing at the beginning of a meeting.

Review is not a rehashing of any part of the meeting. It should bring to light aspects of content, processes, and interactions that can benefit from greater awareness on the part of individuals and the group. A perceptive facilitator will vary the means of review and offer questions to elicit information that might not otherwise be brought to light. "Where did we experience gratitude in the meeting?" "Were there any moments of unresolved tension?" "What did we do that might be of interest to our spiritual helpers?" Review in the form of an earnest question is the best kind of invitation to spirit beings.

X. Prepare and follow up. If we recognize that our meetings are a kind of ritual, then preparation and follow-up are as important as the meeting itself. Preparation requires more than a quick glance at a copy of the agenda. When individuals come to a meeting having thought about the issues and their colleagues the night before, the spiritual ground has already been tilled.

How we carry the questions as well as the tasks from one meeting to the next can make a difference in whether the seeds sowed will sprout healthily in the coming weeks. How each individual carries the group in between meetings will also make a difference. Working rhythmically with time has both a physical and a spiritual aspect. When we consciously release into the spiritual world ideas that have arisen in the group, it is possible that they will return in a more complete or archetypal form.

These are some of the realities that we may wish to take into consideration as we build a vessel for the spiritual aspect of our work, just as we pay attention to earthly realities in constructing a physical home for our schools.

MEETINGS AS ART

The Artistic Process

The arts, according to Rudolf Steiner, were experienced in earlier civilizations as more integral to life than is the case today. Artistic creativity, he said, was experienced as a transcendent spiritual activity, flowing out of the "spirit-attuned state" in which the human being lived in those times. Only since the rise of materialism has the status of art changed from necessity to luxury.[5]

Rudolf Steiner also observed that in our era a longing for the arts comes out of the recognition of the limits of abstract thinking. Ideas alone are not able to illuminate the world in its full richness; they can only point the way to a deeper reality. Artistic feeling, Steiner said, arises when we sense the presence of something mysterious, such as certain secrets of nature, which can be revealed only through our feeling. Knowing is a matter for the heart as well as the head. To discover a whole, living reality, we need to create, to practice art. He saw the fructification of the arts in our time as an important task for Anthroposophy, and he took up various artistic projects himself during the latter part of his life.[6]

The present-day artist engaged in the creative process moves back and forth between sense perceptions and intuitive visions—awake, but in a somewhat dreamlike feeling state. Steiner described the subtle changes that occur in a person engaged in aesthetic activity (regardless whether the person is creating or enjoying an artistic creation) such that the sense organs are reenlivened and the bodily life processes are lifted to soul-like processes.[7]

In artistic activity we use our heightened sense of feeling rather than our everyday sympathies and antipathies. The artist, consciously or unconsciously, approaches the threshold between the sensible and supersensible worlds and brings something back from the supersensible world into the world of the senses. The resulting creation is a specifically experienced reality lifted into a universal expression.

As Waldorf teachers we understand the importance of the arts and our own creativity in the work with our students. Can we also imagine applying a consciously artistic approach and a heightened sense of feeling to our work with our colleagues in our meetings?

Social Art

In the series of lectures *Art as Seen in the Light of Mystery Wisdom*,[8] Steiner connected each of the arts with the various members of the human being. The laws of the physical body, he said, are expressed in architecture, the etheric in sculpture, the astral in painting, and the ego in music. The still developing Spirit Self he connected to poetry and the Life Spirit to eurythmy. The highest art, according to Steiner, is social art.

The first three arts—architecture, sculpture, and painting (including drawing)—are the spatial arts. These are derived out of formative processes and past evolutionary cycles. They are connected to sculptural forces working out of the past and, in the context of education, help children come into their bodily constitution.

In contrast, the time arts—music, speech and poetry, and eurythmy—are connected to impulses coming out of the future. As Waldorf teachers we work out of our higher bodies and what Steiner called our musical forces in order to guide our students properly into their present life. Social art also belongs to this group of time arts, but is younger, less tangible, and even less developed than eurythmy. How can we study and practice this least tangible of arts?

My own experience is that working in any of the other arts can serve as a basic "instruction manual" for social art. Being grounded in an artistic practice makes it easier to apply the principles of creative activity to *any* aspect of life, including social situations.

As an early childhood teacher, when I had a particularly satisfying day in the kindergarten, I felt as if the children and I had spent the whole morning moving to an exquisite piece of music. When I was responsible for meetings, I began to plan agendas as if I were composing or painting and, during the meeting, I tried to pay attention to compositional elements like repetition, variation, contrast, harmony, balance, focus, surprise, and reprise.

In addition to the writings of Rudolf Steiner, we can also learn about social art in certain traditional texts in which the renewing or healing spiritual element is represented symbolically: the "water of life" from the world of fairy tales, the Grail in the legend of Parsifal, the philosopher's stone of the alchemists, and conversation in Goethe's tale "The Green Snake and the Beautiful Lily."

In North America we owe a great debt to Marjorie Spock, who brought Steiner's concern for community-building to us. She translated Steiner's *Awakening to Community* lectures into English and wrote two pamphlets entitled *Group Moral Artistry*, which are a continuing inspiration for many people. "Goethean Conversation" was the term she used to characterize the process by which a group could invite truth into their midst like a guest. She began with Goethe's framing of conversation as the art of arts and described Goethean conversation as a form of the reverse ritual and an appropriate means of practicing social artistry.

Artistic Meetings

Our artistic sensibilities and an artistic approach to our work in a meeting can enhance the possibility of lifting ourselves into the company of angels, if only briefly. Meetings can be artistic in a number of ways.

A meeting can become artistic when we consciously include an artistic activity in the agenda and allow what flows out of that activity to enhance the rest of our work together. It can also be artistic in the way we use imaginative pictures to enrich our conversations or moments of silence to invite creative inspirations. When the meeting itself is seen as an artistic process, the facilitator and the group will be more likely to strive for a palpable sense of aliveness and wholeness. Finally, if we take our work in the social art seriously, whatever we are able to achieve in the special situation of our meetings has the potential to strengthen our relationships overall and may even have a healing effect on other relationships in the community.

Conscious Conversation—An Invitation

We swim in a sea of spirit. Our matter-bound everyday consciousness, however, easily forgets the reality of spirit living in and everywhere around us. In this age of Michael especially, we have to wake up in those places where we are sleepily swept along with the materialistic tides of existence. It is not easy to push aside pressing everyday concerns again and again to make space for encounters with spirit in one another and with spirit beings on the other side of the threshold.

As Waldorf teachers, this is a task we have taken on not only for the sake of our students but also because the conversation with the spirit is the source of our own strength, inspiration, and creativity. In our meeting life and through an artistic practice of conscious conversation, we have an incredible opportunity to enter as a group into the realm of spirit-sensing. Our own work as individuals—likewise the whole Waldorf movement—needs this renewing spiritual force as it continues to grow and proliferate in far-flung corners of the world.

NOTES

1   Rudolf Steiner, *Awakening to Community* (Spring Valley, NY: Anthroposophic Press, 1974), p. 97.

2   Ibid., p. 157.

3   For a description of the Imagination, see *Foundations of Human Experience*, pp. 45–48 [or the appendix to Roberto Trostli's article in the previous issue of the *Research Bulletin* (vol. 16, no. 2)—ed.].

4   Marjorie Spock, *Group Moral Artistry: Reflections on Community Building* (Spring Valley, NY: St. George Publications, 1983), p. 18.

5   Rudolf Steiner, *The Arts and their Mission* (Spring Valley, NY: Anthroposophic Press, 1964), lect. 2.

6   Rudolf Steiner, *Art as Spiritual Activity*, ed. Michael Howard, ch. 5: "The Two Sources of Art: Impressionism and Expressionism," Munich, Feb. 15, 1918 (Hudson, NY: Anthroposophic Press, 1998).

7   Ibid., ch. 4 ("Sense Organs and Aesthetic Experience," Dornach, Aug. 15, 1916).

8   Rudolf Steiner, *Art as Seen in the Light of Mystery Wisdom* (London: Rudolf Steiner Press, 1984).

↯

EURYTHMY IN THE WORKPLACE

BASED ON CONVERSATIONS WITH BARBARA RICHARDSON

In the Platonic dialogues (*Cratylus*) one can find descriptions of movement, as paraphrased here: What would you do if you couldn't speak? I would make movements with my hands and arms... R like horses running, O is rounded and so on. In the book *Rudolf Steiner's Mission and Ita Wegman,** there is a description of how these archetypal Greek indications were picked up in a modern form. Questioned by Socrates about the essential nature of sounds, Cratylus gives the following indications: "that through the construction of the tongue, the pronunciation of the sounds D and T are formed, for instance: in *D* there is a suggestion of 'binding,' in T on the other hand, a suggestion of stability. In the pronunciation of L, a gliding movement is suggested—smoothness, semi-liquidity; O indicates roundness, R, all movement, the sound-gesture of I (Iota) suggests subtlety, delicacy."

The very first eurythmist, Lory Meier Smits, worked in her husband's button factory and she did movement, an early form of eurythmy, with the workers during their breaks. Steiner visited and observed these exercises, and then helped with new inventions. Annemarie Ehrlich in the Netherlands, a Waldorf student herself, did the eurythmy training, taught in schools and then trained eurythmists. The director of the company wanted to do a training of new employees in one week instead of the usual three weeks, and thought that eurythmy would reach them in such a short time. She used the money she received from teaching to buy

---

*   Margarete and Erich Kirchner-Bockholt, London: Rudolf Steiner Press, 1977.

some copper balls, which she found makes people less self-conscious, to carry out some of the exercises. These copper balls are now a major feature of the activities done in eurythmy in the workplace.

What happens when the copper balls are used? First of all, being copper they do not take away from human warmth as do many other materials. Instead, they give back warmth as many hands come into contact with them. But the chief reason for using them is that they are so visible, and thus they help us notice other people as the balls move. Participants can observe the movement of the copper balls in space, which in turn becomes a way of seeing the interactions of individuals in groups. One could say that group dynamics become visible. Through this heightened visibility the activity becomes a subject of observation, and by sharing observations after an exercise is completed members of the group can learn from their collective experiences. In fact, unlike artistic eurythmy performed onstage, or pedagogical eurythmy done with children, eurythmy in the workplace uses a highly differentiated process of doing, reflecting, refined doing, reflecting etc. This means that every so often the lead eurythmist will stop the activity and ask for observations. At the end of an entire session participants are often encouraged to do quiet journaling to capture some of their experiences. I [Torin Finser] have found this process to be exceptionally helpful in support of adult learning, and we have applied these exercises to develop many skills such as communication, taking initiative, working conflict or building group dynamics.

Annemarie Ehrlich traveled to the United States in 1994 and did a week-long introductory session for eurythmists. She then started a full training in 1995 and graduated a group of eight in 1996. These graduates then went out and applied what they learned in various professions.

So for example, Barbara did exercises from eurythmy in the workplace with the council of the Anthroposophical Society in America to help balance their long days of sitting and enhance their discussions. They found that they got through their agenda faster when they did these sessions twice a day. On a practical level, these exercises can help groups get their work done. Then she worked with the Chicago Waldorf School board, starting with a figure 8, a lemniscate, each person holding a copper ball.

A new board member, experienced with many not-for-profit boards said afterward: It usually takes three to six months of board meetings to get oriented and focused, but here we have done it in thirty minutes.

These applications grew to other places of work such as: the University of Illinois Nurse Midwives, Make-a-Wish Foundation of northern Indiana, daycare providers and an electric company in Alaska. Barbara worked with the board of the Esperanza School in Chicago and a restaurant called Villa Kula, involving everyone from chef to owner, to waitresses to dishwashers. She also did work with an international paper company, vice presidents and CEOs...powerful people who totally got one of the first eurythmy exercises given by Rudolf Steiner (I, A, O) as ever so helpful in understanding the different levels of meeting people, from uprightness (I, pronounced "eee") to receptivity/listening (A) to participation (O).

Why is eurythmy in workplace so effective according to Barbara?

"You are doing something you don't usually do, you are lifted out of cubicle life. You learn to work with others in a way that builds communication. You access your own will and motivation to do things in freedom. Eurythmy, as performing art, exists only in time, it is an activity that flows in time and space. As a participant one does things again and again and understanding builds trust and self-confidence. You meet people you do not usually have much contact with. 'I feel a lightness in my body, feel joyful and connected to the group' said one participant. 'Energy and warmth are streaming through my whole body...moving as a group, mistakes and all, connects us, and connection seems to be what helps us deal with conflicts,' said another. We are called to bring attentiveness to the other, something that is so needed in the workplace today."

An electrical lineman in Alaska found that arriving at solutions with top brass was easier afterward, and that he saw others in a new way as a result. You learn to respect other peoples' talents.

People who have done eurythmy in the workplace often feel energized, expanded and focused. Right and left brain are stimulated to work together. People are made aware of their surroundings and yet can zero in and focus with new perception.

Barbara continues: "The exercises are very simple in the first instance...passing a copper ball around the circle etc. But the process intensifies as the activity progresses, the bar is raised in small increments until at the end many are incredulous at what is achieved in complexity and grace.

Participants are also in a different situation from their usual roles in their place of work. The individuals participate freely, understanding the intention of the exercises, then doing the exercises in space and time. They develop rhythm, harmony and synchronicity with each other. The goal is apparent, success is apparent and if not reached, we try again. Groups learn to learn together, and the skills are directly applicable to everyday situations.

Afterward, we check in with ourselves, "How do I feel compared to when I entered this room?" and "How does this relate to my work, myself and my workplace?"

The most frequent comment is, "Now I feel energized and focused!"

In describing the session in one or two words, almost every time the words are completely different and yet no one finds disagreement with anyone else's words: *Collaboration, Responsibility, Acceptance, Trust, Fun, Becoming Connected, Awareness, Joyful Movement.*

In a recent week-long workshop where eurythmy was done twice a day with directors of small and medium-sized organizations (ten to fifty staff) some comments were:

> Integrating all skills and new tools turns out to be fascinating. Here is a metaphor for the conflict resolution work. As we negoiate who will pass what ball to whom and how, we are learning to integrate the very skills of listening, reflecting, leading and following.

> Creating awareness of the people we work with. Every person is of equal importance. Every person is part of the whole. One person can affect the whole.

> Eurythmy helped me to integrate my thoughts by giving me space and breath. I realized that my body needs more physical movement on a daily basis.

We need to be in tune with one another, lead together and know in which direction we are going.

Moving individually in a group toward a common goal.

To move as a group you must attend to the group, not just the self.

Are there any challenges that Barbara has faced in doing eurythmy in the workplace? "Yes. Often the CEO gets it and has to then sell it to his managers, but they do not understand it in the abstract. It has to be experienced. In one company with many Polish workers, the rank and file caught on immediately thanks to their long traditions of dancing. It was middle management that objected the most. Managers are often afraid of losing face. Many CEOs, once convinced, want everyone to do it. Workers are often just plain grateful for a change of pace to the daily routine."

After an opportunity for the majority of workers to experience eurythmy in the workplace three times over the course of a few days, participants can fairly decide if they want to participate on a regular basis and managers can decide if they want to offer it to their workers. Then an organization or company can schedule blocks of time such as two weeks every six months, or three weeks each year, where eurythmy in the workplace would be offered each day for small groups (ten to twelve) for half-an-hour.*

Schools and nonprofits can benefit even from a half-day of the exercises. Expenses are minimal, mostly involving travel costs and a small honorarium. The materials used are copper balls and rods (which give an immediate return on warmth) and a large space in which to move.

✤

---

* The study done for the booklet by Michael Brater, et al., *Eurythmy in the Workplace: One Company's Story* (Spring Valley, NY: Eurythmy Spring Valley, 1998) measured the time taken for eurythmy along with measurement of electricity, water, and production showed that no production was lost due to time taken for eurythmy. Workers were noticeably more social in their interactions with each other. *Eurythmy in the Workplace: One Company's Story*, is a condensed version of *Personalentwiklung durch Eurythmie* written by Michael Brater, Ute Buchele and Hans Herzer and published in Germany, ISBN 3-924346-23-2.)

3

PAUSING

BY *CLAIRE M. STANLEY, PHD*
CENTER FOR MINDFUL INQUIRY

Most teachers walk into their classrooms at the last minute, close the door at the start of the class, and begin their two hours, or one hour and thirty-five minutes of teaching without any pause. There is a dashing, breathless quality that drives each day. Get up, get dressed, cup of coffee, drive to school or university, say hello to one or two people, walk down the hall, walk into classroom, begin teaching. No space divides the time of everyday ordinary mind from the time of extraordinary mind, the time when learning begins, the time for the teacher as the vessel, teacher as the impetus, teacher as the firing neuron to place the spark of learning into the students' hands.

What would it be like to pause, even just for a moment to mark a change in time? Like the ships that put up sail when they cross the International Date Line in the Pacific Ocean, is it possible to mark the moment when one has changed from the ordinary mode into the extraordinary? Tara Brach and others talk of a "sacred pause" and although it sounds like something grand, it is but a moment taken intentionally before one begins anew. It is but a breath, felt deeply in the body. It is but a breath that fills the lungs and allows the body stop, to step out of time, out of rush, and into the timeless. The sacred pause and just one breath interrupts life on automatic and brings with it purpose, clarity, wholeness.

Think back on any time you have attended a music concert. The conductor walks onto the stage to the sound of applause. She turns her back to the audience. She does not begin haphazardly, flying into the piece of music as if she has just dashed out of her car, coat dangling off her left arm, cup of coffee in the hand, and briefcase dragging her along through the corridor. She does not ask the orchestra to start playing, or the chorus to begin singing, or the soloist to lift his voice in a way that might suggest that they were running a marathon. She does not send forth a signal to begin a marathon and then simply ask everyone to start dashing toward the end of the time, the end of hours and minutes together until all the time is used up.

No, the conductor stops and pauses. There is a silence in the audience and in the whole space of the opera house or the intimate salon or the theater. Anticipation then mounts in the minds and hearts of the listeners. Awareness and attention arise in each member of the orchestra, or each member of the chorus. Notice how their faces turn upward toward the conductor, notice how they stop, breathe, anticipate the opening of this glorious work of music with joy. Then the conductor lifts her hands, raises the baton and on one beat, moves everything forward. And in that moment, everyone is there, everyone is present, pulsing, muscles in arms and shoulders, muscles in throat and lungs moving in the present moment to create the beauty of the piece, to lift up the hearts of all listeners.

It is possible for a teacher to pause at the beginning or in the midst of teaching in a similar way. Teachers can walk into the classroom and stop, pause to put down their books, briefcase or papers. They can stop, just breathe and be silent for just a moment. They can look out at the students as a conductor looks at each member of a chorus or orchestra. Then they, the teachers, can draw the students into their sphere, touching them with a sense of presence.

Some teachers I know also ask their students to come into a moment of silence before the class begins. This is nothing special but it is extraordinary. Everyone in the room simply sits in silence for one or two minutes. How many minutes of the day are taken in silence? There is a chance for everyone to stop and breathe, to take a sacred pause out from life in the fast lane, to get off of the treadmill, to drop into the moment, and in so doing connect with the timeless.

This pausing is worth its weight in gold, a golden moment as it were, something that says to all those present, "What we are about to do is important. What we are about to do matters. What we are about to do is going to be done with care and joy." So much is communicated by the tiniest of gestures. I once saw a ballet dancer command an audience of thousands by the pointing of one finger. I once saw His Holiness the Dalai Lama speak to eighty thousand people in a sports stadium and command everyone's attention by taking a moment to stop and simply look out into the crowd with a beaming smile on his face, as if he were meeting with a small group of friends in his living room. I once saw a teacher walk into her classroom and then just stop and stand facing her students for a moment. With this simple gesture, the students also stopped and began again from a place of clarity and purpose.

Try this: Practice pausing several times each day, at the beginning or in the midst of your teaching. One of my teachers says, "Being mindful is not difficult to do, it is difficult to remember to do." Take the time to leave the ordinary and take a journey into the extra-ordinary. Take the time to leave the rush, interrupt it, by simply stopping right in the middle of some fast-paced, moving-forward moment in the hectic swirl of your teaching life. Take just a moment; pause to reconnect with mindfulness of breath, sounds or body.

And when you have paused, then take that moment to breathe. Know that as you have taken that one breath, so have your students. See any one person in front of you and know that he or she too is a fragile being just like you whose life depends on just one breath. Know that when there is no more breath, there is no more life. Feel the life in you right now surging and rolling in and out like the waves of the ocean. Feel the space of all of life and then begin again to connect with all that is ordinary in your teaching life but in a fresh and mindful way.

🌱

4

The Birth of the First Waldorf School

BY MILAN DALER

" A people without the knowledge of their past history, origin and culture is like a tree without roots."
—MARCUS GARVEY

If we think of Anthroposophy as a tree, we can imagine the concept of the Threefold Social Organism as being one of its major branches and Waldorf education and its living pedagogy a tender green shoot sprouting from this branch. To make this image consistent with what Rudolf Steiner had to say about the development of Spiritual Science, however, we have to picture this tree as growing upside down, with its roots embedded in the sky and its branches and buds reaching toward the ground. For this is how Steiner once described Anthroposophy: "It is like an upside-down plant, with its roots in the heavens (the world of the spirit) and its blossoms and fruit in practical life on Earth."

As any gardener knows, for blossoms and fruit to mature, the conditions—soil, climate, rainfall—have to be just right. And this exactly describes the circumstances surrounding the origins of the first Waldorf School in Stuttgart, Germany, at the end of World War I.

Those of us who currently enjoy the good fortune of working as teachers and administrators in Waldorf schools and institutes throughout North America are now entrusted with tending these still new and fragile blossoms and fruits, and with this trust comes also a solemn obligation, perhaps even duty, to all those who were there at the very beginning in Stuttgart and Dornach. Without their immense enthusiasm and sacrifice for the realization of what Steiner called the threefold social organism, we and our students would have no Waldorf schools to enter every morning.

For this reason alone, among many others, we owe it to our founders—the "forerunners of the forerunners"—to make ourselves familiar with their story (which is also our story) and always to remember our roots.

To tend our precious inheritance wisely and effectively, we must continuously renew our own relationship to Anthroposophy and to Waldorf pedagogy. And we also need to remind ourselves that we are not alone in this venture but a part of a thriving worldwide movement with far-reaching goals.

In a few years' time, we will celebrate the hundredth anniversary of the opening of the first Waldorf school in 1919. How did that happen? How did the school come into being? What led up to this event?

To explore these questions, it is important to appreciate the significance that Rudolf Steiner's idea concerning what he called "the Threefold Nature of Social Life" has for us and for our schools. It is most certain that the Waldorf Movement would not be here today were it not for the great wave of hope and enthusiasm that was felt across Europe between 1917 and 1922 by those who participated with Rudolf Steiner in the gradual unveiling of his blueprint for social renewal so sorely needed at the end of World War I. It was the first time—indeed, the only time—that Rudolf Steiner engaged in a full-scale political campaign, sensing clearly a one-time window of opportunity opening to rescue humanity from continuing on a path of conflict and destruction.

In this context, then, the stage was set for the inauguration of the first Waldorf school in the aftermath of the tragic events wrought by the First World War, sometimes referred to as the Great War, with casualties and atrocities on the scale humanity had never seen before. In the words of Karl König, founder of the Camphill movement and a devoted student of Rudolf Steiner, World War I was one of the most powerful historical events in the entire development of humankind.

Before Waldorf education could enter the world, three distinct streams had to flow together simultaneously:

1. An Austrian (Eastern) stream in the person of Rudolf Steiner
2. A German stream (the realm of the Middle) in the person of Emil Molt, "Father of the Waldorf School"
3. An American (Western) stream in two persons: William Waldorf Astor (1848–1919) and his cousin John Jacob Astor IV (1864–1912), who died on the *Titanic*

As my dear colleague and friend Christof Wiechert pointed out recently, this earthly constellation beautifully mirrors the words of Rudolf Steiner in the Foundation Stone Meditation:

> *Let from the East be enkindled*
> *what through the West takes on form.*

Indeed, a golden thread of anthroposophic pedagogical renewal was gradually taken up, first "from the East" by Rudolf Steiner—who already in 1906 said, "Should Spiritual Science be called upon to work pedagogically in a practical sense, it would be able to communicate every detail"—and then 13 years later by Emil Molt, who through the infusion of Western-Astorian cash gave Waldorf education its inaugural home in the Uhlandshoehe school building in Stuttgart.

"What does the United States have to do with the origins of Waldorf education?" you may ask. "Didn't it all start in Stuttgart?" Actually, it all began indirectly with a tobacco plantation in North Carolina, without which the conditions necessary for the birth of the Waldorf school might never have occurred.

Our story begins, then, with the first American aristocratic dynasty—and one of the richest. This was the Astor family, started by Johann Jakob Astor (1763–1848), a butcher's son from a village called Walldorf (meaning "village in the valley") set deep in the Black Forest of southern Germany. Young Astor, who emigrated to the U.S. in 1784, made his fortune in fur trade and real estate, becoming the first multimillionaire in U.S. history; by the time of his death he was worth about $20 million (110 million in 2006 USD). His descendants included two cousins, William Waldorf Astor and John Jacob Astor, who really did not like each other. In fact, they fought so bitterly that each decided to build his own huge hotel on 34th Street and 5th Avenue in New York City, one right next to the other. They were to be called Hotel Waldorf and Hotel Astoria. First one was made bigger than the other, then the other was made taller than the first. Finally, business sense prevailed and, by the time the hotels opened, they were combined into one behemoth called the Waldorf-Astoria Hotel.

This is where the North Carolina tobacco plantation comes in. It was originally a part of a dowry belonging to one of the wives of these cousins, and soon it became the source for expensive cigars that were sold to high-end clientele in the hotel's Waldorf-Astoria Cigar Store. The tobacco business prospered, and the cousins decided to try their luck selling their cigars and cigarettes in their ancestral Germany. But since they were no longer Germans themselves and did not understand the intricacies of German markets, their venture went bust and they put up the brand name Waldorf-Astoria and its logo for sale.

Here our story picks up the thread of Emil Molt, a highly paid general manager of Germany's United Cigarette Works, a tobacco expert, and a keen businessman. He was also a spiritual seeker already acquainted with Theosophy, and always on the lookout for new ways of spiritual self-development. In 1902, when the Waldorf-Astoria brand appeared on the market, Molt immediately sensed a great opportunity. He loved the brand's elegant logo and cigarettes. The American style was bold and contemporary; the cigarettes had names like "Chicago," "New York," "Boston," and "Washington"—so different from European cigarettes! He persuaded his partners in United Cigarette Works to make the purchase. It resulted in a huge windfall for the company, and Molt became one of the three partners in the new Waldorf-Astoria Cigarette Company of Hamburg/Stuttgart.

At about the same time as he acquired this new company, Molt met Rudolf Steiner and began to attend, together with his wife Berta, as many of Steiner's lectures as his business commitments would allow. Meeting Rudolf Steiner was truly a pivotal event in Molt's life. He became a close pupil of Steiner in his Esoteric School, adopted a vegetarian diet, and stopped drinking alcohol. He hosted Rudolf Steiner as a family guest every time he visited Stuttgart.

The Waldorf-Astoria factory thrived under Molt's skilled and careful management, his two partners giving him a free hand. By 1906 Molt, barely thirty years old, had oversight of some 1,200 workers and managers. He thought of his workers as members of his extended family, and for as long as the factory flourished—it closed in 1929 almost exactly 10 years after the founding of the first Waldorf school—he endeavored to take care of them and their dependents, including their children. The year 1913 saw a big expansion of the factory, and new buildings were built in hopes of further business expansion. Then came August 1914 and everything changed as Europe's monarchs sleepwalked their way into World War I.

A large number of Molt's workforce was drafted into the army and shipped off to the trenches, but before they went he assured them they would still have their jobs when they returned from the front. To maintain production at the factory, the absent soldiers' wives and daughters were trained to carry on the work. Molt kept in touch with soldiers in the trenches by sending them packets of Waldorf-Astoria cigarettes, which also included cards on which were printed brief excerpts from the basic books of Rudolf Steiner. When at the end of the war the soldiers began coming home and turning up at the factory gates, Waldorf-Astoria all of a sudden had a great surplus of workers, since Molt refused to let anyone go. To keep everyone engaged, the factory started offering adult education classes in many subjects during the work days, which meant that the workers were actually paid to learn. Other employee benefits offered by Waldorf-Astoria included free recreation in factory-owned vacation homes and an in-house savings bank paying more than five percent interest.

Then one day, in the early spring of 1919, one of the workers proudly told Emil Molt how his young son had been offered a place in a prestigious private high school, but sadly would not be able to go because the family couldn't afford the tuition. The story deeply touched Molt, and since by this time he was already very active in the Movement of the Threefold Social Organism, speaking on the subject to large audiences, an idea came to him to start a factory-sponsored school for the children of his employees. With great excitement he shared this idea with his wife Berta, who wholeheartedly supported the initiative.

On April 23, Rudolf Steiner came once again to visit the Molts, and with feelings of some trepidation Molt asked Herr Doctor what he would think of such an idea. Steiner's enthusiastic reaction was, "Yes, yes, I have been waiting for it!" Molt revealed that he had already set aside a tidy sum of 100,000 Marks for the project. Steiner's reply—that this was a very good sum to begin with—must have made Molt's jaw drop. Indeed, by the time the school opened in September 1919, a little more than three months later, this amount had been spent many times over, personally financed by Molt mostly, and partly by Waldorf-Astoria, as well. Steiner agreed to become the school director, Molt received the title Father and Protector and Berta Molt was called school mother. E. A. Karl Stockmeyer set out to find teachers, all of whom were vetted and approved by Steiner and hired as employees of the Waldorf-Astoria cigarette factory.

We need to return now to the story of the threefold social organism. While the armies of the world powers were destroying each other and everything in their path, Rudolf Steiner was working tirelessly as a counterbalance to their attacks. In 1916, while holding many lecture cycles, traveling across Europe, and overseeing the building of the first Goetheanum, Rudolf Steiner wrote a slender volume entitled *Von Seelenraetseln* (*Riddles of the Soul*), in which he first elaborated his idea of the threefold human being.

In this book, he describes the human being in terms of three different spheres: a nerve–sense organization, a rhythmic organization, and a metabolic-limb organization. These are not to be thought of as being independent of one another, but rather as three distinct systems with interpenetrating functions. Similarly, Steiner characterized society as complementing this organization with three social spheres: cultural–spiritual, law and rights, and economics.

In terms of the human being, on this view, the nerve–sense organization, concentrated in the head, receives impressions like a mirror. The metabolic–limb organization is essentially active and transformative, with its defused center in the lower portion of the torso. Creating a balance between these two organizations (one centered above and the other below) are the functions of breath and heartbeat that constitute the rhythmic organization of the middle.

In this way we recognize the nerve–sense organization as the bearer of thinking, the rhythmic organization as the bearer of our feeling life, and the metabolic-limb system as the bearer of our life of will. In our head consciousness we are awake (at least for a portion of the time), in our rhythmic system lives dream-consciousness, and in our metabolic–limb system we are lastingly asleep.

Experiencing these three systems as a synthesis within the individual human organism is prerequisite to gaining any kind of understanding of the idea of the threefolding of the social organism since the one is the reflection of the other. According to Steiner, the renewal of social life will emerge gradually—and only from the spiritual–cultural life, not from the economic or the rights spheres.

In 1917, Rudolf Steiner was approached by Count Otto von Lerchenfeld, one of his closest students, with the question of how Germany could extricate itself honorably from the war and save the world from further senseless destruction. Steiner had been waiting for this question and, already on the next day, presented Lerchenfeld with a brief and beautifully handwritten memorandum containing the very first description of the threefold structure of the social organism and its lawfulness. Lerchenfeld, who was highly connected in the German government, promptly delivered this memorandum to Crown Prince of Baden, the Chancellor of the German Empire.

In the senior Austrian circles, a similar initiative arose from Count Ludwig Polzer-Hoditz (also a very close friend and pupil of Steiner), who had access to Austrian Emperor Karl through his brother Arthur. Another memorandum was promptly dispatched, this one hand-delivered to the royal court in Vienna by a future Waldorf teacher, Walter Johannes Stein, who was convalescing in Dornach from the war. Since at that time it was highly illegal and risky to be transporting written documents across the borders of war-torn Europe, it is reported that when asked to deliver the memorandum, Stein promised that if captured he would swiftly eat the document. Similar memoranda were delivered to many other leading personalities of the time, but none of them was willing to give it serious consideration.

We know what came next. In 1918 Germany and Austria capitulated, an armistice was signed, and the disastrous consequences of the Treaty of Versailles were set in motion. An exhausted and decimated Europe was hungering for change. All of its emperors had been toppled by revolutions. Great power vacuums opened up among the fledgling new democratic governments. Into this turbulent milieu Rudolf Steiner and a few of his colleagues stepped with a bold and even desperate push to gain support for a Threefold Commonwealth. Steiner knew that the clock was ticking and that to avert future disasters, it would be necessary "to get the threefold ideas into as many heads as possible" before it was too late.

In 1919 Steiner wrote his widely circulated "Appeal to the German Nation and to the Civilized World," again detailing a way to resolve social unrest, but as with the memoranda of 1917, few people were interested. In its conclusion, he wrote:

> We must be clear about this, however: Either we will make the effort to face the reality, or we will have learned nothing from the misfortune [of World War I]. Then what was unleashed by this disaster will continue and will proliferate into the boundless.

We know now that, despite great efforts and personal sacrifices, this valiant effort did not work out, and that, by the end of 1922, this window of opportunity had firmly shut. The people of Europe took up the nation-states ideas of Woodrow Wilson and began their blindfolded march toward World War II. Indeed, Rudolf Steiner warned, "Should not the Michaelic Thought of Social Threefolding be taken up at this time, Europe will be laid waste within thirty years."

What is this threefold structuring of social organism? Just as every person on Earth has needs, rights and talents, so, too, does human society have three dimensions:

- An economic dimension, serving the sum of an individual's physical needs;
- A political dimension, guarding the sum of individual rights;
- A cultural dimension, embracing the sum of individual talents and abilities, including all that we bring with us to Earth as intentions, qualities and characteristics.

By the *economic dimension* we refer to all that is involved in the production, distribution, and consumption of commodities, drawing upon the transformed substance of the Earth's mineral, plant, and animal kingdoms. If we look at all we possess and use during our lifetime—in terms of housing, transport, food, clothing, heat, power and so on—we will see that it all originates in nature and has been transformed by human activity. Of ourselves we produce almost nothing. We come to realize that, in the most basic and practical ways, we utterly depend on one another. Even setting aside moral considerations, we arrive at the need for brother/sisterhood in economic life. The more altruism enters in, the more efficient economic activity becomes. In our economic dealings we are not free, since no one can survive without the basic necessities of life; nor in our economic life are we all equal, since some of us need more than others and the weak cannot produce as much as the strong. When it comes to work, people simply have different strengths and abilities.

As a second consideration, if we are to remain human, we need to have a "place" within the order of other human beings. Within such a community we have rights and must be treated equally with others. Out of this need the sphere of law and democratic state has arisen. Everything that is established as law, regulation, code of conduct, and agreed-upon behavior is the proper sphere of the *political dimension,* of the democratic administration or government. In this sphere *every person's opinion is of equality value and importance.*

In the future we will begin to awaken to a perception of the other— the divine in the other human being. Rudolf Steiner offers an eloquent picture to help this realization: If you stand on the shores of the Pacific

Ocean and scoop up a beaker of water, you can't say, "In this glass, I have the Pacific Ocean." And yet your beaker does contain something of the Pacific Ocean. By the same token, you can't say of another person that he or she constitutes the divine. And yet, in every human being there is a drop, so to speak, of divinity and by virtue of this drop each human being is equal to every other human being. When we awaken to this perception of the divine in the other, when humanity evolves to the point where this reality is recognized, then the realm of law, the realm of the state, will no longer be needed because we will no longer harm one another, we will no longer steal from each other. We will have established an ordering of our society out of this recognition—an ordering arrived at not from without, but from within the human being.

Finally, everything within the social life of the community that promotes human development, nurtures the life of the soul, develops individual skills, searches for knowledge, or fosters the striving for individual achievement and excellence falls within what is referred to as the *cultural dimension* of the community. All education, art, religion, science, entertainment, training, and the work of the judges belongs here. In this sphere of social life, human *freedom* of the individual must be considered as the guiding ideal. We need freedom to be ourselves, to develop the capacities we've brought with us; in short, we could say that the supersensible aspect of the human being must be free.

These are the three spheres or realms of social life that, in their interweaving, each working according to its own inner law and nature, form the unity of human social life in its unfolding through evolution.

It is important that each of these three spheres finds its own center, its own direction. At the moment, economic life is extremely dominant and tends to control much of our cultural life. To a certain extent, it controls the state, too, in that it controls the forming of laws. But these three spheres must be held distinct. Economic life has to find its own ordering; the realm of the state, the realm of rights, must find its own center; and our cultural life must be free, must find its own center also.

Toward the end of his life, Rudolf Steiner was asked what he would say was his most important contribution to humanity. Without a moment's hesitation, he replied that it was his proclamation of the threefold ordering of the social organism.

Can we as Waldorf teachers and administrators, in appreciation of this statement, work together to quicken the coming of this ideal? Yes, most definitely, we can. We can begin simply by occupying our thought life with these ideas on a daily basis, perhaps using them as a lens or a diagnostic tool to view and understand the problems of our contemporary civilization.

As a simple exercise, we can begin taking in the news through this lens and asking questions such as: Which domain(s) of society is (are) involved here? Is there an issue of unlawful interference in one domain by another? A common problem these days, for instance, involves commercial (economic) interests attempting to influence legislation (rights) with the intention of creating greater profits.

So far, the threefold idea has never enjoyed a laboratory in which it could be worked out in practical life. Since it has to do with the arrangement of the whole of social life, it is not possible for a solitary organization to manifest all the principles of a threefold social organism or to be fully threefolded. Only when, in a given geographic region, a sufficient number of individuals and organizations working in all three realms of life—cultural, political, and economic—harmonize their actions in line with threefold principles, will it be possible to have the requisite cooperation necessary to establish the beginnings of a threefold social organism.

↓

NOTE

There are numerous worthy initiatives and movements already taking place, though they continue to work separately. These include:

- community supported agriculture (CSA)
- biodynamic (BD) agriculture
- organic foods
- permaculture
- community land trusts
- sustainable communities
- living wage initiatives
- socially responsible investing and philanthropy
- fair trade practices
- intentional communities
- alternative medicines
- Waldorf education

Implementing Threefold Structure in a High School Community

BY REA GILL

Why do some schools evolve while others dissolve? As it approaches its hundredth anniversary, the Waldorf school movement is still a revolutionary force for social change with not only an educational mission but a social one. After a millennium of much experimentation in self-governance, the movement is now poised to further transform itself and ultimately all organized social life, by modeling a structured "living systems" approach to self-governance. Why is this approach still news? The answer is that, so far, the new approach, referred to here as Threefold Dynamic Governance, has been difficult to implement. Many people are surprised by what they perceive as its rigid structure. Creative people, who happen to be naturally drawn to the Waldorf movement, are apt to balk at the notion that strong will, love and a common vision will not suffice, that formal architecture is needed to enable an effective way of working and decision-making.

The living systems approach of Threefold Dynamic Governance is intuitive and easy to understand as an idea. After all, a social organization can be seen to possess the characteristics of a living organism and so it would follow that you have only to treat it as such and it will emerge, thrive and maybe even have a positive evolutionary effect on the rest of society. Indeed, supported by a specific structure, an organization can become not an amorphous assemblage of warring egos but a reflection of the threefold human being with systems that mirror the same three dynamic sophisticated ones that give life to the human form.

In its highest form, the social organization is semiautonomous (much as the automatic functions the human body perform) and feels somewhat like of a phenomenon. Though it is never perfect, the threefold social organization is a wonder—created by human beings in service to human beings and using inherent and divine architecture. It is perplexing then, to many people, that examples of it are rare in our world.

A School on the Cusp

In October, 2010 I began as executive director at High Mowing School, the oldest Waldorf high school in North America and the only Waldorf boarding school. I could see evidence everywhere of a beloved but beleaguered school lingering on the cusp of its maturity; talented faculty and staff were hard at work despite less-than-plentiful resources and a vague (or not-so-vague) feeling of "stuckness." The students (about 100 of them) were engaged in creating and learning in small classes with devoted teachers and well-formed curriculum and, for the most part, fiercely in love with their school, but feeling an unevenness in the way the school dealt with itself—and them. There was an expressed need for change from many at the school; in the way people communicated with each other, how decisions were "handed down" and the feeling that many voices were not being heard. The consensus was that the school was being hindered by these nagging challenges. It is significant that it was the student council, out of a wish to be more effective and engaged in the running of the school, that first expressed interest in a more effective way to govern themselves and they ultimately adopted the Threefold Dynamic Self-governance structure. The faculty took notice and soon expressed a wish to follow suit!

A process of deconstruction, reconstruction and redifferentiation of the existing structure began. Within two years we had adopted a leadership and operating structure that utilized principles of threefolding with the important addition of principles and processes of a circle-governance structure I had recently discovered. As the structure took hold, a time of measuring the results of our efforts ensued. "What was working and what wasn't?" we asked. Since then, the school has been engaged in the process of fine-tuning the structure. We eliminated the decision-making circles that were the result of overdifferentiation, and consolidated some of the groups, a process that is ongoing and ever-shifting to meet the school's needs but always informed by threefold principles. A survey of teachers and staff (taken in 2013) revealed a sense of relief and even joy, mixed with some anxiety about the sustainability of the change. In 2014, the board of trustees began the process of adopting the new form and operating using the same principles.

Threefoldness and Threefolding

What are they, really, and how do they actually work? People have endeavored for years to establish a clear understanding of the actual practice of utilizing the principles of threefoldness (or "threefolding," as Steiner called it). Because it works at many different levels in a socio-organizational setting and is subject to different interpretations, the insights, benefits and results of threefolding in an organization can be difficult to realize. It is helpful to think of *threefoldness* as similar to a pattern or structure in nature, in which outer layers mirror the inner ones and the whole is a sum of divided and interconnected parts, each reflecting the same structure as the whole. Similarly, *threefolding* can be understood to be a practical way of ordering structure and processes in an organization to consist of the three realms in all levels, such that each is unique to itself and its function, and in the image of and touching the rest, or threefolding upon threefolding within threefolding. The table on the following page illustrates aspects of threefoldness.

Society itself possesses three forming impulses that give life to the three social systems or spheres of activity—the cultural, political (legal-financial) and economic spheres. Understanding the development and differentiation of the three human physical systems and getting a sense of the nature of the forming forces that guide the development of these systems, along with how these unseen forming forces also are at work at a social level in the differentiating organization and in the threefold society, can help people effectively serve and provide stewardship for the developing organization.

THREEFOLD PRINCIPLES AT WORK IN LIFE			
exists in society as	cultural–spiritual sphere	political (legal–financial) sphere	economic sphere
exists in the human being as	spirit	soul	body
exists in the human body as	head	heart	hands
exists in human systems as	nerve–sense	rhythmic (respiratory–circulatory)	metabolic–limb
exists in human activity as	thinking	feeling	willing
exists in a school community as	teachers	trustees	parent body, friends, donors
exists in school departments as	pedagogical	governance (legal–financial)	community and resource development
exists in school leadership circles as	pedagogical leadership circle or a college of teachers	general school circle	community and resource development circle
exists in management staff as	pedagogical administrator	school director or administrator	director(s) of community and resource departments
exists as an impulse as	freedom	equality/rights	cooperation/ brotherhood
exists as an essential activity to	enhance the freedom and creativity of the individual	administer the law and the legal norms; monitor financial health; distribute finances equitably; oversee and regulate effective governance and operations	provide goods, services, human resources and capital that serve needs
exists in a Waldorf school to	administer to the pedagogical life	administer to good governance and legal-financial business	administer to the community and resource development activities

Creating a New Superstructure

A unique form of organizational governance called Dynamic Self-governance was first developed in the 1960s in the Netherlands by Gerard Endenburg—a Quaker entrepreneur familiar with the work of Rudolf Steiner and other philosophers, scientists and educators—as a way to reorganize his family's engineering firm. Endenburg applied the physics of mechanical and electrical systems and the principles of social systems to create a new approach to governance. Sociocracy or Dynamic Self-governance was further developed in the United States and documented by John Buck and Sharon Villines in their book, *We the People: Consenting to a Deeper Democracy*. The method is as it sounds; democracy in a deep, true, humanly plausible sense.

Combining the principles of threefolding with the principles of Dynamic Self-governance, or Threefold Dynamic Governance, results in a sophisticated and elegant structure that functions as an integrated three-fold living system mirroring those of the human being. At High Mowing it has been implemented in all three domains of activity: the *Pedagogical, Legal-Financial* and *Community and Resource Development* (CaRD) areas. Policy-setting circles have been established within various domains of activity. Within the Pedagogical domain, these include the Collegium Circle (or College of Teachers), Pedagogical Leadership Circle, Pedagogical Human Resource Circle, Academic Departments and related student life and other pedagogical committees. There are five academic departments: Humanities and World Languages, Math and Science, Studio Arts, Performing Arts, and Movement and Athletics and Student-life committees. Other groups include the Academic, Social-emotional Support, Standards and Cultural Life Committees, as well as the Residential Life Circle.

The circles and groups are interconnected with members in specific positions who provide a double link between circles. These positions include the circle Operational Leaders (downward or feedback link) and Representatives (upward or feed-forward link). Each circle has clearly defined membership, which includes participants who work in

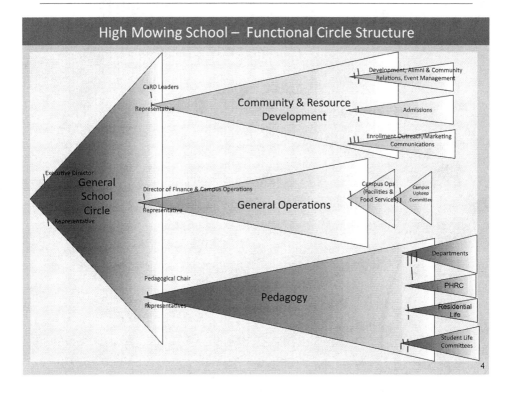

At Work in Life
Threefold Dynamic Governance "Circle" Structure

and have a vested interest in the defined realm, Elected Representatives from the next level circle, an Operational Leader and an appointed Circle Facilitator and Circle Administrator (secretary). Every circle has a unique and specific aim and articulated domain of responsibility. Each circle or group has regularly scheduled meetings with agendas prepared in advance and minutes that record the meeting. Each Circle Administrator (secretary) records decisions, communicates the decisions to the appropriate people or groups and tracks and notes when those decisions need to be reviewed by the circle at some point in the future. The school's student government (Student Council) also operates with a Threefold Self-governance circle structure, which interfaces with the Pedagogical structure.

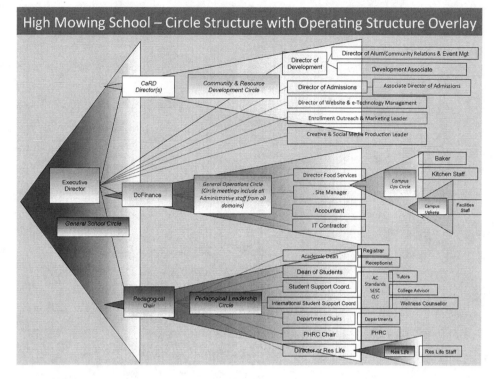

At Work in Life
Operating Structure Overlay—Threefold Dynamic Governance "Circle" Structure

All of the established internal groups meet as full circles when setting policy. When addressing operational issues, operational leaders (not necessarily all circle members) meet to address the day-to-day business as it arises. This is one of the most important principles of a Threefold Dynamic Governance structure: Circles set policy; Operational Leaders oversee the implementation of the policies set by the circles. In other words, rather than the policy-setting circles becoming bogged down dealing with day-to-day operational issues, regular meetings of various operational leaders are convened to address day-to-day issues in a timely way, guided of course by the policies set by the appropriate circles. Operational issues are also resolved in various other ways including within a bracketed session within the regular circle meeting, or in ad hoc meetings, conversations and stand-up, or informational meetings.

Communication and Transparent Information System

High Mowing School currently uses Google Drive (or Google Docs) as the primary system in which to store and share agendas, minutes, reports and other information—this creates an institutional memory for all nonsensitive material. In the interest of transparency, all High Mowing School employees and trustees have access to view all of this material. There is also a weekly all-school report distributed to the entire community, which contains snapshot reports about work being done, announcements, and decisions made by all circles, groups, committees, and operational leaders.

Operating Structure

In addition to the circle structure that provides the form in which the setting of policy, guidelines and direction for the various areas takes place, as mentioned above, there is a corresponding operating structure, which provides the form for how the school implements policy in day-to-day operations. This allows for the smooth operation of the school by empowering the operational leaders, as well as all of the people in operational positions in all realms of activity and departments, to act. This ensures they can accomplish their daily tasks while guided by the *policies set by the circles*—not only in the pedagogical domain but in fact, across the entire organization. This creates a complete picture of ordered and sensible overall governance and day-to-day operations, which is the result of interconnected circles of empowered individuals, whereby all employees are engaged as equals in decision-making around policy-setting within their specific domains of activity defined by threefold principles. Ultimately, every employee serves, with equal influence—or equivalence—on at least one policy-setting circle, and every operational leader is authorized by the appropriate circle to ensure the policies set by the circle are implemented in service to the circle's aim.

Circle Processes

This dynamic threefold self-governance circle and operating structure epitomizes the well-known phrase by Aristotle "The whole is greater than the sum of its parts." It is an elegant and effective way to tap into the power of the circle and utilize processes in which everyone is equivalent where appropriate (i.e., policy-setting). It gives operational leaders access to the wisdom of the membership of the entire organization and empowers processes that think smarter than any one individual operational leader can think. In addition, equivalent and collaborative processes in the circles provide opportunities for self-knowledge, knowledge about and appreciation for the others and a transformative and continuous learning process.

The *Circle-structure Diagrams* illustrate a two-dimensional, flat representation of the circle structure, with each circle represented by a triangle. The triangle is an expression of the activities of the circle— *Lead-Do-Measure*. Each level of circles represents a level of abstraction or domain of activity and not necessarily a hierarchy of authority. The work of each domain becomes more concrete moving from left to right through the circle levels, and more abstract moving from right to left. If you were to only look at these diagrams you would perhaps think High Mowing School was structured in a traditional autocratic pyramid power structure. This is *not* the case. To understand the circle and operating power structure as a threefold holistic living system, you would have to translate the entire structure into a three-dimensional model of overlapping differentiated spheres that could be viewed from all angles. But since that is difficult to do, what can be said is that the structure is a network of semi-autonomous circles, which does *not* constitute an autocratic power structure, but rather a *natural* hierarchy with a power structure that is defined by *function* or domain, similar to how human systems work in relation to each other. Each circle consists of membership determined first by the domain of activity, with operational leaders appointed or hired by the next "more abstract" circle plus representatives selected by the next "more concrete" circle(s). The operational leaders and the representatives provide the double links ensuring each circle is connected in two ways to both the next "more abstract" and the next "more concrete" circles. Each circle of people conducts and controls its own processes as people work together to achieve their goals within their specific domain of responsibility, while guided by the broader aim and policies of the whole organization. The circles are also responsible for their own development and for each member's development facilitated by the use of the "measure" principle in the Dynamic–Self-governance approach described by John Buck and Sharon Villines. Each circle, at each circle meeting, conducts a closing round where feedback is gathered from each member about the effectiveness of the meeting and the work done in the meeting. This allows for growth, improvement and development of the circle, and the individuals, and therefore of the entire organization. The diagrams above help to illustrate the difference between the *policy-setting activity* of the circles, and the *implementation of policy* by the people in operational positions.

OVERVIEW OF THE CORE PRINCIPLES OF THREEFOLD SELF-GOVERNANCE

*Core Principle of a Threefold Social Structure**

The use of the term *threefold* when characterizing a social or governance structure is reference to a principle that describes organizations as dynamic living social entities—responsive, changing, growing and learning—created by human beings and therefore reflections or projections of the same archetypes that exist in the human being. Beginning with this foundational idea, living organizational social systems can be intentionally modeled on mental pictures formed out of a study of the formation of the physical living systems in a developing human being. In this way, such a correlation (not a direct equation) can be drawn between the development of human systems and the development of organizational systems. Understanding the development, differentiation and functioning of the interconnected and interdependent human

---

* For a more in-depth description of threefold principles at a socio-structural level, see my book *A School as a Living Entity*.

systems can provide insight into how an organization develops and functions as a living entity.

Core Principles of Dynamic Self-governance*

Dynamic Self-governance guiding principles describe practical methods and mechanics, which can work in conjunction with a threefolded structure with three independent, interconnected realms of activity. The guiding principles, practices and processes of Dynamic Self-governance provide the practical tools for how the various independent interconnected circles of activity, and the human beings within them, can work within and in relationship to each other, which ultimately enables an effective and functional organization.

Principle 1: *Consent governs decision-making.* Consent means that there are no argued or paramount objections to a proposed policy decision. Policy decisions need to be made with the participation and consent of those they most affect (Note: this is very different from consensus). It is important to define the method of decision-making for all proposed guiding policies. Maintaining consent for guiding policies reduces friction and inefficiency. It maximizes creativity and productivity and ensures that decisions will be made in ways that respect the needs, capabilities, and limits of all who are affected by them. While *policy decisions* are made by consent, day-to-day operational decisions are NOT necessarily made by consent. Rather, the people responsible for implementing policy at an operational level within a specific domain—the operational leaders—decide how various *operational decisions* will be made (autocratic, consent, majority vote etc.).

Principle 2: *A circle is a semi-autonomous and self-organizing unit with a unique aim.* Policy decisions are made within the defined domain of the circle; the leading, doing and measuring functions are delegated to the circle's own members; the memory system is maintained by the circle; circle development is planned by circle members. The structure of an organization needs an adequate number of defined circles or domains

---

*   The principles of Dynamic Self-governance are summarized from the description in the book *We the People* by John Buck and Sharon Villines. It offers a description of how the principles are applied within an organization.

Threefold Human Being

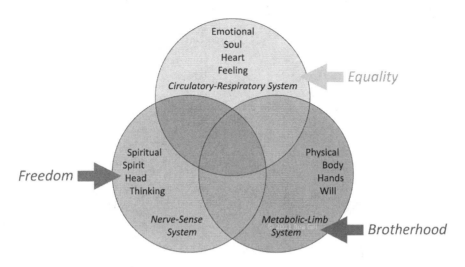

Steiner's Threefold Social Order

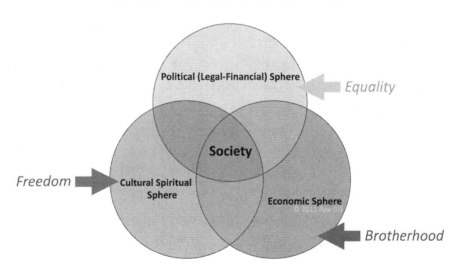

Threefold Organizational Structure Threefolded

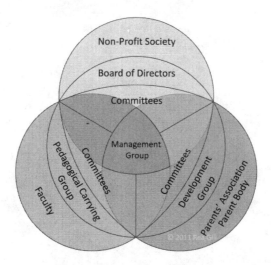

of responsibility that meet regularly, with clearly defined aims and objectives, with responsibilities defined so that those aims can be accomplished. Work processes and procedures must be articulated so that the work of the spheres of responsibility is uniformly guided. Election of members to functions and tasks must take place and those functions and tasks must be designed and defined.

A circle, or domain of responsibility, consists of an elected or appointed group of people assigned to a set of tasks determined by the aim, which is defined by the circle at the next higher level of abstraction. The circle is a semiautonomous, self-organizing, organic entity capable of responding to the environment, according to need, as the circle functions in service to accomplishing the defined aim. Each circle of members has three functions:

1. a "leading function" in that they determine what they are going to do in service to the aim
2. a "doing function" that determines how they will do it
3. a "measuring function" that determines what data is needed in order measure their success and to ensure they are going in the right direction.

The *leading* (planning, scheduling, assessing and setting criteria), the *doing* (delegation and assigning of tasks) and the *measuring* (progress toward accomplishing aims and objectives) functions are clearly defined

242

and assigned (see Principle #4), a memory system is maintained (log book and minutes), and a program of ongoing development of the circle is designed. Each circle determines and executes their own policy within the limits that have been set, with their consent, by the larger organization. It must be clear where *policy* decisions that govern day-to-day work are made, versus where daily *operational* decisions are made.

Principle 3: ***The connection between two circles is a double link*** formed by 1) the operational leader and 2) one or more representatives who participate fully in the decision-making of the circle at the next higher level of abstraction. Connections are created (double-linking) between the defined circles or spheres of responsibility via *representatives* who give feedback to other circles about the needs of their circle (feedback), and through *operational leaders* who give guidance to their circle about the needs of the larger organization (feed-forward steering). Operational leaders are appointed by the circle at the next higher level of abstraction, and representatives are appointed by the circle to serve on the circle at the next higher level of abstraction.

Principle 4: ***Circles elect people to functions and tasks by consent after open discussion.*** When it is time for the various circles to elect people to functions and tasks, circle members define the associated responsibilities, qualifications, and term of service. Nominations are made and discussed openly with all members of the circle present. Discussion focuses on the job requirements and each nominee's ability to fulfill them. The process is complete when membership consents or, in other words, when there is no expressed paramount objection or when all paramount objections have been resolved.

CONCLUSION

Now in its seventy-third year, High Mowing is a vibrant school of 110 students that gathers her breath in the draft of her rich history and sings out her delight in the moment—and her excitement for the future. The mood is hopeful, collegial and expectant. There is a collective sense of forward direction and a feeling of openness, though tempered a bit by residual disappointment and a mild apprehension, especially by faculty who remember less-stable times when the school struggled to prevail in the absence of its founder. Challenges such as those facing all boarding schools—around enrollment and really meeting the educational needs of young people in today's world—and like in any social system human differences and conflict continue to arise, although there is a new awareness of a practical, "safe" way to address them.

Everyone has suffered in some way the expected shortcomings and mini-collapses of a new governance structure. During busy times it can seem overly time-consuming, but there is a feeling that everyone is involved in decision-making and that everyone's voice is being heard if they are willing to speak up as opportunities arise. This has been especially evident in the work in the pedagogical circles, where for the past two years the High Mowing School faculty, with input and participation from the student council and the support of the new circle governance structure, has redesigned the programming to contain the necessary elements of an effective, purposeful, twenty-first century high school education resulting in innovations and a unique schedule—an organic step toward further innovation and growth going forward. The lead, do and in particular, measure activity of the circles in the school structure have enabled an ongoing transformative process to take place. The curriculum and program at High Mowing is now on the cutting edge, along with the governance and operating structure.

Because it is a new democracy, the school's new governance is somewhat fragile. My hope, beyond the success of the continued effort to integrate all of the benefits of Threefold Dynamic Governance at High Mowing, is that the school will be able to provide for its ongoing maintenance someone or a group appointed to coach, retrain and refresh circle members and watch for reemerging old patterns to keep the process alive and vibrant and continuously evolving for years to come in service to both the educational and social mission of Waldorf education.

🌱

6

PUBLIC WALDORF

By Rainbow Rosenbloom

When I first met Waldorf education as a college student, I recognized it as a revolutionary movement, bringing change to the dominant paradigm that education was simply a process of transmitting and receiving information. The notion of creativity as central to the educational process was crucial, as well as understanding the human being differently, and not simply a blank tablet to be written upon or an empty vessel to be filled; rather, it is a complex individual with a unique destiny, as well as having numerous capacities requiring development, guided by renaissance men and women called Waldorf teachers.

The complexity of Waldorf education allows for observers and practitioners alike to select an aspect to trumpet loudly, and can even define Waldorf itself. For example, some are drawn to the beautiful and artistic aspect; for them, Waldorf *is* art. The lovely blackboard drawings, main lesson books filled with beeswax crayon drawings, wet-on-wet watercolor paintings, clay modeling, daily singing and recorder playing, school choirs and orchestras and, of course, class plays—these activities differentiate Waldorf from other educational approaches.

Others will emphasize the developmentally appropriate curriculum, leading the child from the immediate in space to the distant, while beginning with the distant in time to the modern. Recognizing sequence, not only in history and geography, but in science; beginning with the closest in the animal kingdom, progressing through the plants, minerals, and finally into the far-reaching elements of outer space brings a magnificent intelligence to studies.

Still others will focus on the role of teachers, those who stay with their classes for several years, meditating nightly on the children, working with the unique temperaments of the children and collaborating with the parents. Tirelessly preparing for each main lesson block, attending weekly meetings with colleagues, and serving on countless committees all combine to create a loving and devoted teacher, attentive to the needs of the constantly evolving child.

Yet is it then true, that one need only apply these strategies, these *methods,* to a school program to create a Waldorf school? This is the question facing many teachers, administrators and parents as the public-charter movement embraces Waldorf education.

BEGINNINGS

There are public-school districts that have initiated Waldorf programs, most notably the Milwaukee Urban Waldorf School in 1991 and Sacramento Unified with Alice Birney, Carver High School and A. M. Winn. For the purposes of this chapter, however, I focus primarily on the nearly-fifty charter schools inspired by Waldorf education. The charter schools are tied to the mission, vision and the answers to the elements given when the charter was granted. Thus, the commitment to the tenets of Waldorf education can be more easily determined, as well as the probability that the school will continue to exist after the founders have moved on. There may be many individual teachers in U.S. public and private schools employing Waldorf strategies and methods; there may also be schools integrating aspects of a Waldorf approach in their curriculum and/or pedagogy. This is a growing trend that will only increase as Waldorf education becomes more widely known. However, *charter schools* with a defined commitment to Waldorf education will be emphasized for this chapter.

Ever since the first Waldorf charter was granted (Yuba River) in 1994 in Northern California, the groups forming these schools all had these same basic characteristics:

- commitment to bringing the Waldorf curriculum and pedagogy into the public sphere;
- commitment to staffing the school completely with Waldorf-trained teachers;
- desire for universal accessibility to the school regardless of finances.

One could say that these three tenets are held by founders of independent Waldorf schools as well; yet the accessibility aspect has become exceedingly difficult as the burden for financial stability continues to fall upon the shoulders of the parents. Even well-intentioned schools with tuition assistance programs depend upon wealthy families to insure the viability of the school. In fact, many of the charter school steering committees are populated with parents who cannot afford even part of the tuition costs of the private Waldorf schools.

PUBLIC AND PRIVATE WALDORF DIFFERENCES

Thus, independent Waldorf schools and public charter schools inspired by Waldorf education may arise out of similar impulses. Yet they are also quite different, and these differences need to be outlined. I'm going to focus on four major differences.

First, and most importantly, tuition cannot be charged in public charter schools. The state funds the schools in the same way that traditional public schools are funded, though the formula for specific dollars allotted will vary from state to state.

Second, children cannot be denied admission. If they satisfy residency requirements, and register during the enrollment period, they are admitted. If the school is oversubscribed, a lottery is held, and the registration will then include a random drawing. In many schools siblings of enrolled children, as well as children of staff, are given priority.

Third, the students in charter schools must take the standardized tests required of all public school children in the U.S. In addition, the integrity of the state content and Core Curriculum standards must be maintained in each grade. Thus, most of the public Waldorf schools work actively to align these standards with the Waldorf curriculum.

Finally, governance often looks different in a charter school. There is usually a director or a principal who oversees all aspects of the school. Transparency and accountability are mandated by the authorizing school district, and the director is expected to ensure that all processes are held to high standards. In addition, many schools include another administrator who specifically oversees the delivery of instruction. This pedagogical leadership person is sometimes called Director of Instruction or Ed Director and may provide mentoring and establish an evaluation protocol that informs retention and termination of faculty.

So the question arises then: Are these charter schools really Waldorf schools? The differences are clear, but what about the similarities? All the charter schools that join the Alliance for Public Waldorf Education strive to have a faculty filled with Waldorf-trained and state-credentialed teachers. Main Lessons are presented, often with a block rotation exactly like the one given in that grade in an independent Waldorf school. The children work on Main Lesson books, recite poetry, play recorder, sing, and participate in concentration activities each morning. Handwork, foreign language, painting, drawing, gardening, play, and even eurythmy classes can be found in many of the charter schools. The faculty study together, plan the festivals, and collaborate with administration in much of the business.

Nonetheless, one important distinction my colleagues from the independent schools emphasize is that regardless of the appearance of a Waldorf program in the public sphere, we still operate under the authority of school district officials, many of whom do not understand the Waldorf impulse. I have had to defend the use of Old Testament stories in the third grade to one superintendent who was convinced that the study violated the separation of church and state. We called the study *Stories of Hebrew Culture*. I couldn't understand his objection; I reminded him that he had no problem with stories of the Norse gods in the fourth grade, or the Greek and Egyptian gods in the fifth grade, so what was wrong with the Jewish God in the third grade? He eventually relented. So some Waldorf advocates feel that such government interference creates instability and chaos; I believe that it actually builds bridges. This superintendent was now able to appreciate the Waldorf approach as multicultural, exposing children to the narratives and great stories of many cultural traditions. He recognized that this could build capacities for tolerance. For if we develop an understanding and feeling for other cultures through celebrating their stories and rich heritage, we may also appreciate and understand our differences.

In another school district, I had to present the middle school Waldorf science curriculum to the Directors of Instruction for approval. The school I consulted with was only approved up to the sixth grade, and it was now time to expand to seventh and eighth. The conservative district was concerned about science instruction. I brought examples of Main Lesson content for chemistry, physics, astronomy, and physiology, colorfully represented in an imaginative style that was new for them. Their enthusiasm was evident; one director hoped that their traditional science teachers could meet with us to learn to bring more freshness to their lessons.

I can certainly understand this question: Why should we need approval to do what we know is best for the children? Why should we have to defend our approach? However, defending our methods increases exposure to Waldorf education and allows children and families more opportunities to experience it. This is what inspires so many of us in the public Waldorf movement. We are committed to widening the exposure and increasing accessibility so that Waldorf is no longer the best-kept secret in education, but rather a cutting-edge movement that builds important capacities in children, enlivens their imagination, creates curiosity and interest in the world, and builds deep respect for themselves, their peers and all whom they meet each day.

ADMINISTRATION IN WALDORF CHARTERS

The following summarizes four areas of effective administration pertaining to Waldorf charter schools:

- Gate-keeping
- Personnel
- Evaluations
- Becoming a leader

Choice is paramount in public Waldorf, and leadership must understand how to frame it. Parents are choosing this education for their children. Teachers are choosing this approach for their careers. Thus, school developers and administration must ensure that teachers and parents know what it is they are choosing. I call this the "Art of Gate-keeping." In private Waldorf schools, teachers can choose who fits and doesn't fit in their classroom. In public Waldorf, parents choose, but leadership can help the right choice to be made. I remember one specific case many years ago when I was a Waldorf charter school administrator.

A woman came into the office wanting to enroll her five-year-old grandson into our kindergarten. She was the guardian, as his father was in prison and his mother was a drug addict. The poor little boy had already been kicked out of five schools, so the grandmother was just searching for an alternative program. I had no doubt he could thrive in our Waldorf program if she provided the requisite support at home, and if indeed she knew and was enthusiastic about what Waldorf could bring to her grandson. She came in to enroll and, as a public program, we would have to accept him. But first I wanted to make sure she knew what she was choosing, so I described the Waldorf approach. Then I asked her what she was really looking for, what she thought would be most helpful for her grandson. She said that she felt what he really needed was a classroom with a very small teacher–student ratio. I agreed, but then told her that our school did not have such a small ratio but that the Montessori charter down the road did. I suggested that she visit that school, and if she preferred ours, to come back the next day and we would enroll her grandson. I never saw her again, and I'm sure she made the right choice for her grandson.

Gate-keeping is definitely an art. One should always leave the parent or guardian with the impression that they are the one making the decision regarding enrollment, because, in truth, they are. However, it is the responsibility of administration to be transparent about what is being chosen. A public Waldorf program can teach, actually must teach, what it says it will teach in its charter document, or in the agreement with the district. Thus, if the document clearly states the subjects to be taught in each grade, in addition to the Common Core, and it is articulated to the parent, they can make a decision about what they want for their child. When enrolling a fourth-grader once, I remember going over the block rotation with the parent, asking her to initial each block that was to be taught in the course of the year. There would then be evidence that each was discussed and communicated adequately. This parent happened to be a Jehovah's Witness, and when it came to the block on Norse Mythology and my explanation, she disclosed that she didn't want her child to be exposed to such a topic. I told her I understood, and that I would certainly support her in making such a choice for her child, but that at our school, we clearly state that Norse mythology is part of our fourth-grade curriculum. I told her she may want to reconsider enrolling her child in a program where she objected to a subject we were chartered to teach. She ended up choosing a different school but left feeling respected and understood.

It is incumbent upon administration to be informed about all the other choices in the district. Larger district meetings with many directors and administrators serve both to discover what else is being offered and to be an ambassador for what public Waldorf is providing. This bridge-building allows for the public Waldorf administrator to learn about local options, thus informing the recommendation given to parents searching for the right place for their children. Please do not mistake this art of gate-keeping to be a disguised way of selecting only "Waldorf" families for the program! To the contrary, diversity is the life-blood of public Waldorf, and we want as wide a cross section as possible. However, it is actually loving and kind to ensure that the choice being made is arising from an understanding of what a child will experience; it is a function of leadership to try to minimize disappointment as much as possible, while at the same time trying to understand the best possible fit for a family.

PERSONNEL

Trained and experienced Waldorf teachers are extremely hard to find, yet they are critical for a school's success, private or public. Successful administration must recruit actively, throughout the year, and engage a process that is intelligent, thorough, and transparent. Because parents are more actively involved in charter governance, hiring committees will be composed of administrators, parents, and teachers, working in a collegial way to arrive at a decision through consensus.

More often than not, faculty candidates will lack the requisite teacher preparation in Waldorf curriculum and methods. Most states require teachers to have a state credential, and Waldorf charters will support the ongoing training of its faculty to gain Waldorf certification. The puzzle for charter administration is to imagine how quickly a new-to-Waldorf faculty member will take up the work with mentoring and support. I have personally witnessed experienced public school teachers encounter Waldorf and tell me it felt like "coming home." They take up the well-known strategies as though it were natural for them. The key is to devise interviews where such "naturals" can shine.

Administrators in public Waldorf schools provide the accountability required by districts. It is important to visit classes often, unannounced, to monitor both the excellence in teaching and the class management expected. Building the right kind of trust with the faculty will ensure the welcome in each class, right down to the children who happily greet the visiting administrator.

The rich promise of Waldorf unfortunately brings expectations that are sometimes difficult to meet, especially in a new public school. I have seen far too many crises evolve out of personnel issues. Most often it surrounds the new teacher struggling with discipline and not understanding how significant it is to build a community within the classroom. Parents may clamor for a change, and it becomes especially sensitive when governing board members have children in the class. It is one of the most important jobs of the public administrator to listen to parents' concerns and then create a process filled with respect and accountability.

EVALUATIONS

Evaluations are a critical piece in monitoring excellence and providing accountability. Charters must do what they say they are going to do or risk intervention at the district level. The curriculum offered and methods promised are part of the charter document. Administration is tasked with the requisite oversight. Thus, when a problem in a class is noted, immediate measures are required to help bring stability. If evaluations are part of the rhythm of the school, there is a greater chance that early detection of needs will be observed, and that a healthy process that brings confidence to the parents and the board can be engaged.

If the evaluation process determines that a specific teacher requires additional support, that teacher may be put on a "plan of improvement." This plan will stipulate benchmarks to be met by a prescribed time, often in the course of the following year, unless the situation is dire. Outside evaluations, peer reviews, and parent surveys all contribute to the general picture of success or challenge in the classroom. Every part of the process must be documented. Teachers and parents must be assured that the best interests of the children take priority.

BECOMING A LEADER

The last aspect of administration I will address involves the character of the director/principal in a Waldorf charter school. Public Waldorf includes some rather complex relationships. First, the administrator reports to the board, often called the Charter Council, or the Governing Council. This is largely a group of parent volunteers, though some schools have created a professional board of educators and community members. The administrator serves at the pleasure of this group, attends the monthly meetings and reports on the entire organization. This group will also evaluate the administrator and decide upon salary, continued employment, or ending the relationship.

The other administrators (special ed, early childhood, business or operations, and ed director) all report to the executive director, if the school is large enough and organized in such a way. And the teachers report to the ed director and the executive director or principal.

Thus, the administrator of the school must be somewhat of an expert in human relations. One listens with a conscious heart, self-reflects throughout the day, and acts decisively primarily through facilitation of process. Instead of solving problems and fixing things, the successful administrator guides process. This talent is actually the key to becoming a true leader. Curbing one's own reactive tendencies and refraining from blaming others, the public Waldorf administrator can seamlessly provide the leadership arising from selfless striving, modeling the kindness, courage and insight that a community can rely upon.

THE FUTURE

Many groups all over the country are forming to explore the possibility of gaining a charter for a public school inspired by Waldorf education in their communities. The first one on the East Coast, Circle of Seasons, an hour north of Philadelphia, opened in 2013. The excitement is palpable. Neighborhood schools with an inspired curriculum, infused with the arts, emphasizing community in the classroom, and supporting a pedagogy rich in movement, rhythm, and imagination are being developed collaboratively by teachers, parents, and community leaders who want something innovative for their children, literally all over the country.

Enthusiasm is leading to unique development as well. The Kona Pacific Charter School in Hawaii began in 2008 with a threefold purpose: to weave the separate strands of local agriculture, Hawaiian culture, and Waldorf education into a single school, available to all families who wanted to participate. This school now has a lunch program featuring local and organic choices; nearly seventy percent of the children are being fed for free, qualifying as part of a federal program for free and reduced lunch. And most impressively, each morning the entire school gathers in the sacred center of their campus, led in Hawaiian chants and blessings to begin the day. The charter movement is birthing originality far and wide.

Waldorf education belongs to all children, families, and teachers seeking schools with spirit that emphasize enlivening capacities in their students. The need is great and is growing. Recently I spoke with a mother new to Waldorf who only found out about it by searching online for tech-free education. She was desperate for a change. She lives in an afflu-ent suburb of one of the largest U.S. cities, and her local school now has each pupil using an iPad for lessons. The teachers retreat in favor of the iPad doing most of the instruction. This concerned mother has noticed frayed social interactions since this development. The last straw was, however, when her ten-year-old daughter was "caught" reading a book. Her teacher told her to read it on the iPad; she then had to actually sneak the book home to read.

Many predict an explosion of interest in public Waldorf in the com-ing years. It's hard to know just how many small groups are forming to develop schools, but if enquiries to the Alliance for Public Waldorf Education are any indication, steering committees for new charters are arising in many U.S. cities and states. A new Stanford University study praising public Waldorf is about to be released; this will certainly add to the interest and ensuing demand.

We can now only hope that young, vibrant leaders emerge to tackle the challenges of opening and sustaining these new schools. Waldorf edu-cation offers an important and vital alternative to mainstream public education, and it deserves to be accessible to all who recognize its spirit.

Yes, Waldorf education offers an important and vital alternative to today's approach to schooling, and it deserves to be accessible to all who recognize its spirit.

$$\psi$$

7

DIALOGUE AND RESTORATIVE CIRCLES

BY JOHN CUNNINGHAM

"When you stand as a conceiving, thinking human being in the presence of another person, it is a strange fact that the reciprocal relationship that comes about between one person and another brings into existence in your subconsciousness the tendency to be put to sleep by the other person. You are actually put to sleep—'lulled' to sleep—by the other person. You are actually put to sleep in your subconsciousness by the other person. This is the normal relationship between two human beings." —**Rudolf Steiner**, Dec. 12, 1918

With the stage set for the human encounter, each of us brings into the meeting our social and antisocial forces: forces acting only in sleep and forces inherent in the activity of thinking. We defend our thoughts and awake. We rise up conceptual and seek, through our thoughts, to lull the other's thoughts to sleep. Of course, this is all playing out subconsciously, instinctually. And, of course, this is normal! When we meet, we say: "Hi, let my lullaby begin!" to which we respond, "I don't feel like sleeping. You sleep!"

> Thus, when you come into the presence of a person, that person puts you to sleep; that is, your thinking is put to sleep, not your feeling and willing. (Steiner, Dec. 6, 1918)

Here is an important clue. What is it that we mutually seek to put to sleep in the other? It is their thinking, and not their feeling or willing. When the other seeks to put us to sleep, if we wish to remain active in our thinking, we must assert ourselves to wake. Only in this awakening in our thinking can we free ourselves from what the other wills to do. Here

is where conflicting entanglements begin, in a mutually reciprocal asser-
tion of thinking and an equally mutual resistance to sleep.

> We are in great measure antisocial beings with regards to our concep-
> tual life, our thinking, and can become social beings only by educat-
> ing ourselves...it is of utmost importance for us to realize perfectly
> clearly that it is possible to become social beings, to become such
> through self-discipline. (Steiner, Dec. 6, 1918)

Whereas our antisocial forces arise as an evolutionary imperative, we can
only become social through self-discipline.

What can we draw on to understand Steiner's use of the metaphor
sleep? Within the waking state of consciousness, we can find all three
conditions with which we are familiar: waking, dream and sleep. In the
light of everyday life, we are most awake in our conceptual life. In our
feelings, we dream. In our life of will, we are no more awake than we
are in deepest sleep. It is to this realm that we must look if we wish to
become *consciously* social.

To become social, one must be *willing to become other*. In fact, as we
enter into this idea, it opens up worlds. Ron Brady, the philosopher of
Goethean science, characterizes the intrinsically dynamic nature of life
as "becoming other" to maintain itself. Bob Dylan said it as well—"that
he not busy being born is busy dying." In the human encounter, sleep
implies a bit of both. It is a dying of our own antisocial impulse to allow
the other to come to birth in our willed, empty attentiveness. To honor
the spirit within us, we must never cease in becoming and, in the human
encounter, this is becoming other.

Through dialogue, we create our communal world, and to build
bridges between each other through our willing, our *willingness to
become other*. We do this through interest, through a Goethean plunging
into the senses, through allowing the other's thinking to replace our own
such that the other can be understood as the other wishes. We must allow
the other to "presence" within us. We must give our will unto the other
such that their will can shape ours into understanding. And we must let
go of the past, will ourselves out of the stream of necessity so that we can

attend the other's becoming, the stream that approaches from beyond and out of the future.

The classic formulation for what takes place when we confront each other comes from the lecture of December 12, 1918. In no other lecture nor written work did Rudolf Steiner ever return to this in such succinct form. It's a bit like a haiku:

> Of what does human dialogue in fact consist? We have seen that it consists of one person trying to put the other to sleep, while the other tries to resist and stay awake. This is the archetypal social phenomenon of social science, in Goethe's sense of the term.... None of our thinking about social forms can bear fruit if we do not make the effort to take these things into account.

The dynamic context of dialogue is the oscillatory interplay between the *antisocial forces*, forces of waking, self-assertion and self-expression, and the *social forces*, forces of a special kind of sleep, of becoming other, and of understanding. A betweenness is created whenever we dialogue, a dynamic that is drawn together in our willing to be social and pulled apart through our antisocial impulses.

This immensely complex human encounter we call dialogue is how we create our lives together. In that we dialogue *well* with each other, we nurture our shared wellbeing in community. We feel a sense of confidence in others and in ourselves. When our dialogue breaks down, that selfsame confidence falls away. We find ourselves entangled in misunderstandings, distrust, and the antisocial ways we instinctively think about the situation, the other, and ourselves. "Social sleep" becomes labored.

When this breakdown of dialogue occurs and we distance ourselves from each other, we need the means to return to dialogue so that we can work our way through whatever has happened. It is through the clash of our antisocial impulses that dialogue breaks down. In response, we need social forms that support each of us in getting heard as we'd like, but more importantly, that support us in really sleeping into each other. That, of course, is the challenge.

Given what we have learned about the social and antisocial forces, our social form must address the reality of these "intimate" human impulses and create a space for the conscious enactment of the interplay, but in slow motion, in order to bring the instinctual into the light of day. Only with this slowing down of the interplay can we hope to untangle our knots. We need a form that slows us down so mutual understanding can be re-created.

How might we begin to imagine this form? The dialogue must occur within a form for which those involved are co-responsible. Once we realize that we are co-responsible for the context within which whatever has happened has been able to happen, we will also welcome the opportunity and support coming together to co-responsibly create something new within our community from the "mess" we've made together.

The dialogue process must insure mutual access to understanding within that communal context. It must allow each person to speak and be heard, and guarantee the opportunity to be heard and understood. There must be an unconditioned sharing of power, access and opportunity.

To insure mutual understanding, people must each have their own time to speak. They must have the freedom and support to speak what is true for them. To insure we know they've been heard, someone will be asked to agree to listen and reflect the essence of what was said. We create a call-and-response; people speak and are heard by the others. The others listen and reflect back. The speakers confirm or clarify; they are given the right and freedom to decide whether they have been heard or not.

By allowing each to speak, we give people a space to assert antisocially what is true for them. At the same time, we ask listeners to engage their social forces and to listen, to become willing "sleepers." Then sleepers "sleep-talk," so to speak, as they reflect the essence of the significance spoken. To close the loop, the heartbeat of the dialogue process, the speakers determine whether or not they've been understood. Once that happens, others can speak their mind. We call this the dialogue process. This form and the agreements underlying it constitute the ordering within which the conversation evolves.

Notice how the archetypal social phenomenon is brought into consciousness and becomes subject to our communal will, our co-responsive intention. It then supports our mutual understanding and allows us mutually to re-create the narrative and meaning of what has happened.

The dialogue process can also educate us. By experiencing the pendulum swing in slow motion, we can learn to raise this oscillation of impulses further into our awareness and bring this into future encounters within community.

With a communal dialogue process, we begin to create a new restorative social form. We have a heartbeat to and fro in dialogue. This is the essence of what needs to live in any new social form worthy of being called "new" or "social."

We live time in being human, and within our form we must support the trajectory of communal becoming. To do this, we might mark three stages in this conversation whereby we can re-humanize the present, re-humanize the past and then create something new into the future.

What is the "matter" that sets the trajectory in motion? We must identify what it is that matters such that we come together in our form and invoke the support of our dialogue process. What has been said or done that calls us into a circle?

Before we gather to dialogue, we must identify a doorway into what matters. It must unite us in our entanglement; we must agree on an act, a single action arising from a single choice. It must be observable and cleansed of any evaluative staining. That's the event, the matter why we meet.

Who determines the act? It can only be the one who initiates the circle. That's the event, the matter at hand, the reason why we meet. How do we do this? With the guiding question of each stage or round. When we come into the circle, we want a chance to speak to *how we are right now* in relation to the event and its consequences. Here we speak to the present. Then we want to speak to *what we were looking for* at the moment we chose to act, in whatever actions we took. Here we speak to the past. And finally, we want to offer what we'd like to see happen next and enter into agreements with one or more other people in the circle. This satisfies our need to take some steps *to create something new* out of what has been revealed. We want concrete actions and, especially if they come in the form of one-to-one agreements, we set up the possibility that confidence, trust, and deepened connection may also be restored.

We began by speaking of context and now we return. As we enter these restorative circles, we remember that those invited who come are co-responsible for the context within which whatever has happened has been able to happen. Whatever has happened—what we term conflict—is telling us something, alerting to some way in which our community has not developed sufficiently to handle the increasing individuation—the rising antisocial forces—and that we need to come into a circle to dialogue. If this is true, then the one who facilitates or hosts the circle must bear no responsibility for the outcome. It is those who dialogue who shift their co-responsibility from what has happened to what can be created out of what happened. The host becomes responsible for safeguarding the integrity of the form; the participants are co-responsible for the outcome.

There are many further details to such a form. How is such a dialogue process facilitated or hosted and what is the nature of the support a host might bring? How do we begin to grow these forms? What needs to be in place? What are the resources needed?

The form we've begun to create already exists. It is known as Restorative Circles and has a unique birthplace, one of the most violent pockets of humanity in the world. In the mid 1990s, Dominic Barter was an Englishman living in Rio de Janeiro. He found jarring the contrast between the world he inhabited in Rio, and that of the semiautonomous shantytowns run by drug lords. The *favelas* were a world unto themselves and suffered one of the highest murder rates among young men in the world. Despite being warned against it, Dominic was drawn to venture into these enclaves; he entered and sought to engage in dialogue. He had no agenda nor outcome in mind; he allowed the situation to guide him. He survived, and returned time and again. Relationships were formed and he was presented with their struggles.

Foremost among them was their justice system, or more to the point, their justice-by-killing-system. What they needed more than anything was an alternative. Dominic listened and, in a mysterious way, began to midwife a new form of justice. Through trial and error—and enormous courage—the form began to educate him as to what it needed to survive and serve in this harshest of environments. Restorative Circles were born.

Before closing, I want to share a couple of examples. I mention its birthplace to show how robust the form can be. It has shown it can handle extremely conflicted, violent situations. My first example is at the other extreme. It can adapt and support us across the whole spectrum.

In a K–12 urban Waldorf school, I was asked to introduce Restorative Circles. The school had been buffeted with a series of social conflicts and crises over the years, and wanted to be more proactive and create systems school-wide to respond to conflict. Together with my wife, Cat, we gave an introductory training to the staff and faculty of about forty individuals. As follow-up, they asked us to return to a series of staff meetings to facilitate further practice with semi-simulated circles—a form we use to learn the process. As we met before our third visit, the chairperson expressed frustration that key members in the group had begun to push back against the time within the weekly meetings that was being devoted to Restorative Circles. She wanted our help in working with the situation. We proposed that we use a Restorative Circle itself to engage with the situation, and hold it as a fish bowl within the larger group.

It turned out to be a profound experience for all of us. Using the dialogue process with the circle of five, we heard from each person there. Surprisingly, the dialogue revealed that all shared the same longing. They all wanted to develop new capacities to engage with conflict within the school. It turned out there wasn't resistance to Restorative Circles. Rather they wanted confidence that the effort would be sustained over time. They feared that there wouldn't be sustained interest and effort. For those in the wider circle, the experience was compelling and illuminating. The process allowed a dialogue that was safe and more direct than usual to discuss an internal tension or conflict that was beginning to affect other members of the staff. In the end, agreements were entered into and their work with Restorative Circles became even more united. It also showed us that what might appear to be a minor matter on the surface, when engaged with directly, can reap unexpected benefits.

Cat and I hosted a different circle at another Waldorf school. In this case, it was at the end of the school year and within the tight circle formed by the administrator, college chair and faculty chair. Over the course of the year, tensions and rifts and distrust had built up and were impacting the staff as a whole. The three of them approached us asking that we host a circle. In this circle, it was enormously helpful to have the form and slow down what was being shared. Slowly we worked through the antisocial thinking of each of the threesome, both what each wanted understanding around and what was triggered by what an other shared. The form brought to light habits and where they were stuck in their own thoughts. As we proceeded—and we spent nearly two hours in dialogue—gradually things began to shift and move. In the end, there was great relief and a kind of guarded optimism and hope. Agreements were entered into going forward. It is in this process, the making of simple, time-sensitive, concrete agreements, and then the honoring of these agreements, that new social substance can be created. It is this *will* activity that can renew and strengthen community and become a source of resiliency and creativity.

✤

8

SLEEP

BY LYNN JERICHO

Sleep on it. We all know the truth of the benefit of a night's sleep to making a decision or getting a clearer perspective on a question or a concern. Why does this work? How can we actively use the mystery of sleep to live richer lives? Here are some of my thoughts.

The Mystery of Sleep

What is sleep? What happens to consciousness? Where do "I" go when I go to sleep? When I was a little girl, my mother would tuck me into bed and tell me I was going to Lily White's party, which referred to the white bed sheets. I loved the idea because it seemed to make sense that when I went to sleep I was going somewhere where others would be interacting with me. However, my living body was there in the bed so how could I be going somewhere else?

When we fall asleep there is a separation. Our soul and spirit separate from our living body and from the world and life of our senses to enter what is called the spirit world, the supersensible realm of Source beyond time and personal story. There we are refreshed and restored.

Each time we sleep we cross the threshold between waking and sleeping twice. Once when we fall asleep and then when we wake up. The thresholds of sleep are similar to a death and birth of earthly, sensory consciousness. Thresholds hold rich meaning for us. We cross thresholds when we enter into different space or begin something new and we reach thresholds of magnitude or intensity that must be exceeded for a certain reaction, phenomenon, result or condition to occur or be manifested.

When we sleep on a decision, question or concern we seek a new or intensified sense of selfhood. We reach and cross thresholds. Sleep is a spiritual activity. In meditative practices, we essentially work to create the phenomenon of sleep without sleeping, while remaining awake.

There are three spiritual activities during sleep:

1. We spiritually "digest" all that has entered our consciousness during the previous waking time.
2. We offer the spiritually digested, morally alive content of our earthly day to the spiritual, "akashic" records.
3. We receive insight, guidance and comfort from spiritual beings inspiring new thoughts and understandings, clarification of feelings and directions for impulses for actions and deeds for the future.

While we are sleeping and in this state of separation, our living physical bodies are also actively regenerating. Healing and (re)growth take place during sleep. Consciousness (thinking, feeling and willing) uses up the resources of our living physical bodies. The brain is only two percent of our body but uses at least twenty percent of our energy. If you think a lot, are emotionally intense or very active, you are using far more than twenty percent. When your soul or consciousness is finding its resource in the spirit world and not depending on your brain, heart or gut, your living body can use the creative, renewing energy of life to restore, heal and grow itself. Ideally, every night your living body becomes a better earthly home, servant, vehicle for your consciousness and your inner divinity.

Preparation for the Spiritual Activity of Sleep

We can certainly just fall asleep in simple physical exhaustion. In this case, we still go into the spiritual world, we still get inspirations, and our living physical bodies still restore, heal and grow. However if we consciously prepare for sleep, the benefit is much more powerful. Preparation for sleep is a discipline requiring self-awareness and self-regulation, which can challenge your tired soul. You would prefer to brush your teeth, read a few pages and fade into dreamland. However, beginning a practice with the following preparations you will find sleep is much more restorative and inspiring.

These preparations are best done sitting up on the edge of your bed. I keep thinking about them once I am under the covers when it is all too easy to fall asleep in the middle of the exercise (which I often do). As I write this, it's occurring to me to use my meditation timer (I use the insight timer app on my iPad—it announces that time is up with the sounds of a variety of Tibetan gongs.)

This preparation is not prayer or supplication, nor is it meditation. You are opening a particular pathway in your soul to the guidance available during your sojourn in the spiritual realm of sleep.

Sleep Preparation Practices

Review of the Day: This is a slow methodical review of the day. You do the review backward as if you were unwinding something you just wound up. Essentially, you are recollecting, reviewing and releasing the sensory perceptions and the material expressions and impressions of the day.

You are undressing the day and getting it ready for bed. You wouldn't go to bed with your clothes on, would you? If you did you probably wouldn't feel like you'd had a good night's sleep. So undress your soul from all it put on during the day. Here are some of the ways you can undress your soul:

- Think of your interactions with others during the day (you might include all the people you thought about).
- Think of all the activities of your day—work activities, home activities, the things you did and the things you thought about doing. Try not to load them with emotions but keep your judgments neutral.
- Think of your experiences of nature.
- Think of your experiences of material things.
- Think of your feelings during the day—anxiety, annoyances, delight, sadness; try to do this with equanimity.

Now put on your soul pajamas.

Ask a Question: Each night before you go to sleep, ask an open question. You are not asking for a specific outcome when you ask an open question. How can I resolve my confusion about...? How can I find an organized structure on which to find clarity and certainty? I am concerned about my child (or another person); is there something I can say, do, feel or meditate on to support that person's life? I feel I must make a decision or take action in a particular situation; how do I make the right choice, do the right thing, make the right change and let go of my anxiety?

The gesture must be open. Imagination, inspiration and intuition come only to those who are free. If you have an agenda, you will block your development during sacred sleep.

Speak with the Dead and the Unborn: This is also the time to speak to members of your karmic community that have crossed the threshold of death. Imagine them with warmth and light, then ask them a question or invite them to help you. If you are aware that your deed is significant to the future, you can also reach out to those unborn human souls that are close to a new incarnation. Ask these souls for direction for your will as your waking life will be shaping the world they are born into.

I have found that it may take perseverance in your questions to find the response to them. You may need three or seven or twelve or twenty-eight repetitions of the questions, asking the questions in different ways, before you find your soul hearing the response. Be patient and be devoted.

Have a good night's sleep in the spirit world. You will wake up to a new you, a new perspective, a new understanding and a good day's waking.

🌱

9

THE ROLE OF TEACHER–ARTISTS
IN THE SEVENFOLD WALDORF SCHOOL

BY REG DOWN

Education is a cultural affair. Waldorf schools pursue a holistic, child-centered ideal: to maintain and engender creative capacities within children. It does this via art. Not that the goal is to be an art school, but to permeate the curriculum with artistic activity. This means that all Waldorf educators, regardless of subject taught, must be artists.

Waldorf schools, however, are made up of more than just teachers and children. They are institutions whose function is to create a space for the teacher and child to meet. Clearly, the relationship the teachers hold vis-à-vis the children cannot be quite the same as that held with the school organization. How can we understand the role the teachers play within the organization of a Waldorf school as cultural institution?

The words addressed to the teachers by Rudolf Steiner at the founding of the first Waldorf school in Stuttgart, which has subsequently been used as a meditative picture within colleges of teachers, gives us an image of what stands behind a striving group of educators. Behind each individual stands their angel; above that is the working of the archangels; above that again is the wisdom-working activity of the archai. Steiner was reminding the teachers they were not alone; that collegiality includes more than their personal selves. In principle, this picture can become a working reality for any progressive group. For a college of teachers who guide a school culturally it is of especial importance.

The description Steiner gives in this "meditation" is a familiar one [10]: human beings, angels, archangels, archai. Directly connected with this hierarchical picture is one relating to the higher members of the individual human being: "I," spirit self, life spirit and spirit body (sometimes called spirit man).[1] When we have fully achieved spirit self we will be (like) angels; when life spirit is achieved, archangels; when spirit body is achieved in the far-distant future, archai.

When visiting a Waldorf school we meet the *faculty,* getting to know them as individuals and sensing how they relate as a group. We experience how the character of the school is affected by who they are, and how they work together.

If we return a few years later faculty members may have left and the group working changed; the school, however, has retained its essential personality. What we are now recognizing is the element *unique to each individual Waldorf school.*

Visiting a number of schools, we perceive each school as part of an educational *movement,* which includes more than just the schools themselves: national associations, colleges, teacher trainings, foundations, publications, and so forth, are all involved in maintaining and developing the Waldorf education movement.

Looking further afield, we see the Waldorf school movement as only part of a much larger phenomenon symptomatic of a *global awakening.* This presents itself in an almost overwhelming variety of initiatives within civil society, resurgent or freshly minted religions and philosophies and attempts to grasp the world in an integrated synchronistic manner. As part of this global awakening, the practical endeavors and spiritual-scientific worldview of Anthroposophy and its daughter movements finds its place.

We can summarize our brief overview thus:

Archai	Spirit body	Global Spiritual Awakening
Archangels	Life spirit	Waldorf movement
Angels	Spirit self	Individual Waldorf school
College	"I"	Faculty

Although these three overviews are put side by side, in reality they overlap and are part of a unified whole.

So far we have only looked *upward*. What then of the other half? Taking the human being as our archetype we can add astral body, etheric body, and physical body as three members below the "I," just as spirit self, life spirit and spirit body are three members above it.[2] We can connect the astral body to the fact that we have internalized *organs* with their various functions or tasks. [3]

Streaming through the organs, and spread throughout the whole body, the actual *life activity* occurs in conjunction with the etheric body. The *results* of the life activity and processes are made visible in the muscle, bone, tissues, and so forth—in brief, the physical body.

The Waldorf school movement is part of a larger awakening to global awareness and spirituality. Within the Waldorf movement are the individual schools with their faculties. The teachers present a variety of *subjects* to the children. Each subject forms a different organ of perception and mode of consciousness within the children. Within the "organ-forming" subjects the actual *activity of teaching* and learning occurs.

The *results* of the teaching and learning forms within the students what we might characterize as an "educational body," which then goes out with the children into the world. What is this "educational body" that lives inside each Waldorf student? If we bring all that there is in Waldorf education, all that is brought to the child; the subjects, verses, festivals, everything, and synthesize it all into a single picture, what do we see? A human being; not a particular, ordinary person but the archetypal human being.

We can also find other organs within the school—the festivals committee, for example. Their function is to arrange the *which, where,* and *how*. The individual festivals are then celebrated in the course of the year. This activity strengthens the etheric bodies of the children, which, in turn, becomes part of their "educational body" and is carried out into the world.

The college "meditation," in looking "upward," points to the angels, archangels and archai as being the "outer" spiritual source of strength, courage and wisdom for the school. Looking "downward," (in name only), we find organs within the school directed not to the "outer" spiritual world but to the outer material world. Board, administration, fund-raising and finance committees all have the function of sustaining the school legally and economically. They also interact with and administer the non-pedagogical functions within the school itself.

Within each administrative organ, differentiated according to function, are the actual activities or "life processes." These will also involve the general parent body to greater or lesser degree and through their activity keep the school viable and alive. The results of the activity of the school's various administrative organs are visible in the buildings, property, capital items, and so forth. We can now complete our overview:

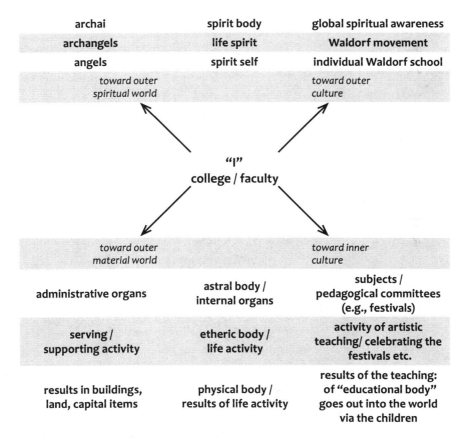

archai	spirit body	global spiritual awareness
archangels	life spirit	Waldorf movement
angels	spirit self	individual Waldorf school
toward outer spiritual world		*toward outer culture*

"I"
college / faculty

toward outer material world		*toward inner culture*
administrative organs	astral body / internal organs	subjects / pedagogical committees (e.g., festivals)
serving / supporting activity	etheric body / life activity	activity of artistic teaching/ celebrating the festivals etc.
results in buildings, land, capital items	physical body / results of life activity	results of the teaching: of "educational body" goes out into the world via the children

A Waldorf school is a seven-membered being participating in the spiritual and material worlds. Like a beehive it is partly visible, partly invisible. This is potentially true for all institutions. The difference, however, in those institutions arising out of Anthroposophy, is a striving to consciously connect in a spiritual-scientific way with progressive spiritual beings. When this view of the school is synthesized into a single image we see, once again, the archetypal human being standing before us. Waldorf schools strive to be *human*, in the fullest sense of the word.

❦

We can now, in part, answer the question posed at the beginning of the article: How can we understand the role the teachers play within the organization of a Waldorf school as cultural institution? The teachers are the *"I"-principle.*[4]

This sheds light on why Rudolf Steiner did not designate a headmaster or board of directors to direct the teachers' activity. It is a question of freedom. Teacher–artists require a free space for their activity as a prerequisite for the unfolding of a healthy educational and cultural life. They cannot be given a program or curriculum from "above" or be dictated to, for instance, just as Beethoven could not have been given a program of action to be an artist by some "higher" authority. This element lay within his individuality.

This picture is not to be understood as a lessening or downgrading of the role of board, administration and parents—on the contrary. In a culture inimical to what lives in Waldorf education, their role of creating and protecting the free space needed for the healthy educational development of their children is vital, even a prerequisite. Nor does it mean that teachers live aristocratically on the pedagogical mount; open lines of communication and mutual understanding are necessary for healthy functioning.

We also see how the board and administration not only perform the role of allowing a school to function within society, but, in addition, mirroring the activity of the angels, protect and shelter the essential Waldorf nature of the school.

The activity within the administrative organs constantly bears in mind the values and ideals held by the individual school and the

Waldorf movement as a whole, yet connects itself meaningfully to the rest of society. When this is successful, the results of their activity make visible in the world the striving of the beings connected with a spiritually awakening humanity; for instance, through the buildings and their architectural style. In the end we can say that this work "is love made visible."[5]

↓

We have now established, albeit briefly, the "what" of the teachers within a Waldorf school. The other half of the question is the "how" of their role. How do the teachers perform their function as "I"-principle?

The "I" is a unity, and a unified faculty is necessary for healthy functioning. The teachers who unite their destiny with a school can choose to work *together* as a college. Doing so provides a focus for working with the higher members of the school along with issues of administration and pedagogy. While it is desirable for each individual or sub-group to carry the whole picture of the schools' being, their working will, perforce, remain partial and ineffective unless it occurs within the context of a united faculty who carries the same picture.

On the surface a college generally does two things. It occupies itself with a meditation and, time permitting, spiritually enlivening studies or activities; the lion's share of the meeting time is then given over to administrative and pedagogical issues. In reality, as with any artist, spiritual working and practical working go hand in hand and do not fall into two distinct and separate activities. It is easy to understand a group working with administrative and pedagogical issues, but it sounds rather daunting to work with angels, archangels and archai. How does this actually occur? Through what avenues do the imaginations, inspirations and intuitions of these beings appear within the group?

↓

We have an inner "physical" ego (point-centered in the physical body, gazing and acting outward), and an "outer" spiritual "I," ("periphery-centered," acting from the circumference). What proceeds from within ourselves we consider our own. Harder, and often more reluctantly grasped, is understanding that what comes to us from outside is also part of ourselves. Our outer spiritual "I" lives within all that surrounds us, and our ego-path through life, our biography, is made up of what we do out of ourselves *and* what approaches us as destiny. Together they form a total picture. Our inner "physical" ego is *exclusive*, and our "outer" spiritual "I" lives *inclusively* within nature, in the spiritual world and in other human beings.

We have all experienced how a single sentence, word, or even gesture from someone can change our life direction. If we attribute this new impulse in our lives as proceeding solely from the individual who spoke we would, usually, be subject to maya, appearances. In reality our outer spiritual "I," in the broadest sense of the word, is speaking to us. When it is we ourselves who have spoken the word that changed the direction of another's life, it is well worth recalling in detail what happened in that moment—especially those words and gestures that seemed insignificant to us at the time.

Becoming aware of the outer spiritual "I" is one of the tasks of the consciousness soul.[6] The consciousness soul is active in two directions, one outer and one inner; this has direct consequences for how the college works.

First, the college takes careful note of all that passes in its environment. It knows the spiritual world is just as capable of speaking through a student, parent, visitor, board member or event as it is of speaking within the college. In this respect the college is a self-aware sense organ; receiving impressions or perceptions and adding the necessary concept to the percept. [7]

Second, the college looks within, and a more intensive activity is possible: *focused listening*. To what are we listening? Our colleagues! Because our outer spiritual "I" lives within the spiritual world *and* within each other, we listen carefully to what our colleagues have to say to each other, to their *conversation*.

A remarkable passage, spoken by the character Maria, appears in one of Rudolf Steiner's mystery plays, *The Portal of Initiation:*

> When many people join in conversation,
> their words present themselves before the soul
> as if among them stood, mysteriously,
> the Archetype of Man.
> It shows itself diversified in many souls,
> just as pure light, the One,
> reveals itself within the rainbow's arch
> in many-colored hues.

It can come as an inner jolt to realize, when meeting with colleges of teachers in different parts of the country, that *the same being* is present in each one. On becoming familiar with the experience the mood is more one of homecoming.

Conversation consists of discussing a subject held in common. A college, in addition, can choose to include what lives invisibly in their midst. This element expresses itself to the group via the word. Inwardly, we open up and listen attentively. We become conscious of what needs to be said via the thoughts that light up in us. Where one person cannot grasp what needs to be said, the other can. In this way a single stream of thought is expressed; not necessarily by one person, but by different members of the group. A communal conversation occurs. What is striven for is no longer personal opinion, but the thought-that-lives-among-us. The thought element should not be taken as cerebral, but in the mood of the above quote. Thought is only the more consciously grasped aspect.

Initially, conversation seems too prosaic, too ordinary to be of such importance. The problem with the spiritual world is not that it is so far away, but that it is *so close.* We fail to see in the seemingly ordinary the extraordinary revealing itself. It really should not surprise us, however, that progressive spiritual beings manifest themselves in our conversation. They approach us with the utmost respect for our freedom; neither impinging on our will, nor overwhelming our feelings. They approach us delicately, through our thoughts, which we are free to accept or reject.[8] Nor do they approach us with a prepackaged idea or thought content. Their thought is above individual language, and we must struggle to mold it into a form suited to our own situation.

The scope of this way of working does not confine itself to a closed group of college members and spiritual beings. The higher selves of the children, parents, and all those connected with the school may, at any moment, be involved in the process. Indeed, this approach can be especially fruitful in discussions around a child in difficulty, for instance.

What is the nature of the activity we engage in when listening with all our soul to our colleagues and strive to grasp the thought-that-lives-among-us? Creative, artistic activity. It is no different from the way a composer listens to the music he is about to set down, or the eurythmist listens for the source of her movement. The teachers must work with no less artistry, are no less artists within the college, than they are within the classroom. Indeed, a successful college *is* an artist; is as much a creator being as the archetypal human being of which the school is an image.

NOTES

1. See Dr. Johannes Tautz, *The Founding of the First Waldorf School in Stuttgart,* transcript of lectures given in Spring Valley, New York, 1982; published by the Council of the Pedagogical Section of the Anthroposophical Society in North America.

2. Extensive material is to be found on the spiritual hierarchies. The reader who is unfamiliar with the subject will find numerous references to the spiritual hierarchies in Rudolf Steiner's lectures and writings. See *An Outline of Esoteric Science* (Hudson, NY: Anthroposophic Press, 1997); *The Mission of Folk-Souls* (London: Rudolf Steiner Press, 2005); *The Spiritual Hierarchies and their Reflection in the Physical World* (Great Barrington, MA: SteinerBooks, 2008).

3. See Rudolf Steiner, *Theosophy: An Introduction to the Spiritual Processes in Human Life and in the Cosmos* (Hudson, NY: Anthroposophic Press, 1994), as well a numerous references in Steiner's lectures.

4. See note 3.

5. This is meant in the general sense that an internalized astral body is necessary in order to have internalized sense and metabolic organs. See, Rudolf Steiner and Ita Wegman, *Extending Practical Medicine: Fundamental Principles Based on the Science of the Spirit,* London: Rudolf Steiner Press, 1997.

6. Lest there be unclarity on this point, there is no automatic conferring of "I"-status on any individual or group of teachers. Just as a person can have a weak ego, or even, in certain circumstances, no "I"-presence at all, so, too, can a school be in this position and yet continue to function—even, seemingly, quite well. It is entirely possible to have all the accoutrements of Waldorf education and yet be a shell.

7. Kahlil Gibran, *The Prophet* (Prague: Albatross, 2015).

8. See note 3.

9. See Rudolf Steiner, *Intuitive Thinking as a Spiritual Path: A Philosophy of Freedom* (Hudson, NY: Anthroposophic Press, 1995), as well as numerous other authors on Anthroposophy.

10. While the college "meditation" refers to strength, courage, and wisdom in connection with the angels, archangels, and archai, Steiner's "Foundation Stone Meditation" connects "thought" and "spirit vision" with those beings.

10

The Wisdom of Geese

by Angeles Arrien

This fall when you see geese flying back south for the winter, flying along in "V" formation, you might be interested in knowing what has been discovered about why they fly that way. It has been learned that as each bird flaps its wings, it creates an uplift for the bird immediately following. By flying in a "V" formation, the whole flock adds seventy percent greater flying range than if each bird flew on its own.

> *Basic Truth #1: People who share a common direction and sense of community can get where they are going more quickly and easily because they are traveling on the thrust of one another.*

Whenever a goose falls out of formation, it suddenly feels the drag and resistance of trying to go it alone and quickly gets back into formation to take advantage of the lifting power of the bird immediately in front.

> *Basic Truth #2: If we have as much sense as geese, we will stay in formation with those who are headed in the same direction we are going.*

When the lead goose gets tired, it rotates back in the wing and another goose flies point.

> *Basic Truth #3: It pays to take turns doing hard jobs with people or with geese flying south.*

The geese honk from behind to encourage those up front to maintain their speed.

Basic Truth #4: We need to be careful about what we say when we honk from behind.

Finally, when a goose gets sick or is wounded by gunshot and falls out, two geese fall out of formation and follow it down to provide help and protection. They stay with it until it is either able to fly again or until it dies, and then they launch out on their own or with another formation to catch up with their own group.

Basic Truth #5: We need to stand by on another in both good and tough times.

11

WELLSPRINGS OF THE ART OF EDUCATION
THREE REVERSALS IN THE WORK OF THE WALDORF TEACHER

BY CHRISTOF WIECHERT

From the very beginning, much depends upon our ability to correctly address our work and to understand that we must give ourselves a particular direction appropriate to our time," says Rudolf Steiner in the first lecture of *Foundations of Human Experience*.[1] He then gives a picture of the prevalent role that egoism has to play in the development of humanity now. At this point in evolution, he explains, inner attention and self-realization are necessary. At the end of the lecture he returns to this, painting an unusual situation: "There can be a great difference, and it does not depend simply upon whether one teacher is more clever than another in superficial pedagogical techniques. Rather, the main difference in the effectiveness of teaching comes from the thoughts the teacher has had during the entire time of his or her existence and brings into the classroom."[2] He goes on to point out how thoughts that are directed toward a child's development, for example, work differently on the child from thoughts that do not.

What happens when a teacher forms such thoughts? "At the moment you have such thoughts, something within you fights against everything that is merely personality. At this moment everything that forms the basis of your personality is dampened. Something of what predominates in people because they are physical human beings is quelled."[3] We could say this basically brings us to the question of inner substance. The strength and quality of the Waldorf impulse depends on whether we confront ourselves inwardly or not and are able to engage in an inner struggle with "mere personality." Are we as Waldorf educators able to give ourselves that direction? Viewed this way, we simultaneously deal with the question of the contemporary relevance of the Waldorf school, for this does not depend on systems or new forms (although they certainly have to be there as well), but on ourselves. The way we relate to ourselves and to the world is what counts. This can give rise to some confusion. An attempt will be made here to characterize different types of this confusion.

Three Types of Confusion

A first type of confusion lies in the temptation to interpret the Waldorf impulse as a system: a set of actions, established forms, habits, and even a body of convictions or anthroposophic knowledge. We may call it Anthroposophy, but that may only be true to an extent. There is a certain manifestation of Anthroposophy that is rejected more and more by younger colleagues and parents. An example of this is the use of anthroposophic knowledge as a weapon to argue a *personal* point. Many people instinctively recognize this as a form of ideology that needs to be questioned, no matter who the person representing the ideology is.

A second type of confusion arises because Waldorf schools have taken on certain forms, for example, a fixed curriculum. This is necessary, otherwise the schools would not be able to exist. The confusion over the opinion that this is everybody's private business arises when the outer form is taken for the thing itself, even when the original impulse no longer has anything to do with it. For example, when a colleague does not want to do the class play in the eighth grade but in the seventh grade, this sets up conflict with the traditional form: "without an eighth grade play it is not Waldorf." This is, of course, an innocent example. There are certain forms, right into matters of pedagogy, which are no longer the expression of a true impulse of the art of education, but of a habit that can often not be traced to a specific origin anymore. When this is the case, people will have a hard time recognizing the true intentions of the Waldorf school.

A third type of confusion arises because Anthroposophy rightfully values individual freedom very highly. Without the free human being there would be no Anthroposophy at all. This "freer climate" is exactly the reason why many new colleagues find their way to Waldorf schools. In practice, however, it can easily happen that this freedom is confused with license, or even stamina, in pushing something through. Waldorf schools offer a lot of opportunity for this. We pay dearly for this confused notion of freedom because on average we are more prone to social conflicts than other schools. Put in a different way, the potential for conflicts in our schools is high, not because of Anthroposophy, and also not because of the way we are organized, but because of ourselves.

Three Reversals

In the final analysis, these areas of confusion stem from the way in which we do our inner work. How do I take myself in hand? How can I help myself in such a way that I come closer to my true self? I need help. A first way to bring about a reversal is to start asking questions and become a seeker instead of someone who has the answers and is all-competent. This is actually a first step on the path toward Anthroposophy, whether one wants to recognize it as such or not.

Not so long ago many Waldorf teachers were led toward this question by destiny and had started this process of inner transformation. It was a time when the inner path was not so much spoken about in schools, but individuals actually did walk the path of self-development and this, moreover, was a private matter.

Nowadays, many colleagues find their way to the schools without destiny having brought them to this point (and we leave aside here what the cause of that may be). It is part of being a teacher, however, to arrive at the realization, *"I can only teach when I learn to change myself."* People may stick to that is true in the sense that nobody can demand of me that I go on a path of inner development. But I must honestly demand this of myself when I practice the profession of Waldorf teacher. At the beginning of the first lecture of *Foundations of Human Experience,* Rudolf Steiner puts it this way: "Dear friends, we can accomplish our work only if we do not see it as simply a matter of intellect or feeling, but, in the highest sense, as a moral spiritual task."[4] This implies a second reversal. But how does one go about this?

By way of example, let us look at the way the teachers' meeting is structured. The structure of the meeting can itself be a source of confusion, as we all know. But this meeting is also the heart and soul of the school. The heart perceives, gives impulses and direction, and is an organ that is always learning. The same holds true for the teachers' meeting. Rudolf Steiner calls it "continuously evolving education." Today that implies that colleagues not only take up the question of continuing education together, but also that all colleagues get the opportunity to discuss these questions of transformation. Specifically, questions such as the following would be asked: How does a new colleague learn about the teachers' meditations? Is the way one practices these professional meditations a scheduled topic of conversation? Is it possible to talk about this theme in the meetings?

This will obviously only be possible when the circle of teachers has practiced establishing the right *mood* in the meetings. Such a mood can only come about when colleagues agree to look upon the meeting as something that is just as important as the teaching itself. It is necessary to remind one another to practice the virtues of real listening (What does my colleague really want to say?), of active silence (not being silent out of a lack of interest), and of keeping one's speaking in check. (Is it really necessary for me to say something now? Do I speak to the point or do I automatically raise my hand to speak?)

When this happens, a space will be created in which all colleagues can feel safe, because their contributions will be heard and taken up. When this safe space is established and when one can talk about inner questions, it will also be possible to find a fruitful way to deal with anthroposophic content within the meetings. This is the third reversal: When the periphery creates a center that will radiate out again to the individuals, a common instrument for a common aim will have been created.[5]

A circle of teachers that strengthens itself in this way will break down the first type of confusion and Anthroposophy will actually be something living, working between individuals. Next to all the depth. But one phenomenon should be described. Important things a circle of teachers has to achieve together, a *new commitment* is asked of us.

Renewal through Reenlivening

Let us now look at the second category of confusion. Schools are by nature conservative, and Waldorf schools are no exception. This is, of course, a general judgment that needs to be qualified.

When we survey the development of the past twenty-five years, we see that considerable progress has been made in many areas. Movement education has experienced a strong impulse, ranging from juggling to complete circus shows. Strong developments have arisen through various attempts to connect schools with the world of work by means of doing practica, and by other means. The artistic quality and craftsmanship in the handwork subjects have attained nearly professional standards. Steps have been taken to introduce experiential studies. There are schools that devote a whole evening every year to show the work done in eurythmy. Education in technical subjects has seen many outstanding achievements as well. Special-needs teaching has undergone several developments, ranging from various tutorial arrangements to the founding of independent, special-needs schools. Initiatives have been taken toward more integration and diversity. In connection with that, a particularly promising initiative is the founding and recent opening of an intercultural school in Mannheim, Germany. The search for alternative ways to do final exams and grading has resulted in various new forms. Furthermore, models have been developed to tackle the middle school anew, and new forms for high school are being created by many circles of colleagues. This list is by no means complete, but it demonstrates a strong power of initiative, worthy of the Waldorf schools.

Most of these initiatives are extensions of Waldorf pedagogy. In and of themselves they are very valuable, but they have not essentially touched the *core work* of the Waldorf school, the education in kindergarten through high school. The question arises: How can this energy, which is obviously there, also be turned inward? To a certain extent, the core work is at a disadvantage, because existing tasks have to be performed anew every day. In this case, one cannot speak of renewal. But one *can* speak of reenlivening, which is an inner renewal.

Let us return once more to the topic of meetings. One often hears that what happens in the Thursday meetings takes teachers' last strength. It behooves us to look into the causes of this, and we must find solutions for this phenomenon.[6] It is not our task here to answer these questions in detail.

Rudolf Steiner often pointed out the necessity of self-knowledge as something that continues to build strength when one is on the path of self-educating. "Picture yourself rightly." One often experiences that the energy that enables one to know oneself (or criticize oneself) is actually there, but gets directed outward and becomes criticism of people or the world in general. It is as if we are dealing with a shadow thrown by the prevailing mind set. The result of directing criticism outward onto others, however, is that one is no longer capable of really meeting one's fellow human beings, and this applies to both colleagues and parents.[7]

Our ability to meet others becomes shrouded, and, as a consequence, colleagues become estranged from one another.

We have many opportunities to turn this situation around. Such a reversal can be brought about when we inwardly activate our *powers of recognition and appreciation*.[8] Without this, a college of teachers will never become a community that gives energy and orientation to the individual. When that has been accomplished to a certain degree (something that is definitely the case in a number of schools) the way is open to the real questions that concern our daily interaction in the classroom. Then one can tackle questions such as: "How are we doing? Where do our strengths and weaknesses lie? What can we improve or change? Where do we fall short?" In this way our daily tasks will come to stand in the light of development. Teachers and school will become a living and developing organism. Here, too, we see a reversal. A reversal of direction away from the ordinary. That is what anthroposophic practice actually is. It demands self-awareness and conducting oneself morally, and it is up to each individual to initiate that.

When steps have been taken to establish such a foundation, the need arises to look anew at everyday practice and the application of the curriculum from the viewpoint of pedagogical relevance. We can ask ourselves, for example, if we are able to give our teaching the necessary freshness by the way we relate to the material and the students. Such activity will lead to our students later remembering not only the class trips, class plays, and other highlights, but also the core work: the liveliness of everyday school. Inner initiative enlivens everything and counteracts the second type of confusion. Here, too, a new commitment is demanded of us.

The Search for a New Sense of Commitment

We should now look briefly at the third type of confusion. Teachers who administer a school themselves and who have to use their inner resources in teaching, standing up for all they do, develop a understand anew what a blessing it is for a circle of stronger relationship to themselves. Being involved in an anthroposophic way of working *can* throw a shadow: It may result in a strong form of self-centeredness. And this, in turn, will hinder *community* development in our schools. At the close of the first course on Waldorf pedagogy, Rudolf Steiner summarized the inner prerequisites for being a teacher. Teachers have to work on harmonizing the following four attributes: *initiative, interest, devotion to the truth,* and the imperative *not to turn stale or sour.* It has been pointed out in another article that these four attributes correspond to the transformation of the temperaments, which do not properly serve self-education unless they have been worked on.

There is no mention of a fifth prerequisite, namely, "building a community of teachers." This may seem strange today, but will become understandable when one looks back and apprehends the historical setting of the founding of Waldorf pedagogy. The personalities whom Rudolf Steiner addressed were practicing inner development. Apart from that, he had pointed out the enormous implications for social life at the opening of the first course for teachers. Furthermore, community building is contained as a seed in the above-mentioned four requirements, because the second one runs as follows: "The teacher should be a person who is interested in the being of the whole world and of humanity."[9] No one would like to admit to being a person lacking in interest. We experience *interest,* so to speak, as something that every human being is basically equipped with in our time. And yet it is formulated here as a fundamental requirement for teachers. This is obviously something that needs conscious tending. Therefore, there must be some part of us that needs to be educated to develop interest. When I observe what I do at those moments when I find myself not being interested in something, I can notice that I want to stay in my own little circle; I feel as if I have enough to deal with when I keep to myself. I close myself off. But when I persist and try to develop interest, I will experience something like a freeing from the narrow bonds of myself. This happens when I turn toward something else. I open up.

Imagine that one practices this newly discovered capacity with a colleague whom one usually shuns. Something new will open up. Persisting in this will lead to rich and new discoveries. Not only will I get to know myself anew, but I will also gain the sense of how I help to build community. This opens up a new appreciation of the necessity for all colleagues to partake in child study, not just those who know the child or just the "specialists." One will also have this when the kindergarten teachers take part in the meetings. It should be a matter of course. When this comes about, we will have started to tackle the third type of confusion. But the same thing holds true here also—namely, that we have to find a way toward a new sense of commitment.

These remarks cannot lay claim to offering solutions for the way things are in individual Waldorf schools. They merely try to offer a few examples of the *inner practice of Anthroposophy.*

🌱

NOTES

1–4. Rudolf Steiner, *The Foundations of Human Experience*. Great Barrington, MA: Anthroposophic Press, 1996; Aug. 21, 1919.

5. Rudolf Steiner, *Anthroposophical Leading Thoughts: Anthroposophy as a Path of Knowledge: The Michael Mystery*. London: Rudolf Steiner Press, 1998, "The World Thoughts in the Working of Michael and in the Working of Ahriman," Nov. 16, 1924.

6. Heinz Zimmerman, *Speaking, Listening, Understanding: The Art of Creating Conscious Conversation,* Hudson, NY: Lindisfarne Press, 1996.

7. Hartwig Schiller, ed., *Innere Aspekte der Konferenzgestaltung* (Inner Aspects of Shaping the Teachers' Meeting). Stuttgart, 1990.

8. Jörgen Smit, *Lighting Fires; Deepening Education through Meditation.* Stroud, UK: Hawthorn Press, 1992.

8. Rudolf Steiner, *Discussions with Teachers,* Hudson, NY: Anthroposophic Press, 1997, p. 180.

12

ADVICE FOR ADMINISTRATORS

BY SIEGFRIED E. FINSER

Hello Torin,

Ever since you asked whether I had any advice to give to administrators in Waldorf schools, I have been struggling for an answer. I have reached the age when all advice that seems so sensible turns out to be turned upside down by real events.

I am sure of one thing. The basic administrative duties involving financial management, office management, communications and support, school scheduling and substituting, parent relations and all regulatory matters like licensing, report filing, insurance etc. are pretty much covered in manuals and other programs. I think the Independent Schools Association has excellent programs and literature on those matters. I don't see any necessity to comment further on them.

Administration is one of the functions I personally always did poorly. That's the reason I can give administrators such good advice! I am not confused by the reality. What I have to say comes mostly from observations. Observing, listening, admiring and suffering have given me my credentials.

Given the truth in the old saying "Free advice is worth what you pay for it," I have resisted the temptation to pretend I know something about Administration. Instead, I'd like to share a few of my observations.

1.   From what I have experienced, it seems the greatest likelihood of success comes from *picking the right school*. Each one is unique, an administrator may fail in one and be a relative success in another. The

reason I say relative is because administrative success is very elusive in a Waldorf school. The faculty have one picture of what that means, while the Board of Trustees may have a completely different one. The parents always have a third view on any subject, except for those who end up on the Board or the Finance Committee.

Every Waldorf school is not only unique, it is also at a particular stage in its development. As a result, an administrator may be just right for the school at one stage of its development, but then as it reaches another stage, may no longer be the right fit. There is nothing sadder than seeing someone cling to a job for which they are no longer the right person. There is so much work to be done in the world and life is so precious, why fight the current when the signs are usually easy to read? I would get out, let someone else work at it, and I'll go on to find the right work for my particular capacities. It is healthier for the school and for me. Each of us needs to be among the people with whom we share karma, purpose, culture and timing.

How do I know when I am in the wrong school or the wrong job? If I am lucky, my coworkers will let me know. If I notice that I no longer have the support of my colleagues in the faculty, on the Board, in the committees and my own staff, it's time to move on. There will always be a few who love me, but my healthy sense of feeling tells me my time is over. Moving on is a good thing, especially if it comes after some years of working well together. It shows me that both the school and I have developed, have grown. In a way I worked hard to advance my school organizationally and now it needs a different set of capacities. I did it to myself and that's good. If I stay on, I will only be holding the school back from further development. Some schools are stuck in their development by persons or groups of persons hanging on for dear life!

Of course, there are a few schools that just don't develop. I don't know why! They go through recurring cycles, seducing new generations of parents, new teachers and new administrators into their own familiar cycles of crises and successes. In that case an administrator may manage through one cycle or maybe two and then simply have to leave, usually feeling guilty for something they were only part of, but not solely to blame. It is sometimes good for the soul to be somewhere else.

One of the reasons often given for trying to outlast a departure is that it is supposed to be healthy for our karma to settle differences while we are still alive. This might be so in some cases. It would be easier if we had the perspective of a few more past lifetimes to work with. In their absence, I generally characterize it as banging your head against a wall and hoping something good will result.

What would I do? This may seem strange to anyone working in a Waldorf school, but here's what I would do. At least once in every three years, and certainly after the first year as an administrator, I would (on an individual basis) force my colleagues on the board, the faculty, also a few parents out of their social hiding places. I would ask one or two, every now and then, "How am I doing? What can I do better? Have you seen me do anything really well?" The best way to do this is not all at once. I'd take one person at a time and get at least an important handful done in a matter of a few weeks. Of course, this only works if I really want to know.

This is not a statistical evaluation exercise. I'd be looking for tidbits, little signs that reveal to me how people feel. I would look for pregnant pauses in the answer, a shift of the eyes to the right or left before answering...and such other signs of hidden feelings and thoughts. I have to make it clear *I really want to know!*

Isn't what I am suggesting asking for criticism? Is that wise? Don't I get enough without asking for it? My feeling is that only by asking is permission really granted to work together productively. I know that administrative work requires the support of colleagues and that without it, sooner or later, my work will suffer. I would make a conscious decision to find out sooner rather than later. It also gives me a chance to do something about it. After all, should the children be the only ones in a school growing and developing?

2.   Another thing I've noticed is that administrators often like to take on a certain role they are comfortable with. Such a role might be "the Expert" or it could be "the exhausted overworked servant" or still

another role might be "the facilitator." I have enjoyed watching how each individual in that job gradually tailors the job to suit their favorite personality. The only role that is rarely taken on openly is "leader." For some reason, in Waldorf what still escapes me is that such a role is a definite no-no! It might not even be anthroposophic, even though the role in the beginning of the Waldorf school movement was always clearly specified.

3.   What is usually not realized is that the school as a total personality also creates the "role" for the administrator. It shapes the administrative role to suit its angelic psyche. So, between the personality of the school and the personality of the administrator they give birth to a unique way of functioning.

Is that a good thing? Isn't it natural? Maybe it can't be helped! The answer is yes to all three. Nevertheless, administration in its essence has to be "situation" determined not personality based. In other words, there are times when an expert has to force a decision. There are other times when a lot has to get done with not much help. Still other times a good listener is really needed for the problem to go away by itself. At still other times—or better, all the time—leadership must be active.

Some people might think this is being all things to all people. I call it doing what the situation requires. Administrative action must always be "situation based." There, I've said it.

How do I know what the situation requires? That's an easy question to answer. I don't! That's where I have to step out into the unknown, where all my capacities are called on to do the right thing in the right moment with the right people. Administration in its essence is facing every situation creatively, calling on inherent imaginative capacities and daring to act responsibly with various degrees of certainty. Administration in a Waldorf school is not for the faint of heart.

4.   Perhaps the last important observation I'll mention might have come first. I have noticed that Waldorf school offices often miss opportunities to shape and document routine procedures. Facing a blank slate every morning forces creativity, but it is also tiring. Creating good habits

for the whole school community is a function of administration that sometimes gets over looked.

When I wake up in the morning I follow a given routine. I don't sit down each morning on the side of my bed and try to creatively decide what to do next. "Should I first comb my hair for a change? Maybe, since it is Wednesday, it is more appropriate that I first brush my teeth? But washing my face feels so good." I have habits that get me into life without soul searching. That's why we create habits. The body social needs them, too!

To establish a healthy performance improvement program for teachers and staff, one that achieves the right goals and is accepted by all involved requires enormous creativity and procedural acumen. Once it is accepted and operational, the trick is to follow it religiously. I can promise anyone reading this letter that not establishing it and leaving it to be creatively done each year is the best way of ensuring that it will never get done. I have been around too long to be fooled any more by high-sounding intensions without creating the habit structure (procedure) that goes with them.

Once it exists, there is no earthly reason why the procedure has to remain a secret. Just knowing the procedure and that it exists often solves problems waiting to surface, before they do. The results of a particular evaluation is usually best kept confidential but recorded in the personnel file. The program description, the procedures, the criteria, the principles followed can be shared openly. It can actually instill confidence where suspicion once ruled.

5.   As a postscript, I need to mention the issue of confidentiality. There are actually very few matters that need to be confidential in a Waldorf school. Nevertheless, an aura of secrecy tends to move into the entire administrative functioning of the school like a dense fog punctuated by an occasional foghorn.

The soul of administration is the act of communicating. How many times have I heard either a person or a group taking on a task for the school or for the faculty and reporting now and then that they are "working on it?" That is the most popular explanation imaginable. It actually says nothing, seems to satisfy no one and usually does great harm to the social atmosphere. I list a few alternatives below:

1. *"We have not yet met but scheduled our first meeting for.... At this point we are probably going to determine a schedule for ourselves, decide whether we have the right people, the right mandate and also a clear understanding of what we are charged to accomplish. We plan to report our progress back to you at the next meeting."* This is a truthful report. It allows the chair to make a note to follow up at the next meeting and gives people a feeling the assignment is being taken seriously.

2. Suppose we've had two meetings and are struggling with a variety of opinions and how to sort them out. This is not a shameful situation. It does not need to be hidden. The most outstanding conclusions have sometimes been reached in groups with diverse perspectives. The report needs to be positive, not apologetic. It might be *"We have met together for two meetings and brought to the surface as many of the different perspectives on the issue as we could discover. They naturally overlap considerably, but the five main points we are considering are: (1, 2, 3, 4, 5)."* Now that's a report. As a rule, in many schools it would be simply "We're working on it."

3. "We've already met six times and agree on several aspects, but are completely deadlocked on one issue. We agree on the following issues: (1, 2, 3) We are not yet ready to report on (4) but will keep you informed as we continue to work."

4. "We're ready to submit this first draft of our conclusions. We would like feedback from you prior to the next meeting so that we can consider your suggestions and comments in drafting a final report."

5. "Attached to this email is a copy of our final.... We plan to share it with parents at the next all-school meeting. Even though it is a final ... X ..., it is not cement and we plan to use it as a living document as we work with it over the coming year."

The idea is to communicate with real substance along the way, not as a surprise at the end of years of secret work. Secrecy breeds suspicion and suspicion breeds antagonism that loves conflict and incubates politically correct hatred.

Those are my comments, Torin, about what I have observed in administrative functions in the Waldorf schools. There are hundreds and thousands more comments that applaud what occurs in them as well. I have not mentioned them, since they are well known. I mean such things as:

1.   The remarkable dedication of almost all administrative staff. Very few schools would have survived without the remarkable service and long hours devoted to them by administrative personnel. In many cases this has been with little or even no compensation. We would also have to factor in the "volunteer" services without which no Waldorf school would exist today. Waldorf is truly a call to service.

2.   The willingness to take on administrative duties by so many untrained and inexperienced teachers and parents. It is unbelievable with what courage and determination various individuals (including myself) plunge into an administrative function they have never done before without a moment's hesitation. It is also incredible how schools allow it, usually out of necessity, and expect miracles. Waldorf is truly a home for magicians.

3.   The astounding way that Waldorf people (if there are such people) grow and learn on the job. There even used to be a school that requested volunteers to serve on the Board. A sign-up sheet was provided on the bulletin board. I used to quip, "From one board to another Board in one easy step." But do you know, for a while it worked? Can you believe that? Waldorf is truly developmental to the core.

4.   The marvelous manner in which so many people in administrative functions throw themselves wholeheartedly into the work without feeling the need to consult with the expertise already existing on the internet and in public and independent school associations and foundations. If anyone can reinvent the world it is bound to be someone in Waldorf administration.

> *Sincerely but also with tongue in cheek,*
> *Siegfried E. Finser*

13

Poems and Verses for Leaders

One might wonder, why end a book with a seemingly random assortment of poems and verses? After all, could one not find these in a variety of texts and downloads? Yes, of course. But these are some of my favorites. And, they are chosen with a purpose in mind.

Sometimes prose just does not do it. Sometimes a poem or verse, if lived with over a period of time, can work on the soul in a way that prose cannot. Since so much of this book is about supporting leadership, I felt compelled to include some of the material here at the end that has most supported me.

I would like to suggest that the reader glance over the selection below and select one or two to "adopt" for a while. If one lives with a particular poem or verse, it has a way of working in on the soul, nourishing, supporting and educating. If the particular selection does not work for you, try another. I have lived with many of these, and they have made ever so much of a difference in my life. I am happy to lend them to my friends and readers.

This first section contains gems from Rudolf Steiner.

🌱

EXCERPT FROM FOUNDATION STONE FOR THE FIRST ADDITIONAL
BUILDING OF THE WALDORF SCHOOL (DECEMBER 16, 1921):

May there reign here spirit-strength in love;
May there work here spirit-light in goodness;
Born of certainty of heart,
And from steadfastness of soul,
So that we may bring to young human beings
Bodily strength for work, inwardness of soul and clarity of spirit.
May this place be consecrated to such a task;
May young minds and hearts here find
Servers of the light, endowed with strength,
Who will guard and cherish them.

🌱

This is healing—
When in the mirror of the soul
The whole community takes shape,
And when in the community
The strength of each is active.

🌱

Moral activities are all acts performed as the
result of wonder, trust, reverence, and faith.

🌱

God's protecting, blessing ray,
May it pervade my growing soul,
That it can perceive
Strengthening forces in the worldwide all.
Resolving to begin to waken in itself,
Life-filled might of love,
Seeing thus the strength of God
Upon its path of life,
And working with all it owns
For God's true purpose.

🌱

Still in seed are the soul's deep longing,
Growing forth are the deeds of willing,
And maturing the fruits of life.

I feel my destiny,
My destiny findeth me.

I feel my star,
My star findeth me.

❧

MICHAEL IMAGINATION

You who are sprung from powers of Sun,
Radiant, grace-bestowing spirit powers,
You are predestined by thought divine
To become the shinning robe of Michael.

He, the herald of Christ, directs in you
The mankind-bearing sacred Will of the World.
You, the light-filled beings of the ether world
Bear the Word of Christ to men.

Thus appears the proclaimer of Christ
To enduring, thirsting souls.
Your flaming Word rays out to them
In the cosmic age of Spirit body.

You, the pupils of Spirit re-cognition,
Take up Michael's wise direction,
Take up the Word of Love as Will of Worlds
In your soul's high aims, actively!
        (from Rudolf Steiner's last address)

❧

WHITSUN

Where senses' Knowledge ends,
There only is the gateway
Which opens for the soul
True/All life-realities.
The soul creates the key
When it strengthens itself
In the battle which world powers

Wage against human forces
Upon the soul's own ground;
When it, by its own strength,
Dispels the sleep, which there,
At senses' frontier,
Surrounds with spirit night
The faculties of knowledge.
The Powers of knowing.

🌱

THE AMERICAN VERSE

May our feeling penetrate
Into the center of our heart and
Strive with love to unite itself
With those Human Beings seeking the same goal, and
With the spirit beings, who, full of grace,
Behold our earnest heartfelt striving;
And in beholding, strengthen us from realms of light
Illuminating our life in love.

🌱

Man needs inner allegiance;
Allegiance to the guidance of spiritual beings.
On this allegiance, he can build
His eternal life and self
And thus allow eternal light
To shine through sense existence.
                    (tr. by Sophia Walsh)

🌱

The light of sun
It fills the day
After night.

The strength of soul
Wakened it is
From restful sleep.

Thou, my soul, give thanks to the light,
In it there shines the power of God.
Thou, my soul, be strong in thy deed.

🌱

We must eradicate from the soul all fear and terror of what comes
toward us out of the future.

Man must acquire serenity in all feelings and sensations of the
future.

He must look forward with absolute equanimity to everything that
may come.

And he must think only that whatever comes is given to us by a
world direction full of wisdom.

It is part of what we must learn in this age, namely, to live out of
pure trust, without any security in existence—trust in the ever-
present help of the spiritual world.

Truly, nothing else will do if our courage is not to fail us.

Let us discipline our will.

And let us seek the awakening from within ourselves every morning
and every evening.

> From the luminous heights of the Spirit
> May God's clear light ray forth
> Into those human souls
> Who are intent on seeking
> The grace of the Spirit,
> The light of the Spirit,
> The life of the Spirit,
> May He live
> In the hearts,
> In the inmost souls
> Of those of us
> Who feel ourselves gathered together here
> In His Name.
> —RUDOLF STEINER, *Verses and Meditations*, p. 195

POEMS AND VERSES FROM OTHER AUTHORS

THE MAN WATCHING

I can tell by the way the trees beat, after
So many dull days, on my worried windowpanes
That a storm is coming,
And I hear the far-off fields say things
I can't bear without a friend,
I can't love without a sister.

The storm, the shifter of shapes, drives on
Across the woods and across time,
And the world looks as if it had no age:
The landscape, like a line in the psalm book,
Is seriousness and weight and eternity.

What we choose to fight is so tiny!
What fights with us is so great!
If only we would let ourselves be dominated
As things do by some immense storm,
We would become strong too, and not need names.

When we win it's with small things,
And the triumph itself makes us small.
What is extraordinary and eternal
Does not want to be bent by us.
I man the Angel who appeared
To the wrestlers' sinews
Grew long like metal strings,
He felt them under his fingers
Like chords of deep music.

Whoever was beaten by this Angel
(who often simply declined the fight)
Went away proud and strengthened
And great from the harsh hand,
That kneaded him as if to change his shape.
Winning does not tempt that man.
This is how he grows: by being defeated, decisively,
By constantly greater beings.
—RAINER MARIA RILKE

AS KINGFISHERS CATCH FIRE

As kingfishers catch fire, dragonflies draw flame;
As tumbled over rim in roundy wells
Stones ring; like each tucked string tells, each hung bell's
Bow swung finds tongue to fling out broad its name;
Each mortal thing does one thing and the same:
Deals out that being indoors each one dwells;
Selves—goes itself; *myself* it speaks and spells,
Crying *Whát I dó is me: for that I came.*

I say móre: the just man justices;
Keeps grace: thát keeps all his goings graces;
Acts in God's eye what in God's eye he is—
Christ—for Christ plays in ten thousand places,
Lovely in limbs, and lovely in eyes not his
To the Father through the features of men's faces.
—GERARD MANLEY HOPKINS

⚜

FROM ROBERT LEWIS STEVENSON, "A CHRISTMAS SERMON"

We require higher tasks because we do not recognize the height of those we have. Trying to be kind and honest seems an affair too simple and too inconsequential for men of our heroic mold: we had rather set ourselves to something bold, arduous, and conclusive; we had rather found a ____ or suppress a heresy, cut off a hand or ____ an appetite. But the task before us, which is to co-endure with our existence, is rather one of microscopic fineness, and the heroism required is that of patience. There is no cutting of the Gordian knots of life: each must be smilingly unraveled.

⚜

COMMUNITY

Danger of becoming ingrown, exclusive. Need to meet and work out community leaders, enter into their projects and concerns.
Teachers need to speak out of world knowledge, practical. Have interest in others!

> I step into this day,
> I step into myself,
> I step into the mystery.

Be patient toward all that is unsolved in your heart and try to love the questions themselves, like locked rooms and like books that are now written in a very foreign tongue.... And the point is, to live everything. Live the questions now. Perhaps you will then gradually, without noticing it, live along some distant day into the answer.

— RAINER MARIA RILKE

Toward thee strives the love of my soul
Toward thee flow my loving thoughts
May they uphold thee
May they enfold thee
In heights of Hope
In spheres of Love.

—RUDOLF STEINER

You who out of heaven's brightness
Now descend to earthly darkness.
Thus through life's resisting forces
Spirit radiance to unfold
Spirit warmth enkindle
Spirit forces to call forth
Be you warmed through by my love
Radiant thinking
Tranquil feeling
Healing willing
That in spirit's heights well rooted
And in Earth's foundations working
You may servants of the World become
Spirit illuminating
Love evoking
Being strengthening.

—RUDOLF STEINER

✤

AGAINST FEAR

May the events that seek me
Come unto me;
May I receive them
With a quiet mind
Through the ground of peace
On which we walk.

May the people who seek me
Come unto me;
May I receive them
With an understanding heart
Through the stream of love
In which we live.

May the spirits who seek me
Come unto me;
May I receive them
With a clear soul
Through the healing light
By which we see.

—ADAM BITTLESTON

✤

DESIDERATA

Go placidly amid the noise and haste, and remember what peace there may be in silence. As far as possible without surrender be on good terms with all persons.

Speak your truth quietly and clearly, and listen to others, even the dull and ignorant; they, too, have their story.

Avoid loud and aggressive persons; they are vexations to the spirit.

If you compare yourself with others, you may become vain and bitter, for always there will be greater and lesser persons than yourself.

Enjoy your achievements as well as your plans. Keep interested in your own career, however humble; it is real possession in the changing fortunes of time.

Exercise caution in your business affairs, for the world is full of trickery. But let this not blind you to what virtue there is; many persons strive for high ideals, and everywhere life is full of heroism.

Be yourself; especially do not feign affection. Neither be cynical about love; for in the face of aridity and disenchantment it is perennial as the grass.

Take kindly the counsel of the years, gracefully surrendering the things of youth. Nurture strength of spirit to shield you in sudden misfortune. But do not distress yourself with imaginings. Many fears are born of fatigue and loneliness. Beyond a wholesome discipline, be gentle with yourself.

You are a child of the universe, no less than the trees and the stars; you have a right to be here. And whether or not it is clear to you, no doubt the universe is unfolding as it should.

Therefore be at peace with God, whatever you conceive him to be, and whatever your labors and aspirations, in the noisy confusion of life, keep peace with your soul.

With all its sham and drudgery and broken dreams, it is still a beautiful world. Be careful. Strive to be happy.

—Max Ehrmann

🌱

It may be that when we no longer know what to do
we have come to our real work,
and that when we no longer know which way to go
we have come to our real journey.
The mind that is not baffled is not employed.
The impeded stream is the one that sings.
—Wendell Berry

Before Thee, Father,
> In righteousness and humility,

With Thee Brother,
> In faith and courage

In Thee, Spirit,
> In stillness.

> —DAG HAMMARSKJÖLD, *Markings* by

"DAFFODILS"

I wandered lonely as a cloud
That floats on high o'er vales and hills,
When all at once I saw a crowd,
A host of golden daffodils;
Beside the lake, beneath the trees,
Fluttering and dancing in the breeze.

Continuous as the stars that shine
And twinkle on the milky way,
They stretched in never-ending line
Along the margin of a bay:
Ten thousand saw I at a glance,
Tossing their heads in sprightly dance.

The waves beside them danced; but they
Out-did the sparkling waves in glee.
A poet could not be but gay,
In such a jocund company:
I gazed—and gazed—but little thought
What wealth the show to me had brought:

For oft, when on my couch I lie
In vacant or in pensive mood,
They flash upon that inward eye
Which is the bliss of solitude;
And then my heart with pleasure fills,
And dances with the daffodils.

> —WILLIAM WORDSWORTH

We look up to you
Through darkness and gloom
To conquer the fears
Of threatening doom
You—giver of strength
Create us anew
To live in your measure
Good, Beautiful, True.

—RUDOLF STEINER

Still in seed are the souls deep longings,
Growing forth are the deeds of Will,
And ripening are the fruits of Life.
I feel my star
My star finds me.
I feel my destiny,
My destiny finds me.
I feel my goal.
My goal finds me,
My soul and the world,
They are but one.
Life, it grows brighter around me.
Life, it grows harder for me.
Life, it grows richer within me.

—RUDOLF STEINER

THE SONG OF THE RAIN

Under the sun
The earth is dry.
By the fire,
Alone I cry.
All day long
The earth cries
For the rain to come.
All night my heart cries
For my hunter to come
And take me away....

Oh! Listen to the wind,
You woman there;
The time is coming,
The rain is near.
Listen to your heart
Your hunter is here.
            —LAURENS VAN DER POST

WAKING

Get up from your bed,
get out from your house,
follow the path you know so well,
so well that you now see nothing
and hear nothing
unless something can cry loudly to you,
and for you it seems
even then
no cry is louder than yours
and in your own darkness
cries have gone unheard
as long as you can remember.

These are hard paths we tread
but they are green
and lined with leaf mould
and we must love their contours
as we love the body branching
with its veins and tunnels of dark earth.

I know that sometimes
your body is hard like a stone
on a path that storms break over, embedded deeply
into that something that you think is you,
and you will not move
while the voice all around tears the air
and fills the sky with jagged light.

But sometimes unawares
those sounds seem to descend
as if kneeling down into you
and you listen strangely caught
as the terrible voice moving closer
halts,
and in the silence
now arriving
whispers

Get up, I depend
On you utterly.
Everything you need
you had
the moment before
you were born.

—DAVID WHYTE

The master in the art of living makes little distinction between his work and his play, his labor and his leisure, his mind and his body, his education and his recreation, his love and his religion. He hardly knows which is which. He simply pursues his vision of excellence at whatever he does, leaving others to decide whether he is working or playing. To him he is always doing both.

—L. P. JACKS

In a gentle way, you can shake the world.

—MAHATMA GANDHI

I long to live in the heart of Peace. I have done my work, and I hope that my Master will grant me peace to sit by Him, not to talk, but to listen to His own great silence.

—RABINDRANATH TAGORE (letter to a friend,
New York, Feb. 8, 1921)

Nothing can be taught to the mind which is not already concealed as potential knowledge in the unfolding sould of the creature. So also all perfection of which the outer man is capable, is only a realizing of the eternal perfection of the Spirit within him. We know the Divine and become the Diveine, because we are That already in our secret nature. All teaching is a revealing, all becoming is an unfolding. Self-attainment is the secret; self-knowledge and an increasing consciousness are the means and the process.

—SRI AUROBINDO

Work is love made visible...
—KAHLIL GIBRAN

Until one is committed, there is hesitancy, the chance to draw back, always ineffectiveness. Concerning all acts of initiative (and creation), there is one elementary truth the ignorance of which kills countless ideas and splendid plans: that the moment one definitely commits oneself, then Providence moves, too. All sorts of things occur to help one that would never otherwise have occurred. A whole stream of events issues from the decision, raising in one's favor all manner of unforeseen incidents and meetings and material assistance, which no man could have dreamed would have come his way. Whatever you can do or dream you can, begin it. Boldness has genius, power and magic in it.

—JOHANN WOLFGANG VON GOETHE

Thoughts from H. H. the Dali Lama

This is what the Dali Lama has to say on the millennium, which begins began January 1, 2001. All it takes is a few minutes to read and think about. Do not keep this message. The mantra must leave your hands within ninety-six hours. You will get a very pleasant surprise. This is true even if you are not superstitious.

Instructions for Life in the New Millennium from the Dali Lama

1. Take into account that great love and great achievements involve great risk.
2. When you lose, don't lose the lesson.
3. Follow the three R's: Respect for self, respect for others, responsibility for all your actions.
4. Remember that not getting what you want is sometimes a wonderful stroke of luck.
5. Learn the rules so you know how to break them properly.
6. Don't let a little dispute injure a great friendship.
7. When you realize you've made a mistake, take immediate steps to correct it.
8. Spend some time alone every day.
9. Open your arms to change, but don't let go of your values.
10. Remember that silence is sometimes the best answer.
11. Live a good, honorable life. Then when you get older and think back, you'll be able to enjoy it a second time.
12. A loving atmosphere in your home is the foundation for your life.
13. In disagreements with loved ones, deal only with the current situation. Don't bring up the past.
14. Share your knowledge. It's a way to achieve immortality.
15. Be gentle with the Earth.
16. One a year, go someplace you've never been before.
17. Remember that the best relationship is one in which your love for each other exceeds your need for each other.
18. Judge your success by what you had to give up in order to get it.
19. Approach love and cooking with reckless abandon.

↓

Fulfilling goes through hoping
goes through longing
willing flows in weaving
wails in quavering
waves veiling
waving breathing in freedom
freedom winning
kindling
—RUDOLF STEINER, speech exercise,
Discussions with Teachers

Forge me with fire a sword for my smiting
Fright to my foes and flame to my fighting
Shape me a shield both forceful and fierce
Stalwart and sharply to fend against fear.
Strike me a spear to speed as a shaft,
Fearless to fly as a shot from the start.
Staunch be my front against fury assailed,
Strong be my soul where the feeble have failed.
—ANONYMOUS

ECCE HOMO

Feeling weaves within the heart,
Thinking radiates within the head,
Willing strengthens within the limbs.

Weaving radiance
Strengthened weaving
Radiant strength:
That is man.

Man, Speak,
And through you is revealed
The World's creation.
The world's creation
Is revealed through you, O Man,
When you speak.
—RUDOLF STEINER

Be patient with all that is unresolved in your heart,
And try to love the questions themselves.
Do not seek for the answers that can not be given,
For you would not be able to live them.
And the point is to live everything.
Live the questions now.
And perhaps, without knowing it,
You will live along someday into the answers.

—RAINER MARIA RILKE

And joy is everywhere; it is in the earth's green covering of grass; in the blue serenity of the sky; in the reckless exuberance of spring; in the severe abstinence of grey winter; in the living flesh that animates our bodily frame; in the perfect poise of the human figure, noble and upright; in living; in the exercise of all our powers; in the acquisition of knowledge; in fighting evils.... Joy is there everywhere.

—RABINDRANATH TAGORE

A POEM BY AN UNKNOWN SOLDIER

Do not stand at my grave and weep,
    I am not there, I do not sleep.
I am a thousand winds that blow,
    I am a diamond glint on snow.
I am the sunlight on ripening grain,
    I am the autumn rain.
When you awake in the morning hush,
    I am the swift, uplifting rush of birds circling in flight;
I am the stars that shine at night.
So do not stand at my grave and cry,
    I am not there. I did not die.

STAGES

As every flower fades, and us all youth departs,
So life at every stage
So every virtue, so our grasp of truth,
Blooms in its day
And may not last forever.

Since life may summon us at every stage
Be ready, heart, for parting, new endeavor,
Be ready bravely and without remorse
To find a new light that old ties cannot give.
In all beginnings dwells a magic force
For guarding us and helping us to live.

Serenely let us move to distant places
And let no sentiments of home detain us
But lift us stage by stage to wider spaces.
If we accept a home of our own making
Familiar habit makes for indolence.
We must prepare for parting and leave taking
Or else remain the slaves of permanence.

Even the hour of our death may send
Us speeding on to fresh and newer spaces
And life may summon us to newer races
So be it, heart: bid farewell without end.

—HERMANN HESSE

Epilogue

Social Architecture as a Foundation

for Collaborative Leadership

"I want to demonstrate to the world, the architecture of a new and beautiful social commonwealth. The secret of my harmony? I alone know it. Each instrument in counterpoint, and as many contrapuntal parts as there are instruments. It is the enlightened self-discipline of the various parts, each voluntarily imposing on itself the limits of its individual freedom for the wellbeing of the community.

"That is my message. Not the autocracy of a single stubborn melody on the one hand, nor the anarchy of the unchecked noise of the other. No, a delicate balance between the two; an enlightened freedom. The science of my art. The harmony of the stars in the heavens, the yearning for brotherhood in the heart of man.

"This is the secret of my music."

—Johann Sebastian Bach

After so many pages we are now back to where we began with the opening quote from Bach. He describes his music as not just a solo melody line or a rush of anarchy, but as a creative act I like to call "social architecture." What is really meant by this characterization? Where can we find examples of social architecture around us, in nature or in human activity?

- Is it to be found in the majesty of a sunset with the rich colors illuminating a cluster of clouds on the horizon?
- Could it be found in a flock of geese flying south in the fall?
- Or perhaps a clump of ferns in a forest glade?
- Maybe it is present in a series of passes that lead to a three-pointer at a crucial moment in a basketball game?
- How about when everyone stands for the sing-along portion of Handel's *Messiah?*

- Could it be present in a group of children singing carols at your front door on a snowy winter afternoon?
- Or perhaps it is evident in the circle of sharing during an AA meeting?
- Is it present in the opening or closing ceremonies of the Olympics?
- Might it be present in the hushed silence after the reading of a beautiful poem?
- Or could it be present in the small knot of people gathered around the coffin of a loved one?

These questions have no end because I find social architecture all around us, wherever there is beauty, truth or goodness. When we leave things in a natural state, let children be children or experience art in all its manifold forms, it can be present. Some of life's greatest triumphs are embedded in social architecture, such as winning the gold in the Olympics. These examples are all about the individual person/impression/event embedded in a larger reality. Examples are all around us, but all too often we disturb the natural order of things though our clumsy attempts to be clever or organized, to overthink problems, and the magic can disappear faster than the setting sun.

All of my books to date are in sum total simply attempts at reaching for a renewal of social architecture. One of the best tools I know is active striving toward collaborative leadership.

The term is used frequently in various settings and is often misunderstood. It is not an excuse for everyone doing everything together, or for blurring lines of authority and responsibility. It is not the same as coordination or simply better communication, although those aspects are valuable to any organization.

One could imagine stages of interaction, going from a more generalized state to one that is more complex:

1. COMMUNICATION—letting others know what you are doing and staying aware of what they are doing;

2. COORDINATION—trying not to get in each other's way such as coordinating schedules and so on and taking on a project that reinforces and supports the efforts of others;

3. COLLABORATION—intentional work that is mutually supportive and highly conscious in intent and direction.

So what are the key characteristics of collaborative leadership? It is often transitory, present in some projects and then not in others. It cannot be institutionalized or fixed in rigid forms. Collaboration resembles the "smell test" in that it is readily identifiable when it is happening based upon some key characteristics:

1. Clarity around roles and responsibilities so individuals can take maximum action independently;

2. A concerted effort to orchestrate the independent actions so they are mutually supportive; example: an outreach effort that entails collaboration between admissions and development so that the messaging is consistent;

3. Regular face to face and online meetings that include reporting, discussion and ending with action items (and follow up in subsequent meetings);

4. Attention to the "navigation" of issues and tasks through the organization, healthy processes;

5. Creating a culture of trust and support for initiative;

6. An organization that values fellowship as well as leadership (we are all followers and at times leaders);

7. Leaders who are selected for their skills, capacities and experience in a field of expertise (not personal or political connections);

8. Leaders who individually and collectively attend to good communication and reporting;

9. Leaders who are self-aware and willing to grow personally and professionally;

10. Regular review, both collectively and individually.

Regarding the last point, it is ideal when everyone knows the cycle of review/evaluation and how it will be done. Those opportunities allow for growth and development. Otherwise, it is best if there is minimal "Monday-morning quarterbacking." Everyone has opinions, but constantly airing them is a luxury most organizations cannot afford. There is a time and place for review. Otherwise it is best to give leaders a chance to lead and collaborate with each other.

There are natural, and one might even argue necessary creative tensions within collaborative leadership. So often people are used to asking others for things, seeking permission, requesting funding etc., all of which play into the old mind set of traditional hierarchy. When asking, seeking permission, requesting we are in fact "voting" for a CEO or someone who can "answer or approve." Old forms are thus perpetuated. In a collaborative leadership structure each leader has to become an "owner" of both the process and the outcomes. One needs to use problem-solving skills, enlisting others for input but steering the process in ways that create conditions for successful results.

One of the challenges of collaborative leadership has to do with overlapping areas of responsibilities. A traditional organizational structure has people compartmentalized: HR, marketing, finance and so on. One still needs departments and clarity around roles and responsibilities, but at the top level of senior management at least, people need to be willing to tolerate some ambiguity in which some roles intersect. In higher education, for example, there is a need for marketing leaders to meet with those involved in programing or academic delivery so that the website reflects both the best practices in web design as well as content that is true to the organization it represents. One has to be willing to have regular and frequent conversations in those areas of overlap and shared responsibility. One aspect of collaboration is thus situational leadership in which the issue, task, or project may call for slight adjustments while in motion, while in process. A good "team" can do this seamlessly.

This then leads to one more salient characteristic of collaborative leadership: all concerned need to work out of images of the whole rather than just see "the parts." Each person in the organization needs to be acutely aware of the mission and vision, but the leaders in particular need to be willing to see the implication for others whenever a decision is made. One needs to be simultaneously aware of the periphery as well as ones own task, conscious of the ripple effect of any action or decision. One of the best ways to do this is to ask ahead of time: How will this affect you? Is there something I have not thought of, can you make any suggestions? If these questions are asked *before* action is taken, it will help others understand and support the subsequent outcomes. Success in collaborative leadership looks like a team effort even when individuals are primarily responsible for certain actions. Each part needs to reflect something of "the whole." This allows for maximum creativity, flexibility, and spontaneity. As Doc Childre and Bruce Cryer say in *From Chaos to Coherence,* "As any jazz musician knows, it takes flexibility and adaptability for improvisation to create beauty."

Collaborative leadership can build a new social architecture that is as beautiful as any temple, mosque or church on this Earth. It is not measured in stones and glass, but in human deeds of love and dedication. The results are at times invisible to our usual sense perceptions. Yet, through the efforts of striving, self-aware leaders can create a new social architecture that can support our deepest intentions to realize our humanity on this Earth today.

APPENDICES

APPENDIX 1

DANA:
DEVELOPMENT AND ADMINISTRATORS NETWORK OF AWSNA

Mission Statement

The mission of DANA is to support Waldorf schools and Waldorf education in North America by fostering healthy and effective organizational, financial, and administrative practices. Through its networking activity, DANA promotes research into Waldorf organizational and administrative principles and seeks to educate and assist Waldorf school communities in the implementation of these principles.

June 2001

APPENDIX 2

STANDING COMMITTEE MANDATE DOCUMENTATION FORM

Name of Committee: DANA, Date: 1-3-07

(Development and Administrators' Network of AWSNA)
Mandated by: AWSNA Leadership Council

Mission:

DANA's mission is to support Waldorf schools and Waldorf tion in North America by fostering healthy and effective organiz financial and administrative practices. Through its networking activity DANA promotes research into Waldorf organizational and administrative principles and seeks to educate and assist Waldorf school communities in the implementation of these principles. June 2001

Authority and Responsibility:

DANA is authorized to:
- Organize and conduct meetings of DANA regional coordinators and others.
- Develop job descriptions for DANA coordinators.
- Select and orient new coordinators.
- Select committee chair (cochairs) and terms.
- Select representative to Leadership Council.
- Develop, grant and review mandates for subcommittees and task groups. Provide input to other AWSNA governing bodies, committees, task groups and members of the Association.

DANA is responsible for:
- Achieving results as described in its Mission Statement.
- Reporting plans and results in a timely manner.

Individual(s) Receiving Mandate: DANA Committee

DANA Committee consists of:
- DANA Regional Coordinators
- AWSNA Executive Committee Members
- Others as deemed appropriate by the committee.

Chair, or Reporting Individual, of Mandate Group:

Chair or co-chairs as selected by the Committee

Time and Frequency of Review:

July 2007, and every three years thereafter.

Resources Allocated to Enable the Committee's Work:

Funding for annual general meeting of DANA Coordinators and some expenses from AWSNA. Funding for special projects and related activities from AWSNA general fund and/or grant sources.

Group Receiving Reports and Responsible for Review of the Committee:

Leader of Programs and Activities and Leadership Council.

Reports also to Delegates and Board of Trustees.

Frequency of reporting:

DANA annual meeting minutes to leader of Programs and Activities and Leadership Council.

Update for delegates and Board of Trustees at June Delegates' meetings.

All parties to this mandate agree to adhere to the guidelines outlined
in the Mandate Agreement and the Principles of Operation

By: _____ for the Mandating Group

Signatures of individuals receiving the mandate

APPENDIX 3

From Facilitation chapter:

Appendix A: Process Agenda Template

Title of Event

Date

Location

Meeting Start and End Times

Meeting Purpose and Objectives:

- Describe the primary purpose of this meeting
- Describe the meeting objectives
- Describe the decisions to be made

Participants: List of participants

Meeting Leader: name(s) of meeting leader

Facilitator: name(s) of facilitator and breakout group facilitator

TIME	TOPIC, OBJECTIVES, AND ACTIVITIES	SETUP AND MATERIALS

Clock time here
 	
Names of people responsible here
 	
Meeting leader, facilitator, time keeper, recorders
	1. Name of activity
	Objective:
	    What you would like to accomplish for this session
	Activities/Interactions:
	    List of specific activities using process techniques
	    and recording methods with times attributed to
	    each step
	Total time =___ minutes
		Room setup
		
		Equipment, materials, supplies needed

Time
 	
Names of people responsible here
	2. Name of activity
	Objective:
	    What you would like to accomplish for this session
	Activities/Interactions:
	    List of specific activities using process techniques
	    and recording methods with times attributed to
	    each step
	Total time =___ minutes
		Equipment, materials, supplies needed

Time	Break—also include activities needed to prep for next session	Food, beverages

Time
 	
Names of people responsible here
	3. Name of activity
	Objective:
	    What you would like to accomplish for this session
	Activities/Interactions:
	    List of specific activities using process techniques
	    and recording methods with times attributed to
	    each step
	Total time =___ minutes
		Equipment, materials, supplies needed

Time	Lunch – also include activities needed to prep for next session	Food, beverages

Time
Names of people responsible here
	4. Name of activity
	Objective:
	    What you would like to accomplish for this session
	Activities/Interactions:
	    LIst of specific activities using process techniques
	    and recording methods with times attributed to
	    each step
	Total time = ___ minutes
		Equipment, materials, supplies needed

Time
 	
Names of people responsible here
	5. Name of activity
	Objective:
	    What you would like to accomplish for this session
	Activities/Interactions:
	    List of specific activities using process techniques
	    and recording methods with times attributed to
	    each step
	Total time = ___ minutes
		Equipment, materials, supplies needed

Time	Adjourn	

MEETING-EVALUATION TEMPLATE

Workshop Title, Date, Location

Thank you for attending the _____ Workshop. We are interested in your feedback about this workshop. Please take a moment to give us your opinion on this evaluation form.

PLEASE COMPLETE BOTH SIDES OF THIS PAGE.

Please indicate the strength of your agreement with each statement below:

The workshop:	Strongly disagree	Disagree	Not sure	Agree	Strongly agree
was a valuable use of my time.					
purpose was clear.					
was the right length of time.					
If not, was the meeting too long or too short? (circle one)				Too long	Too short
	Strongly disagree	Disagree	Not sure	Agree	Strongly agree
I feel that leadership will use my suggestions.					
The workshop format achieved the stated objectives.					
Rate each aspect:					
Workshop location:					
Workshop facilitation:					
Workshop materials:					
What did you like most about this workshop?					
What did you like least about this workshop?					
Other comments:					

BEST AND WORST FACILITATION PRACTICES

Some of the BEST things facilitators can do:

- Carefully assess the needs of the members.
- Create an open and trusting atmosphere.
- Help people understand why they are there.
- View yourself as a servant of the group's needs.
- Make meeting participants the center of attention.
- Speak in simple and direct language.
- Work hard to stay neutral.
- Display energy and appropriate levels of assertiveness.
- Treat all participants as equals.
- Stay flexible and ready to change direction if necessary.
- Make notes that reflect what participants mean.
- Listen intently to understand completely what is being said.
- Know how to use a wide range of discussion tools.
- Make sure every session ends with clear steps for the next meeting.
- Insure that participants feel ownership for what has been achieved.
- End on a positive and optimistic note.

Some of the WORST things a facilitator can do:

- Remain oblivious to what the group thinks or needs.
- Never check group concerns.
- Not listen carefully to what is being said.
- Lose track of key ideas.
- Take poor flip-chart notes or change the meaning of what is said.
- Try to be the center of attention.
- Get defensive.
- Get into personality battles.
- Put down people.
- Unassertively manage conflict.
- Let a few people or the leader dominate.
- Never check how the meeting is going.
- Be overly passive on process.
- Push ahead on an irrelevant agenda item.
- Have no alternative approaches.
- Let discussions get badly sidetracked.
- Let discussion ramble without proper closure.
- Not know when to stop.
- Be insensitive to cultural diversity issues.
- Use inappropriate humor.

(Ingrid Bens, 2005, *Facilitating with Ease!* 2nd Edition.
Jossey-Bass, San Francisco)

ADDITIONAL RESOURCES

Facilitation Training

Interaction Associates *www.interactionassociates.com*
Institute of Cultural Affairs in the U.S.A. *www.ica-usa.org/index.php*
International Association for Public Participation: *www.iap2.org*
International Association of Facilitators: *www.iaf-world.org*

Facilitation Resources

Bens, Ingrid. 2005. *Advanced Facilitation Strategies: Tools and Techniques to Master Difficult Situations*. Jossey-Bass. San Francisco.

———. 2005. *Facilitating with Ease! Core Skills for Facilitators, Team Leaders and Members, Managers, Consultants, and Trainers*. 2nd ed. Jossey-Bass, San Francisco.

Kaner, Sam, Lenny Lind, Catherine Toldi, Sarah Fisk, and Duane Berger. 2007. The *Facilitator's Guide to Participatory Decision-Making*. 2nd ed. Jossey-Bass, San Francisco.

Schuman, Sandy (editor). 2005. *The IAF Handbook of Group Facilitation: Best Practices from the Leading Organization in Facilitation*. Jossey-Bass, San Francisco.

Schwartz, Roger, Anne Davidson, Peg Carlson, and Sue McKinney. 2005. *The Skilled Facilitator Fieldbook: Tips, Tools, and Tested Methods for Consultants, Facilitators, Managers, Trainers, and Coaches*. Jossey-Bass, San Francisco.

Conflict Management Resources

Association for Conflict Resolution, Environment and Public Policy Section: *www.acrepp.org*

Fisher, Roger, William Ury, and Bruce Patton (ed.). 1991. *Getting to Yes: Negoiating Agreement without Giving In*, 2nd ed. Penguin, New York.

Ury, William. 1991. *Getting Past No: Negoiating with Difficult People*. Bantam, New York.

APPENDIX 4

STRESS SURVEY
POTENTIAL STRESS EVENTS
(CHECK ANY THAT APPLY TO YOU WITHIN THE PAST YEAR)

___ Death of a spouse	100
___ Divorce	73
___ Marital separation	65
___ Jail term	63
___ Death of family member	63
___ Personal injury or illness	53
___ Marriage	50
___ Fired at work	47
___ Reconciliation	45
___ Retirement	45
___ Change in health in family member	44
___ Pregnancy	40
___ Sex difficulties	39
___ Business adjustment	39
___ Change in financial status	38
___ Death of a close friend	37
___ Change to a different line of work	36
___ Change in number of arguments with spouse	35
___ Mortgage over one year's net salary	31
___ Foreclosure on mortgage or loan	30
___ Change in responsibilities at work	29
___ Son or daughter leaving home	29
___ Trouble with in-laws	29
___ Outstanding personal achievement	28
___ Spouse begins or stops work	26
___ Begin or end school	26
___ Change in living conditions	25
___ Revision in personal habit	24
___ Trouble with the boss	23
___ Change in work hours or conditions	20
___ Change in residence	20
___ Change in schools	20
___ Change in recreation	19
___ Change in church activities	19
___ Change in social activities	19
___ Mortgage or loan less than one year's net salary	17
___ Change in sleeping habits	16
___ Change in number of family get-togethers	15
___ Vacation	13
___ Christmas	12
___ Minor traffic violation	11

Total (to be filled in by Practitioner)
(If more than 300 points, 80% chance of
serious health change within a year!

(Stress Survey continued)

How satisfied are you with		Function control of self in relationship to	
Self/Life	_____%	Self/Life	_____%
Spouse	_____%	Spouse	_____%
Family/Friends	_____%	Family/Friends	_____%
Work	_____%	Work	_____%
Finances	_____%	Finances	_____%
Community	_____%	Community	_____%
Home	_____%	Home	_____%

Check items true about yourself:

_____ Set realistic goals

_____ Eat the right foods

_____ Avoid caffeine, tobacco, alcohol

_____ At ideal weight

_____ Daily meditation/prayer

_____ Two mindful relaxation times daily

_____ Stable/happy home environment

_____ Relationships all fully resolved

APPENDIX 5

GROUP DYNAMICS-STAGE OF COMMUNITY-MAKING

From *The Different Drum: Community Making and Peace*,
by M. Scott Peck

While he insists that community making does not occur by formula, M. Scott Peck describes four stages of community-making that groups working together commonly experience. They are:

Pseudocommunity
Chaos
Emptiness
Community

Here are these four stages briefly summarized:

Pseudo-community—members attempt to be an instant community by being very pleasant with one another and attempting to avoid disagreement. This is a pretense of community, a necessary stage, but it cannot be sustained forever. The core dynamic is conflict avoidance. Individual differences are for the most part denied. Members tend to speak in generalities, while individuals think to themselves. Community-making requires time, effort and sacrifice.

Chaos—it is not just a state, it is an essential part of any group process. It does not simply go away once the group recognizes it. Differences come right out in the open, members fight for whose norm will prevail. The stage of chaos is a time of fighting and struggle that is neither creative nor constructive. Mature communities of course encounter fighting and struggle, but it often has a rhythm or grace that would not be seen in this earlier stage. The core dynamic in this phase is often despair. Feelings of "hitting a brick wall" or "going nowhere" will prevail. It is no fun, but not necessarily the worst place to be. It is a painful stage, but if well managed, it can be a beginning.

Emptiness—Peck claims, "There are only two ways out of chaos. One is into organization—but organization is never community. The only other way is "into and through emptiness." He views emptiness as the "hard part" of the process and also the most crucial. It is the bridge between chaos and community. In this stage the members of the group need to empty themselves of barriers to communication. During the stage of chaos personal feelings, assumptions, ideas and motives have prevailed. Peck describes, at length, barriers to communication that people need to empty themselves of before true community may be entered. These include:

Expectations and preconceptions
Prejudices
The need to heal, convert, fix or solve
The need to control

To empty themselves individuals must take careful note of what they are carrying within themselves. What prevents them from being truly present with the group and fully accepting others? Peck advises the group share this process of self-examination—stories of personal experience in the group, prejudices, past pain or joy, unfulfilled expectations. Group members begin to hear and see each other more clearly and come together in a new way. There is opportunity for something new to emerge.

Community—Open and empty, a group enters community. Ideally, people experience a deep acceptance of others and find themselves accepted as well. Individuals come to know themselves and others in a new light. Differences still exist but they are addressed, transcended or celebrated rather than suppressed. Respect, appreciation and joy characterize the group.

> *Anthroposophy acts not by means of sermons, exhortations, or catechisms, but by creating a social groundwork upon which human beings can come to know each other. Spiritual Science is the ground of life, and love is the blossom and fruit of a life enhanced by it. Thus Spiritual Science may claim to lay the foundation for the human being's most beautiful goal—true, genuine love for humankind.*
>
> —RUDOLF STEINER, *The four Temperaments*

BIBLIOGRAPHY

Anthroposophy Worldwide (2014). Dornach: Goetheanum, March 2014.

Baldwin, N. (1995). *Edison: Inventing the Century*. New York: Hyperion.

Bolman, L., and T. Deal (eds.). (2013). *Reframing Organizations: Artistry, Choice, and Leadership* (5th ed.). San Francisco: Jossey-Bass.

Buck, John, and Sharon Villines. *We the People: Consenting to a Deeper Democracy*. Washington, DC: Sociocracy.info Press, 2007.

DeGroot, Robert P. (2012). *Effective Meeting Planning and Facilitating*. Seattle: Amazon Digital.

Gladwell, M. (2008). *Outliers: The Story of Success*. New York: Little, Brown.

Clements, Johathan. "Three Questions that Can Change Your Finances...and Your Life," *The Wall Street Journal*. Feb. 27, 2015.

Covey, S. (2006). *Speed of Trust: The One Thing that Changes Everything*. New York: Free Press.

Finser, T. (2001). *School Renewal: A Spiritual Journey for Change*. Hudson, NY: Anthroposophic Press.

—— (2007). *Organizational Integrity: How to Apply the Wisdom of the Body to Develop Healthy Organizations*. Great Barrington, MA: SteinerBooks.

—— (2013). *Finding Your Self: Exercises and Suggestions to Support the Inner Life of the Teacher*. Chatham, NY: AWSNA.

—— (2014). *A Second Classroom: Parent-Teacher Relationships in a Waldorf School*. Great Barrington, MA: SteinerBooks.

—— (2015). *Guided Self-Study: Rudolf Steiner's Path of Spiritual Development: A Spiritual-Scientific Workbook*. Great Barrington, MA: SteinerBooks.

Gill, Rea Taylor. *A School as a Living Entity*, Chatham, NY: Waldorf Publications, 2011

Gladwell, Malcolm (2005). *Blink: The Power of Thinking Without Thinking*. New York: Little, Brown.

Incao, P. Lecture on the etheric and the double (not published.).

Kaner, S. (1996). *Facilitator's Guide to Participatory Decision-making*. Gabriola Island, BC: New Society Publishers.

Kinder, George (1999). *The Seven Stages of Money Maturity: Understanding the Spirit and Value of Money in Your Life*. New York: Dell.

Koteen-Soulé, H. (2014). "The Artistic Meeting: Creating Space for Spirit," in Roberto Trostli (Ed.). *Creating a Circle of Collaborative Spiritual Leadership*. New York: Pedagogical Section Council of North America.

Kotter, J. (2012). *Leading Change*. Boston, MA: Harvard Business Review Press.

Kühlewind, G. "Forgiving," in *Journal for Anthroposophy*, no. 33, 1981.

Nettesheim, Agrippa con, *Sechs Geometrische Figuren uber die Menschliche Gestalt* (Köln, 1533).

NOAA Special Projects Division (2010). *Introduction to Planning and Facilitating Effective Meetings.* NOAA Coastal Services Center.

Prokofieff, S. O. (1991). *The Occult Significance of Forgiveness.* London: Temple Lodge.

Reina, D., and M. Reina (2006). *Trust and Betrayal in the Workplace: Building Effective Relationships in Your Organization.* San Francisco: Berret-Koehler.

Soesman A. (1990). *Our Twelve Senses.: How Healthy Senses Refresh the Soul.* Stroud: Hawthorn Press.

Spock, M. (1983). *Group Moral Artistry II: The Art of Goethean Conversation.* Spring Valley, NY: St. George.

Steiner, R. (1973). *Anthroposophical Leading Thoughts: Anthroposophy as a Path of Knowledge: The Michael Mystery.* London: Rudolf Steiner Press.

—— (1977). *Karmic Relationships: Esoteric Studies,* vol. 3. London: Rudolf Steiner Press.

—— (1984). *Therapeutic Insights, Earthly and Cosmic Laws.* Spring Valley, NY: Mercury Press.

—— (1992). *Reincarnation and Karma: Two Fundamental Truths of Human Existence.* Hudson NY: Anthroposophic Press.

—— (1994). *How to Know Higher Worlds: A Modern Path of Initiation.* Hudson, NY: Anthroposophic Press.

—— (1995). *Intuitive Thinking as a Spiritual Path: A Philosophy of Freedom.* Hudson, NY: Anthroposophic Press.

—— (1996). *The Foundations of Human Experience.* Hudson, NY: Anthroposophic Press.

—— (1997). *The Temple Legend: Freemasonry and Related Occult Movements: From the Contents of the Esoteric School.* London: Rudolf Steiner Press.

Stengel, R. (2009). *Mandela's Way: Lessons on Life, Love, and Courage.* New York: Crown.

Sussman, L. (1995). *The Speech of the Grail: A Journey toward Speaking that Heals and Transforms.* Hudson, NY: Lindisfarne.

Vivian, Pat, and Shana Hormann (2013). *Organizational Trauma and Healing.* N. Charleston, SC: CreateSpace.

Wiechert, C. (2004). "Wellsprings of the Art of Education: Three Reversals in the Work of the Waldorf Teacher," *Research Bulletin,* June, vol. 10, no. 2.

Waldorf High School Teacher Education Program

Douglas Gerwin, Program Chair

A graduate-level summers program leading to a Waldorf high school teaching certificate in:
Arts/Art History — English — History — Life Sciences
Mathematics — Pedagogical Eurythmy — Physical Sciences

Foundation Studies in Anthroposophy and the Arts

Barbara Richardson, Coordinator

Basic anthroposophical principles and artistic exercises that lay the groundwork
for becoming a Waldorf teacher. Individually mentored studies available.

Renewal Courses

Karine Munk Finser, Coordinator

Two weeks of five-day retreats for Waldorf teachers and other professionals
seeking personal rejuvenation and social renewal through anthroposophical study,
artistic immersion, good food, and fun.

For a complete listing of courses please visit ***www.centerforanthroposophy.org***
Summer Programs Located in beautiful Wilton, New Hampshire
603-654-2566 • info@centerforanthroposophy.org

Applications are currently being accepted.

Waldorf Administration & Leadership Program

Designed for:

❖ *Waldorf school staff who have expertise in specific areas of school administration but need more background in Waldorf pedagogy, Anthroposophy, collaboration and group dynamics,*

❖ *Waldorf school leaders such as faculty chair, committee chairs etc. who are experienced in pedagogy but now have been asked to serve in a variety of leadership roles based upon Anthroposophy,*

❖ *Administrators from Camphilll communities and other non–profit ventures based upon Anthroposophy.*

New Program Sessions Offered Yearly

This program consists of five-sessions, balancing face-to-face experiential learning, mentoring, and online learning. The entire program lasts just 13 months with only 10 days required residency (in two 5-day institutes at AUNE) and the renewal course away from work and family. We will foster a retreat-like atmosphere for each residency while at the same time expecting a high level of focus and discourse.

Session 1: A 5-day residency at Antioch University New England in Keene, NH,

Session 2: Summer Renewal course at the Center for Anthroposophy, Wilton, NH,

Session 3: Online independent study will focus on a series of readings targeting one of the two threads (foundation studies or school leadership) with online postings of reflections on the readings,

Session 4: Each participant will be matched with an experienced mentor in his/her field and will spend an hour per week in a distant mentoring session,

Session 5: A final 5-day institute at AUNE in Keene, NH with shared learning and a graduation and celebration. Participants will be awarded a certificate of completion from Antioch University New England.

Primary instruction will be led by Torin Finser.

ANTIOCH UNIVERSITY
NEW ENGLAND

For more information and to apply, visit our website at: www.antiochne.edu/teacher-education/waldorf/ or contact Laura Thomas at the Antioch Center for School Renewal 603-283-2302, lthomas@antioch.edu

The Sophia's Hearth Vision

It is our vision that
Waldorf early childhood education
strengthens caregivers and teachers
to work with joy, courage, and a
spiritual picture of the human being.
Through preparation for their
vocation, they will become guardians
of family life and of the incarnating
child, so that each child will have
a strong foundation from which
to fulfill his destiny.

Join our unique Birth-to-Seven
Waldorf Early Childhood Teacher Education Program,
filled with the wisdom and practical gifts of this
invaluable educational approach.

Our program is recognized by WECAN and IASWECE and
will richly prepare you for a life-changing, fulfilling
vocation in Waldorf schools worldwide.

The Early Childhood Teacher
Education Center at Sophia's Hearth
sophiashearthteachers.org

700 Court Street, Keene, NH USA 03431   603.357.3755